T0295642

A Primer on Critical Thinking and Business Ethics

The post-pandemic world presents leaders with unprecedented levels of dynamism and uncertainty, leaving top management teams no choice but to engage in critical thinking – higher order analyses in which assumptions are questioned and disconfirmation is no less important than confirmation. With critical thinking coming to the forefront of leadership development, we as educators need to reflect on our present MBA curriculum in terms of both content and delivery. These three monographs are a must-read for anyone interested in developing graduate-level critical thinking skills and teaching future corporate leaders how to take a more nuanced perspective on the paradigm-shifting challenges they are likely to face when transitioning into their managerial career.

Peter Bamberger,
Prof Simon I. Domberger Chair in Organization and Management, Coller School of Management,
Tel Aviv University, Israel
Vice President, *Academy of Management*

Organizational leaders continually tell us that what they need most are employees that know how to think and learn. Such skills are necessary for identifying problems, collaborating on solutions, and driving organizational change. Including these monographs on critical thinking in the MBA curriculum will go a long way to providing this essential need for the market.

Dr Kevin Rockmann, Professor of Management,
George Mason University, USA
Editor, *Academy of Management Discoveries*

As someone who teaches business leadership and human values and courses introducing and providing frameworks for analyzing healthcare markets, critical thinking is essential for me and my students. These authors clearly motivate the importance of critical thinking and present techniques to encourage students' development. I could envision these books enhancing my preparation of students, who will become business leaders so they sharpen interpretations and decisions regarding the production and delivery of healthcare services, to create value for those with a financial stake in their organizations' successes and for stakeholders including suppliers, patients, employees, and the community in which healthcare organizations operate.

Kevin D. Frick, Professor,
Johns Hopkins Carey Business School, USA

A Primer on Critical Thinking and Business Ethics: Critical Thinking Applied to Business Management (Volume 2)

BY

FR OSWALD A. J. MASCARENHAS, SJ
XLRI – Xavier School of Management, India

PROF MUNISH THAKUR
XLRI – Xavier School of Management, India

AND

DR PAYAL KUMAR
Indian School of Hospitality, India

United Kingdom – North America – Japan – India – Malaysia – China

Emerald Publishing Limited
Emerald Publishing, Floor 5, Northspring, 21-23 Wellington Street, Leeds LS1 4DL

First edition 2024

British Library Cataloguing in Publication Data
A catalogue record for this book is available from the British Library

ISBN: 978-1-83753-313-8 (Print)
ISBN: 978-1-83753-312-1 (Online)
ISBN: 978-1-83753-314-5 (Epub)

INVESTOR IN PEOPLE

To all teachers who believe in critical thinking as the ultimate differentiator, and to all students who have a penchant for analyzing, assessing, and improving in all that they do.

This volume is dedicated to the late Father E. Abraham SJ, the most well-known Director of XLRI, who held its reins for over 15 years and under whom all three authors were privileged to work.

Contents

List of Tables

List of Exhibits

List of Critical Thinking Exercises

About the Authors

Fr Oswald A. J. Mascarenhas, SJ is a Jesuit Priest from Karnataka, India with priestly training in scholastic philosophy (1959–1962) and systematic theology (1963–1967). He has an MA in mathematical economics (University of Detroit, 1971), an MBA (Wharton School of Finance, 1974), and a PhD in business economics (University of Pennsylvania, 1976). He served as a Professor of Marketing and the Director of Public Systems Research at XLRI – Xavier School of Management, Jamshedpur (1977–1983) and as Charles H. Kellstadt Professor of Marketing Research, in the University of Detroit, Michigan, for 27 years (1983–2010). He last served as the JRD Tata Chair Professor in Business Ethics, XLRI, Jamshedpur (2013–2021). His current areas of research are corporate ethics and critical thinking. He has authored eight books and published over 75 articles in domestic and international business journals.

Prof Munish Thakur is a Professor of strategy at XLRI – Xavier School of Management. He has nearly two decades of experience. Professor Thakur teaches strategy, entrepreneurship, philosophy of research, and research methods. He is passionate about nature, student-centered teaching, and holistic education, especially in management. Throughout his teaching career, he has experimented with a variety of pedagogical learning techniques, such as simulation, case studies, discussions, and reflections. At XLRI, he has been the Chairperson of Xavier's Admission Tests (XAT) and Fellow Program in Management. He is a Fellow of the Indian Institute of Management, Calcutta.

Dr Payal Kumar is the Dean of Research and Management Studies, Indian School of Hospitality, India. She completed her MA from the School of Oriental and African Studies, UK, and Fellow Programme from XLRI – Xavier School of Management, Jamshedpur. She was formerly a Professor and the Chair HR/OB and Associate Dean – International Affairs at BML Munjal University, Gurugram. Dr Kumar is on the editorial board of several prestigious international journals and is a senior reviewer in A category journals, such as *Journal of Organizational Behavior* and *Personnel Review*. She has published extensively, including 14 books, with Palgrave Macmillan, Springer, and Emerald Publishing. Dr Payal Kumar was recently conferred with the Andre Delbecq & Lee Robbins MSR Retreat Scholarship, 2019 (Academy of Management, USA). She is also an Emerald Brand Ambassador and South Asian ambassador for the Academy of Management Discoveries. In an earlier avatar, Payal was Vice President, Editorial and Production, SAGE Publications Ltd.

Foreword

Business schools as *the* major global institution for educating future leaders in business are under fire for at least two reasons. On the one hand, they are accused of not educating their students in a way that prepares them for core management tasks awaiting them in later organizational life. "What" and "how" skills and competences taught in major areas such as accounting, finance, logistics, and marketing are inadequate to help graduates grapple with the problems they face in practice. On the other hand, an arguably more fundamental accusation is the existence of a massive blind spot: the education of leaders fail in going beyond optimizing organizational performance according to traditional items of the balance sheet and take into account the role of organizations as corporate citizens with a co-responsibility to make the world a better place.

A common thread runs through major organizational scandals of the past decade, e.g., German payment processing company Wirecard revealing in 2020 what they argued was an "accounting error" that grossly inflated the balance sheet by about $2.3 billion, German car maker Volkswagen being accused in 2015 of implementing software that could cheat emission tests ("dieselgate"), and international soccer association FIFA being the target of the United States Department of Justice's accusation of money laundering conspiracy, racketeering, and wire fraud in 2015: simply, not only did their upper echelon have insufficient technical skills and competencies to successfully manage their respective organizations, but also made conscious decisions that led their organizations down the dark route of shady business. In a simplistic version of events, finger-pointing, identifying scapegoats, and highlighting personal deficiencies such as greed or lack of a moral compass to navigate the turbulent and dynamic waters of doing business in today's volatile, uncertain, complex, and ambiguous world serves as explanation. However, a more refined effort would point toward the fundamental problem outlined above: the lack of comprehensive education that many future leaders get in business schools and, more broadly, in universities and other higher education institutions around the globe that goes beyond a traditional "facts and figures approach."

A major part of a more comprehensive education involves skills and competencies that revolve around reflecting the status quo, questioning assumptions taken for granted, making choices in ethically charged situations, and thinking out of the box. In particular, this comprises critical thinking and aspects of business ethics addressing various facets of doing business. Typical examples at different levels of social complexity include personal and often contested choices in one's career, such as foreign assignments heavily affecting stakeholders in one's life, interpersonal leadership issues such as in-group versus out-group dynamics that emerge when working in face-to-face groups, organizations externalizing costs by (ab)using natural resources and polluting the environment, grand-scale organizational layoffs affecting whole regions (if not countries), equality and poverty within and between countries, and, arguably, the multiple effects of doing business on the globe and in interstellar space.

The contributions in this book tackle these issues head on. They put critical thinking – in a nutshell "careful goal-directed thinking [whereby...] conceptions of it can vary according to its presumed scope, its presumed goal, one's criteria and threshold for being careful, and the thinking component on which one focuses" (Hitchcock, 2020) – front and center as they explore both the foundation and the application of ways of reflecting on what we find in (and how we construct?) reality, what this means, and how we act accordingly. Of course, critical thinking as such is not new. Some trace it back at least to titans of Greek philosophy such as Plato or Socrates, as well as different schools of Greek skepticism. Others point to the work of John Dewey who has established critical thinking as a potential educational goal. What makes this volume particularly interesting is its comprehensive approach, both in the sense of "horizontally" encompassing a broad range of topics and "vertically" containing phenomena at different levels of social complexity, including the spiritual as well as temporal dimensions of organizing in turbulent and unpredictable contexts (Hitchcock, 2020; Vogt, 2022).

Against this backdrop, the volume is timely and laudable. In it, the authors explore moral responsibility within free enterprise market capitalism through critical thinking, including owning moral responsibility for turbulent markets. They also examine the application of critical thinking to profit maximization and presumptive models of capitalist thinking. In addition, critical thinking is applied to the challenges involved in learning by students and how curricula in business studies should engage students in critical intellectual, ethical, moral, and emotional exercises and standards is also addressed. Further, the authors consider the role of critical thinking in domesticating global social "wicked" problems. They attempt to redesign the MBA program, which will not only address most of its major criticisms but also provide a curriculum framework with basic developmental themes.

I hope the readers will not only better understand critical thinking in its various facets, but also include it organically in their own *praxis* of personal and professional lives. It is a must-read for faculty around the world. My compliments to the authors Oswald Mascarenhas, Munish Thakur, and Payal Kumar, who are all senior academics and authors in their own right.

–Dr Wolfgang Mayrhofer

Dr Wolfgang Mayrhofer is Full Professor and Head, Interdisciplinary Institute of Management and Organisational Behavior, WU Vienna. He is a prolific author-editor, including *Developing Leadership: Questions Business Schools Don't Ask* (SAGE, 2015).

References

Hitchcock, D. (2020). Critical thinking. In E. N. Zalta & U. Nodelman (Eds.), *The Stanford encyclopedia of philosophy*. https://plato.stanford.edu/archives/fall2020/entries/critical-thinking/

Vogt, K. (2022). Ancient skepticism. In E. N. Zalta & U. Nodelman (Eds.), *The Stanford encyclopedia of philosophy*. https://plato.stanford.edu/archives/win2022/entries/skepticism-ancient/

Preface

Welcome to the second volume in the *Primer on Critical Thinking and Business Ethics*. The first volume, as per its title, *Recent Conceptualizations of Critical Thinking* introduced and discussed various definitions, concepts, paradigms, and icons of critical thinking. This volume, *Critical Thinking Applied to Business Management*, will delve into current business institutions where critical thinking is needed the most, such as corporate free enterprise capitalism, its major driving forces, the institution of profit maximization with its effect of turbulent markets and their social externalities. We discuss how corporate executives could be assigned corporate moral responsibility for these externalities. We also probe deeper into the causes of turbulent markets and trace the most likely causes to business schools (over 170-years old as an institution) and their programs of learning. We accordingly suggest that the MBA program needs to be redesigned, with critical thinking informing its new design, structure, curriculum, pedagogy, and delivery of learning.

The Universal Scope, Domain, and Function of Critical Thinking

For over half a century, under various forms and functions, critical thinking has been seeking its rightful place in the domain of human awareness, presence, and application. That is, under the scope and purpose of critical thinking and social analysis, almost every aspect of human civilization, growth, and development has been the object of critical analysis. Especially in generating scientific knowledge and related technological advancements, in the development of health, wealth, and opportunity creation and distribution, and related law-and-order administration, the majority of mankind's progress has been screened, analyzed, assessed, and legitimized through the lens of critical thinking and its critical applications, particularly in schools, colleges, universities, and business schools.

While we all welcome this enviable academic success of critical thinking and its diffusion, its beneficial social impact in critical areas, such as reduction of income and social inequality, gender inequity and discrimination, global environmental sustainability erosion, global animal ethics violation, and cosmic debilitation of nature, has been woefully lacking. Obviously, we need a more rigorous assessment and analysis of our critical thinking tools of social analysis as well as social progress, social development, and social welfare. One such tool relates to profit maximization and the business schools that conceive and institutionalize it via the MBA curriculum, its content, pedagogy, and student learning.

Critical thinking is universal in its potential scope, function, and domain, especially when it relates to evaluating the thinking–reasoning–rationalizing–judging sequence of executive decisions and operations. These in turn, involve value-laden zones embedded in business, economic, or political fields and their theoretical, conceptual, or behavioral underpinnings. While much of this expanding analysis of critical thinking is useful, long overdue, and sociopolitically urgent, it needs to be conceptually more rigorous, robust, valid, and reliable. Axiologically, critical thinking is stimulating and useful when it provokes reflexive and reflexological deliberation.

Socrates (470–399 BC), the Greek philosopher and teacher, is arguably the founder and most celebrated critical thinker of all time. Some 2,500 years ago, he pioneered the tradition of critical thinking through an influential and enduring method of analysis called the Socratic method of questioning. He taught by asking questions, drawing out answers from his pupils to challenge the completeness and accuracy of their thinking. He instituted the critical thinking vision by training his pupils to probe or question common beliefs and explanations of his times, carefully distinguishing those beliefs that are reasonable and logical from those which are not but appealing to our native egocentrism (self-centeredness) and our sociocentric (society-focused) vested interests.

Over the years, critical thinking has assumed multifunctional scope and definitions. Thus, in its earliest and broadest manifestations:

- Critical thinking was *thinking of thinking* (e.g., Socratic methods of questioning and doubting, Baconian method of empirical investigation).
- Critical thinking *included questioning our thinking, rationalizing, believing, and doubting* (e.g., Socratic methods of doubting, Cartesian methods of proving one's existence and operations).
- Critical thinking soon involved questioning our thinking and reasoning processes and judging habits (e.g., Cartesian methods of assumptive and presumptive thinking and reasoning, social structures of discrimination based on natural advantages and disadvantages of race, color, wealth, and nationality).
- Critical thinking assumed even wider and deeper intellectual goals and projects, such as questioning our existence, origin, and destiny (e.g., Thomas Aquinas and the Scholastic methods of dogmatic reasoning).
- The Enlightenment schools pioneered by Immanuel Kant (1724–1804) and his associates Hegel, Fichte, Heidegger, and Schelling questioned the epistemological source of our doctrines, truths, and beliefs; they conceived and designed schools or philosophies of truth based on human reasoning and rationalizing than on human authority (internalized in obedience and submission). In this sense, Kant and his followers founded the schools of Enlightenment some of which are still current and influential. In this context, popular and attractive were Machiavellian critical analysis (see *Prince*) and Bismarck's analysis of political governance structures in the early sixteenth century.

- Martin Luther, who separated from the Roman Catholic Church in 1517, pioneered the Protestant movement which in essence was a pre-critical thinking movement for self-reflection and correction, supported by several second-generation Protestant reformers, such as John Calvin (1509–1564) in France, Zwingli (1484–1531) in Switzerland, and John Knox (1513–1572) in Scotland. These reformers questioned several sedimented doctrines and beliefs of Christian orthodoxy and sought to redefine them so as to liberate them to be relevant and livable.
- Later, critical thinking became primarily social analysis, e.g., Karl Marx (1818–1883) and Friedrich Engels (1820–1895), both German philosophers and economists, were major voices. Marx became the celebrated author of his three-volume opus known to the world as *Das Kapital*, the first volume of which appeared in 1867 with the others being published after his death. Marx founded socialism, later becoming one of the first prophets of European communism. Marx was interested in the revolution itself of socialism and communism rather than in its practical governance and diffusion. His writings became more famous and influential after his death, and his influence continues in the European socialist movements of today. Engels was a close collaborator of Karl Marx in founding and diffusing socialism and communism; they both authored *The Communist Manifesto* (1848), the magna carta of communist socialism. Both spoke of social structures that seemingly divided society into the owner and the owned, employers and the employed, the bourgeoisie and the proletariat, the labor class and its owners, the rich and the poor. Thus, their writings can be construed as the foundational principles of critical thinking as we have them today.

Volume I on Critical Thinking Reviewed

In Volume I, *Recent Conceptualizations of Critical Thinking*, we reviewed several definitions, exercises, and elaborations of critical thinking. In Chapter 1, we reaffirmed the value liberation of critical thinking (not value hibernation); it is freedom from the self-centered rigidity of management orthodoxy and individualism to thinking for others, for the billions of poor people in the world that our capitalist business education or system does not directly benefit or care for. Most global crises today are the unforeseen consequences of uncritical thinking still prevalent in the free enterprise market capital system. Currently, the planet has crossed the threshold point of equilibrium and stability, as global warming, climate change, global pollution, global over-mining, Arctic meltdown, ocean acidity, and global poverty testify. There is a global need for humanity to be engaged in serious critical thinking with immediate remediation policies and measures.

In Chapter 2, we reviewed the history of critical thinking starting from Socrates and Descartes to contemporary contributions. Based on this history we derived several modules and practical exercises for training in critical thinking. Three classic critical thinking models were featured: Socratic questioning method,

Cartesian doubting method, and Baconian empirical method, and we discussed their potential for critical thinking as foundational methods.

In Chapter 3, we characterized the art of critical thinking in terms of its optimal inputs, processes, and outputs. According to great critical thinkers in business management, (e.g., William Deming, Chris Argyris, Stephen Covey, Peter Senge), critical thinking questions or should question the obsessive generalizations, constraints, and the so-called best practices of the prevailing system of management, and try to replace them with more valid assumptions and more meaningful generalizations that uphold the dignity, uniqueness, and inalienable rights of the individual person and the community. We also featured management thinkers on critical thinking, identifying their major models or practical approaches for critical thinking.

In Chapter 4, we focused on our major belief systems, since the way we think and believe influences our behaviors that in turn can either transform the world or negatively affect it. Our mores, paradigms, and worldviews translate into behaviors that in turn even modify the environment. In general, much of our thinking system is backed up by some concept, theory, paradigm, or ideology that our thinking systems generate and interpret as our belief systems of goals and mission statements; our belief systems, in turn, determine our behavior systems (e.g., our strategies, choices, commissions, omissions as implementation systems); our behavior systems determine our impact systems (e.g., impact on us, our families and neighborhoods, cities and villages, our state and country, globe and sometimes even our cosmos). Thus, our behavior systems eventually impact our thinking systems, which we started with, thus completing a circular or spiral loop. We examined the thinking–beliefs–behaviors–impact loop, exploring its internal and external dynamics and structures, as well as the structure and power of our belief systems in business. We applied critical thinking that systematically questions and seeks to redesign our presumed thinking and belief systems.

In Chapter 5, we studied systems thinking, its laws and archetypes that call for a shift in our mindset from seeing just discrete parts to seeing the whole reality in its structured dynamic unity and interconnectedness. Systems thinking fosters our sensibility to see subtle connections between components and parts of reality, especially the free enterprise capitalist system (FECS). It enables us to see ourselves as active participants or partners of FECS and not mere induced factors of its production–distribution–consumption processes. Systems thinking seeks to identify the economic "structures" that underlie complex situations in FECS that bring about high versus low leveraged changes.

In Chapter 6, we introduced the positions of Karl Popper and Nassim Nicholas Taleb, which maintain that uncertainty is our discipline, and that understanding how to act under conditions of incomplete information that creates uncertainty is the highest and most urgent human pursuit. We verify (prove something as right) or falsify (prove something as wrong), and this asymmetry of knowledge enables us to distinguish between science and non-science. According to Karl Popper, we should be an "open society," one that relies on skepticism as a modus operandi, refusing and resisting definitive (dogmatic) truths. An open academic society in which no permanent truth is held to exist would allow counter-ideas to emerge. Hence, any idea of absolutism and Utopia is necessarily closed since it chokes its own refutations. The difference between an open and a closed society is that between an open and a closed mind (Taleb, 2004, p. 129). Popper's idea is that science has problems of fallibility or falsifiability. In this final chapter of Volume I, we dealt with fallibility and falsifiability of human thinking, reasoning, and inferencing as argued by various scholars, as well as the falsifiability of our knowledge and cherished cultures and traditions. Critical thinking helps us cope with both vulnerabilities. In general, we argue for supporting the theory of "open mind and open society" in order to pursue objective truth.

The Design and Structure of Volume II

Closely following the Socratic questioning method of critical thinking, Volume II questions the existence, major principles, and operations of public institutions such as corporate capitalism as a free enterprise market system, and economics-based political systems, we question its major dogmas of sustained profitability and profit maximization drivers and ventures and how to appropriate corporate moral responsibility for the turbulent markets that unbridled corporate capitalism creates with its foreseen and unforeseeable social consequences.

In order to make critical thinking work and reform society, we deliberately chose topics that can and should respond to critical thinking and thereby strive to reform the world. Chief among them is corporate free enterprise capitalism, arguably traceable to Adam Smith's *The Wealth of Nations* (1776). We analyze capitalism's great successes and failures in Chapter 1. In Chapter 2, we trace the causes of capitalist successes and failures, which we believe are the theory, practices, and strategies of profit maximization. Uncontrolled, unexamined, and unbridled profit maximization can easily spin out of market control and discipline and lead to customary abuses of income and social inequalities, the rich and poor divide, poverty and its effects on those who are forced to stay extremely poor and helpless. In other words, profit maximization may be the root cause of corporate greed and envy, which in the long run result in turbulent markets, which is what we address in Chapter 3 of this book.

In Chapter 3, we focus on the human problem of corporate and social morality, in terms of how and when we can assign moral responsibility and accountability to moral persons as agents, actors, corporates, and decision-makers. In particular, we investigate the moral conditions for corporate moral responsibility (such as corporate involvement of rationality, intentionality, freedom, causality, avoidability, and accountability) that can morally justify or exonerate assignation of responsibility to corporate executives involved in creating turbulent markets.

Turbulent markets, though seemingly random and Black Swan events, are manmade and mostly traceable to corporate capitalist markets, especially its financial institutions represented by global investment banks, and the MBA graduates they employ with very attractive salaries, which cause serious income inequalities. Hence, as part of the primary purpose of critical thinking, in Chapter

4, we study the major criticisms faced by the over 170-year-old MBA program, its curriculum, academic structure, content, and pedagogy. We then attempt to design an MBA program that will not only address most of its major criticisms, but will also provide a curriculum framework with basic developmental themes, such as intrinsic motivation management, creativity and innovation management, productivity management, revenue management, and eco-sustainability management. These basic themes are to be researched and discussed in each of its four half-yearly semesters with higher and enlightened forms of learning such as paradigm shifts, analytical learning, experiential learning, and sapiential learning. In this context, Chapter 5 revisits the MBA redesigning project, this time focusing on some "wicked" problems (Rittel & Webber, 1973), with the great hope of eventually taming them, such that we assure our progenies a long overdue legacy of better quality of life, equality, liberty, progress, prosperity, and universal development.

We submit that these four-semester learning modules, if seriously followed, could start reversing the current trends of increasing extraction, encroachment, deforestation, greenhouse gases, ocean acidity, and overgrazed green fodder for cattle food, all of which unwittingly combine to create the current crises of global warming, global industrial pollution, global, climate change, arctic meltdowns, tsunami and hurricanes, earthquakes, and rapidly decreasing terrestrial habitability. One hopes that our commitment to reversing these trends will eventually assure positive long-term effects of global greening, global regeneration, global rejuvenation, and animation of hitherto degraded lands and depleted terrestrial resources. All these positive contributions to cosmic sustainability will inaugurate cosmic restoration, cosmic healing, cosmic justice, peace and human harmony, and solidarity.

Concluding Remarks

To achieve this higher level of humanity and humanizing processes we need transcendent value structures with equally transcendent concepts and theorizing such that we humans progressively abandon anthropocentric thinking and attitudes, that assume everything in the universe is for man and human civilizations, that all non- or sub-humans have only instrumental finalities of serving human development and aggrandizement since presumably man is the center of the universe's purpose of doing, being, and becoming.

Hence, we must also progressively decrease extraction and exploitation of the cosmos for human and infrastructural development which we currently think is normal and ethical, and that cattle, bird, and fish factory farming for table food is natural and progressive, and so on. We must progressively desist from deforesting and indulging in ruthless methods of cattle and chicken factory farming for our food; instead, we could devise creative and innovative methods for reengineering, reinstating, regenerating, renovating, and restoring the deeply depleted planet.

Opposed to this anthropocentric paradigm is the non-anthropocentricism or eco-sustainability paradigm that firmly believes in the equality, democracy, and universality of being and becoming of the cosmos; that all beings (human and non-human) are ends in themselves with no built-in or presumed necessary superiority of humans over non-humans, that the cosmos and its sub-systems are best understood and functioning as connected, networked, and interdependent community of biotic and non-biotic systems. We will delve deeper into some of these themes in Volume III on critical thinking.

Acknowledgments

This book represents the latest research and thinking in the domain of critical thinking as applied to corporate ethics and morals of business management. It has taken several years from conception to execution. The contents of this multi-volume book and the plan for it have been presented and discussed while conducting several graduate courses on *corporate ethics* and *managerial ethics* at various colleges of business administration, such as the University of Detroit Mercy, Detroit, Michigan (1983–2010), T. A. Pai Management Institute (TAPMI) Manipal, Karnataka (2010–2011), St. Aloysius (Autonomous) College School of Business, Beeri, Karnataka (2010–2013), and XLRI – Xavier School of Management, Jamshedpur, Jharkhand (2013–2021).

As the first author, my academic background is philosophy, theology, economics, marketing, e-business, and internet marketing, with an emphasis on ethical and moral market challenges and responses. Several professors molded me during my management studies and over the course of more than 40 years of teaching and research. I am especially indebted to Russell Ackoff, Paul Green, Len Lodish, and Howard Perl Mutter of the Wharton School of Business, Philadelphia, Pennsylvania, where I obtained my MBA. My PhD professors, Michael Bernacchi and Ram Kesavan, were also my colleagues in the marketing department at the College of Business Administration, University of Detroit Mercy, during the 27 years I taught there. I have published over a dozen articles in refereed journals with them, and they have always supported and stimulated my intellectual efforts and research ventures. I regularly use our joint publications in these books, and I am grateful for their friendship and demanding scholarship.

The second author, Prof. Munish Thakur's academic background includes management, strategy, human behavior, entrepreneurship, research, data, and philosophy. He has an MBA from the University of Indore, and is a Fellow of the Indian Institute of Management, Calcutta. He teaches strategy, entrepreneurship, and research methods at XLRI – Xavier School of Management, Jamshedpur, Jharkhand. He is extremely grateful to XLRI for giving him the opportunity to experiment and try new things. His education has been significantly influenced by Nature, mistakes, and failures in life, as well as through exposure to great professors and institutions. He is also grateful to all those who have directly or indirectly influenced his thought process through criticism or support, love or resistance. He would like to thank Father Oswald Mascarenhas for giving him an opportunity to co-author this volume. Although he says his contribution to the book is limited to gathering reading material and having in-depth discussions with me, his impact on the book is no less significant. He would also like to express his gratitude to his wife, mother, children, and the rest of his family for allowing him devote time to this endeavor.

The third author, Dr Payal Kumar is a prolific, prize-winning author, who has published 14 books with Palgrave Macmillan, Springer, and Emerald Publishing and several journal papers. Her research interests include diversity and inclusion, leadership, and followership, and also mentoring. She would like to thank Nick Wallwork of Emerald Publishers for adeptly navigating these three volumes to the publication stage.

Over the last decade, the first two authors had the privilege of teaching at XLRI, the premier school of management in Jamshedpur, India. They have taught more than a thousand post-graduate students, covering all programs of business management. The encouragement and critical feedback from students on chapters, assignments, and cases have helped us rethink and redesign this book to its current level of readability and assurance of learning. We are beholden to them.

We are also grateful to Ms Shruti Vidyasagar, for excellent stylistic editing and proofreading of all the chapters, and Ms Neha Upadhyay, Senior Research Associate at XLRI, who generously served as Google researcher and format editor, liberally devoting a great deal of quality time to check, review, and correct all the references.

We are grateful to the staff at Emerald Publishing for their superb development of the subject indices for the three volumes in this corpus. The third author, Prof Payal Kumar, Emerald's Brand Ambassador, ably negotiated with the Board and Review Editors at Emerald to design and market-position all the volumes.

Chapter 1

Critical Thinking Applied to Free Enterprise Market Capitalism

Executive Summary

This chapter focuses on critical thinking as a new, powerful, and specialized tool and technique for understanding and analyzing the subtle operations of the free enterprise capitalist market system and its ethics and morality. Everything in the world of consumers and market enterprise systems are determined by our supply–demand system that in turn are determined by our presumed limitless production–distribution and consumption (LDPC) systems. From a critical thinking viewpoint, we study the free enterprise capitalist system (FECS) as a dynamic, interconnected organic system and not as a discrete or compartmentalized body of disaggregate parts. Systems thinking with critical thinking calls for a shift of our mindset from seeing just parts to seeing the whole reality in its structured dynamic unity; both mandate that we see ourselves as active participators or partners of FECS and not as mere cogs in its wheels or as mere factors of its production processes. Critical thinking seeks to identify the "structures" that underlie complex situations in FECS with those that bring about high- versus low-leveraged changes in various versions of capitalism. Specifically, this chapter applies critical thinking to FECS as defined by its founder, Adam Smith, in 1776 to its fundamental and structural assumptions, and as supported or critiqued by serious scholars such as Karl Marx, Maynard Keynes, C. K. Prahalad and Allen Hammond (inclusive capitalism), John Mackey and Rajendra Sisodia (conscious capitalism), and others.

Introduction

Economically, free market system or capitalism in the United States has been a grand success. This triumph has partly resulted from natural resources, partly from the United States being one of the largest free-trade areas, and partly from the economic system called "capitalism" by which it is governed. As "standard of living" measurements go, the United States ranks as one of the highest among great nations. In general, this wealth and productivity are widely and equitably

A Primer on Critical Thinking and Business Ethics, 1–29
Copyright © 2024 Oswald A. J. Mascarenhas, Munish Thakur and Payal Kumar
Published under exclusive licence by Emerald Publishing Limited
doi:10.1108/978-1-83753-312-120231001

shared. Hence, capitalism in the United States has survived and been a triumph. But there are problems, mostly manmade, of greed, envy, immediate gratification, wanton consumption, overspending, chronic indebtedness, and the like that have shown the darker side of capitalism. Critical thinking analyzes this darker side in order to cast light on it.

Adam Smith (1976) defined a capitalist corporation as an institution for managing productive skills of the labor force; stimulating, diffusing, and institutionalizing technological innovations; accumulating the nation's human, physical, and money capital; developing a strong and large market that controls itself; and thus, raising living standards sufficiently high among the nation's people.

American capitalism has basically fulfilled this fivefold mission since its founding years. Hence, today, the United States is the best surviving model of free enterprise capitalism and the largest industrial capital base in the world. This incredible success story demonstrates that capitalism works.[1] To the extent that free market system has succeeded for the last 300 years in fulfilling its basic fivefold mission with minimal levels of government intervention, and regulation proves that the capitalist enterprise as originally conceived by Adam Smith (1776) is a viable, valid, and legitimate institution. The US government itself as a democratic capitalist system has been the best when it was the least – that is, when it was least needed to correct the ills of the free market system (Gans, 1988; Kelman, 1987). *This is the capitalist paradox.* Currently, with the US market embroiled in recession or stagflation, some timely government interventions, in terms of appropriate monetary and fiscal policies, are needed.

American capital accumulation is second to none in size, quality, coverage, and relevance (Chandler, 1977; Schumpeter, 1934). Despite enormous federal budget deficits and gaping trade deficits, the massive socioeconomic infrastructure in the United States has been its ransom during the years of uncontrollable recession, technological and corporate restructuring, pandemic recession, and industrial depression. Yet, the same accumulated capital and unbridled progress have created problems (Laudan, 1977; Winner, 1977), such as highly skewed income distributions and social inequalities, ghost towns as an aftermath of massive plant closings, periodic liquidity crises, and low interest rates, which have seriously eroded fixed incomes of the elderly. Regional and national retailing concentrations (e.g., casinos) and giant chain stores (e.g., Walmart) have left neighborhood retailing stores and independents less than fighting chances for survival. The greed for market control has also triggered countless hostile company takeovers that have rendered firms, both big and small, increasingly vulnerable (Ackerman & Zimbalist, 1978; Mascarenhas et al., 2005a, 2005b; Okun, 1975).

---

[1] For ethical defenses of market capitalism, see Acton Institute's journal, *Markets and Morality,* and review Gregg (2007) and Novak (2001). For the *ethical deleterious effects* of capitalism, see Budde and Brimlow (2002), Ma and Eliot (2006), and Miller (2003). For various economic views on the *benefits* of capitalism or the free market system, see Acton (1971), Benne (1981), Boulding (1970), Chamberlain (1959), Dalton (1974), Dorfman (1972), Dublin (1979), Eckstein et al. (1974), Edwards et al. (1978), Friedman (1962), Gutman (1966), Rodgers (1978), Schumpeter (1934), Sedlacek (2011), and Warren (1930).

Christine Lagarde, former Managing Director of the International Monetary Fund (IMF), recognized that, of late, capitalism has been characterized by excesses in risk-taking, leverage, opacity, complexity, and compensation. It has led to massive destruction of value. It has also been associated with high unemployment, rising social tensions, and growing political disillusion – all this in the wake of the Great Recession (2008). One of the main casualties has been trust and trust deficit in leaders, in institutions, in the free market system itself. Her conclusion was that this is a wakeup call (Lagarde, 2014).

In his inaugural speech on January 20, 2009, before a groundswell crowd of over two million people on the Capitol Mall, President Barack Obama, addressing the very same problems faced by the Nation after the 2008 financial crisis, said (*Newsweek*, 2009, p. 28):

> Nor is the question before us whether the market is a force for good or ill. Its power to generate wealth and expand freedom is unmatched, but this crisis has reminded us that without a watchful eye, the market can spin out of control – and that a nation cannot prosper long when it favors only the prosperous. The success of our economy has always depended not just on the size of our gross domestic product, but on the reach of our prosperity, on our ability to extend opportunity to every willing heart – not out of charity, but because it is the surest route to our common good.

Given the massive financial market crisis of 2008 in the United States and its near collapse in the global markets, does the US model of the free enterprise capitalist system (FECS) have a chance to survive and rebound to prove itself? Even if it rebounds, will it ensure the prosperity of all people or just favor the rich and the famous?

Fundamental Structural Assumptions of Capitalism

Like any socioeconomic and political institution, American capitalism has its own strengths and weaknesses.[2] Any free market system makes certain assumptions,

---

[2]For a discussion on the *social costs* of capitalism or FECS, see Ackerman and Zimbalist (1978), Baron and Sweezy (1966), Braverman (1974), Buchanan (1962), Cox, Goodman, and Fichandler (1965), Dalton (1974), Daniels (1970), Eckstein et al. (1974), Edwards, Reich, and Weisskopf (1978), Galbraith (1956, 1958, 1967, 1973), Heilbroner (1970), Hook (1967), Lasch (1978), Marx (1959), Moyer and Hutt (1978), Novak (1982), Okun (1975), Packard (1957), Price (1964), Pursell (1979), Schumacher (1973), and Weber (1930).

Critics of the classical liberal market system note that the optimistic faith in FECS did not actually lead to the prosperity of all individuals and of all nations. Within the nations, the masses became impoverished. Internationally, liberalism led to an intensification of colonialism on the one hand and the hegemonic competition of the great European imperial powers on the other. The result was the great world economic crisis of 1929 with its concomitant mass unemployment, and two World Wars.

some of them are basic and some are derived, which can help us assess the system ethically. We summarize these assumptions in Table 1.1. *Assumptions 1–3* are based on Adam Smith's (1776) theory of free capitalist markets. He maintained, "It is not from the benevolence of the butcher, the brewer, or the baker that we expect our dinner, but from their regard to their self-interest" (see Book I, Chapter 2). In the process of "naturally" seeking one's own self-interest, the individual contributes to the good of the whole society as if by "an invisible hand." Thus, according to Smith, the market determines how society invests its resources, human, and material. It decrees when, where, and how humans should labor. It determines the disposition of capital. The market becomes the regulator of what should be produced, its quality, quantity, and price. The market is called the "sovereign" system.

Table 1.1. Basic Assumptions of Free Enterprise Capitalist System (FECS).

Assumption	Buyers	Sellers	Market Institutions
1	All individuals are self-interested by nature.	All corporations are self-interested by nature.	All market institutions composed of buyers and sellers (corporations) are, therefore, self-interested by nature.
2	All individuals are, by nature, deliberate and calculating in the pursuit of self-interest.	All corporations are, by nature, deliberate and calculating in the pursuit of self-interest.	All market institutions are, by nature, deliberate and calculating in the pursuit of self-interest.
3	Hence, all individuals should be free to pursue self-interest.	Hence, all corporations should be free to pursue self-interest.	Hence, all market institutions should be free to pursue self-interest.
4	Most individuals are, by nature, unmotivated unless awakened by appealing information, products, and services.	Corporations should inform, instruct, and motivate consumers regarding their products and services. This justifies corporate advertising.	Corporations should inform, instruct, and motivate consumers regarding their products and services. This justifies market institutional advertising.

Table 1.1. *(Continued)*

Assumption	Buyers	Sellers	Market Institutions
5	Thus, the moral rule of promoting self-interest (egoism) overrides the moral rule of promoting the interest of others (altruism).	Thus, the moral rule of promoting self-interest of corporations (corporate egoism) overrides the moral rule of promoting the interest of others (corporate altruism).	Thus, the moral rule of promoting self-interest of businesses (market egoism) overrides the moral rule of promoting the interest of others (market altruism).
6	However, individual self-interest should promote common good, without being subservient to it.	However, corporate self-interest should promote common good without being subservient to it.	However, market institutional self-interest should promote common good without the latter dominating the markets.
7	Individuals know best what they want and can best achieve; hence, individual egoism should automatically promote social well-being at the collective level by the theory of the "invisible hand" (Adam Smith).	Corporations know best what they want and can best achieve; hence, corporate egoism should automatically promote social well-being at the collective level by the theory of the "invisible hand."	Market institutions know best what they want and can best achieve; hence, market egoism should automatically promote social well-being at the collective level by the theory of the "invisible hand" and "the State of Nature" (Thomas Hobbes).
8	Hence, the supremacy of the moral principle of enlightened egoism over that of enlightened altruism.	Hence, the supremacy of the moral principle of enlightened corporate egoism over that of enlightened corporate altruism.	Hence, the supremacy of the moral principle of enlightened market egoism over that of enlightened market altruism.

Source: Compiled by the authors.

The free enterprise or free market system is based on the first three assumptions. *Assumption 4* seeks to justify the advertisement–promotion communication system which is an integral part of the capitalist system. *Assumptions 5–8* justify the free market system. They were not proposed by Adam Smith. But several moral philosophers, such as John Locke (1689), Jeremy Bentham (1970), Thomas Hobbes, Kurt Baier (1965), and Henry Sidgwick (1907), have proposed similar or equivalent defense systems of FECS.

Critical Thinking Exercise 1.1

Given the credible and grand success of American capitalism, apply critical thinking to examine its fundamental assumptions as described in Table 1.1, as well as the following concerns[3]:

- The interplay of self-interested suppliers and self-interested buyers will not necessarily result in the good of the individual or of the society (as present market inequalities attest).
- Individual decision-making may not always be well-informed in terms of all personal and social choices and their intended or unintended consequences (as evidenced by current threats of global warming, global climate change, ocean acidity or toxicity, global greenhouse gases, and Arctic meltdowns).
- The marketplace is often dominated by very large corporations (such as the top 10–20 Fortune 500 companies) that are frequently not brought to heel by the forces of federal interventions or consumerist advocacy movements.
- In relation to certain addictive products (e.g., casinos, political campaigns, pornography, fatty fast foods, alcohol, and cigarettes), commercial advertisements may not be the right form of appeal or the right medium to inform and instruct. They tend to misinform, under-inform, or over-motivate such that vulnerable audiences (e.g., children, teenagers, senior citizens) may succumb to subliminal appeals that may have

---

[3]In all the critical thinking exercises suggested in this volume, when the exercise calls for application through the "lens of critical thinking," we recommend that the teacher/student/reader apply the following exhibits and critical thinking models from Volume 1 of this series, titled *A Primer on Critical Thinking and Business Ethics*: Exhibits 1.2 and 1.3 (Chapter 1), Exhibits 2.1–2.8 (Chapter 2), Critical Thinking Models 3.1–3.8 (Chapter 3), and Exhibits 4.1–4.3 (Chapter 4). The choice of a specific exhibit or critical thinking model will depend on the content of the exercise. We also especially recommend the following from Chapter 2: Socratic questioning method (Critical Thinking Exercise 2.1), the Cartesian methodic doubt (Critical Thinking Exercise 2.2), checking critical thinking inputs, processes, and outputs skills (Exhibit 2.5), and foundations for all thinking and critical thinking in particular (Exhibit 2.9).

(*Continued*)

socially undesirable effects (e.g., impulsive or addictive, shopping, purchasing and consumption, behaviors). Ads may often lead consumers to want and buy things that are superfluous (Galbraith, 1968).

- *Expanding consumption is presumed essential to an expanding economy.* Expanding consumption involves more people spending more money for more goods and services to satisfy more needs, wants, and desires. Nevertheless, "civilization, in the real sense of the term, consists not in the multiplication but in the deliberate and voluntary restriction of wants. This alone promotes real happiness and contentment, and increases the capacity for service" (Bose, 1948). Thus, big is not always better than small – indeed, small is beautiful (Schumacher, 1973). In fact, *less can be more* (e.g., advertisements, websites, billboards, aerial, banner, and digital advertisements can be more effective with less information, animation, and graphics)!

- The "deliberate and calculating individual" is not quite as capable when it comes to the wiles of the seller. Today, many products and services are so complex that even a reasonably well-informed buyer needs the aid of the internet, cell phone, blog, Facebook, Twitter, Instagram, or YouTube interaction, a nutritionist, an engineer, or a doctor to make wise decisions about the often bewildering array of possible choices. This is the *tyranny or explosion of choice* (Trout, 2004). This is particularly true, when we have so many "parity products" or "me too" products and so many apparently unnecessary products such as cheap disposable products, artificial products, showy, or show-off products, too many brands of snacks, candy bars, soft drinks, dog foods, children's toys, beers, cigarettes, and tobacco and alcohol products.

- Freedom from tyranny is freedom to make a mistake and the duty to learn from the mistake, as well as the freedom to be right. While, some will have to learn by making mistakes of wrong choices, over-consumption, substance abuse or bankruptcy, others will enjoy their freedom by making the right choices. What advertising does for the children, the elderly, and the economically illiterate, however, is a separate issue that needs further exploration.

During the Great Recession (September–October 2008), when the global economy experienced its worst hit since the 1930s, almost all policymakers sprang into quick remedial action. To stimulate the economy, the US Federal Reserve offered several bailouts and stimulus packages amounting to over a trillion dollars, while other governments spent lavishly, and central banks slashed interest rates. All these measures reduced the severity of the recession crisis considerably. Unfortunately, all these quick and symptomatic Band-Aid solutions quickly exhausted the economic arsenals of governments. Seven years later, in 2015, they remained depleted. Most central banks had interest rates around zero, and government debts and deficits ballooned. Should recession strike again, rich countries may not be strong enough to respond (*Economist*, 2015a, p. 68).

The global economy continues to face many hazards, from the Greek debt saga to China's shaky markets. Few economies have ever gone longer than a decade without tipping into recession. Moreover, most rich countries with their central banks have already used whatever arsenal they had (e.g., lowering repo interest rates when they are already at their lowest, controlling inflation or unemployment when they are allegedly below normal, tax havens have ended with tax deficits with many countries) and may not have the ammunition to fight the next recession. The basic lending of federal funds rate has been virtually at zero since 2008. The Bank of England's base rate is at 0.5%; it had never fallen below 2% since the 17th century. The Euro area and Japan have repo rates stuck at zero. The last time the US Federal Reserve raised interest rates was in 2006. Rich countries have their average debt-to-GDP ratio rise to about 50% since 2007. In Britain and Spain debt has more than doubled. Rarely have so many large and rich economies been so ill-equipped to manage a recession.[4]

In other words, when central banks face their next recession, they may have almost no room to boost their economies by cutting interest rates – a position that would make the next downturn even harder to escape. *Growth, however, is better than austerity as a policy for bringing debts under control.* Governments should instead direct their ammunition toward overdue reforms to product and labor markets. Open-product markets encourage enterprise. *The freedom to hire labor under flexible contracts is the best way to keep unemployment low.* Both reforms can enable an economy better able to cope with the next crisis (*Economist*, 2015b).

American capitalism has survived at least since 1776 and will survive despite abuses. According to Alchian and Demsetz (1972, p. 777):

---

[4]Some economists have resuscitated the idea of "secular stagnation" introduced by Alvin Hansen in the 1930s. This theory explains persistent depressions by asserting that economies fail to recover in terms of a persistent mismatch between the supply of savings and the demand of investment. Reviving this theory, Larry Summers, a former US Treasury Secretary, suggested that demand for investment had fallen because of technological advances that reduce the amount of capital it takes to start a firm. Meanwhile, the supply of funds with which to invest has become plentiful, as a combination of ageing (older people save more) and inequality (rich people save more); also, foreign bond buyers push savings higher. But there are other factors that render the theory of secular stagnation weak: nonresidential investment in the United States was up by 8% in real terms since its peak in 2008 and by 35% since its 2009 trough. As the government's share of gross domestic product shrank following the 2008 crash, investment took up the slack. Despite the phenomenon of falling oil prices and dollar appreciation, business investment in the United States actually rose by an annualized 1%. Corporate investment was bullish: far from weak demand for funds, borrowing soared. Companies issued debt at record rates. Over US$ 609 billion was raised in 2015 (up from US$ 40 billion in 2014), according to Dialogic, a consultancy. Bank lending to business rose by 12% until April 2015, according to Federal Reserve data (*Economist*, 2015a, p. 21).

The mark of a capitalistic society is that resources are owned and allocated by such nongovernmental organizations as firms, households, and markets. Resource owners increase productivity through cooperative specialization and this leads to the demand for economic organizations which facilitate cooperation. When a lumber mill employs a cabinetmaker, cooperation between specialists is achieved within a firm, and when a cabinetmaker purchases wood from a lumberman, the cooperation takes place across markets (or between firms). A theory of economic organization must explain the conditions that determine whether the gains from specialization and cooperative production can better be obtained within an organization like the firm, or across markets, and to explain the structure of the organization.

Critical Thinking Exercise 1.2

Given the debacle of the Great Recession (financial crisis of 2008), apply critical thinking in responding to the following questions that challenge capitalism (*see* Rajan & Zingales, 2014, p. ix).

- Is the American capital system worth saving?
- Is unbridled capitalism still the best or the least bad economic system today?
- Are major reforms needed – where, why, and when?
- Should the system of capitalism be changed completely such that it can survive in the 21st century?
- What are the fundamental strengths and weaknesses of the capitalist system not only in its ideal form but in its historical realizations?
- Is free enterprise capitalism viable, safe, socially progressive, ethical, and moral for other countries, such as India?

Such questions about the viability or the political fragility of the capitalist system, preposterous some 25 years ago, are critical and urgent now, affirm Raghuram Rajan (former Governor of Reserve Bank of India, India) and Luigi Zingales (2014), both professors of finance at the University of Chicago Booth School of Business, in their book *Saving Capitalism from the Capitalists* (2014).[5,6]

---

[5]Dr Raghuram Rajan assumed charge as the 23rd Governor of the Reserve Bank of India on September 4, 2013. Prior to this, he was the Chief Economic Advisor, Ministry of Finance, Government of India, and the Eric J Gleacher Distinguished Service Professor of Finance at the University of Chicago's Booth School of Management. Between 2003 and 2006, Dr Rajan was the Chief Economist and Director of Research at the International Monetary Fund.

[6]In defense of capitalism, also see Mackey and Sisodia (2014).

Our response to these questions and concerns must go beyond the current market financial scams and crises they have created, to the very essence of free enterprise capitalism.

Critical Thinking Exercise 1.3

Apply critical thinking in responding to the following definitional concerns of FECS:

- Capitalism is basically capital accumulation. But capital accumulation does not progress evenly and smoothly since there are both regular business cycles as well as irregularly recurring periods of stagnation and chronic depression. The reasons for the latter economic ailments are built into capitalism: e.g., often capitalists slash wages or attrition labor, thus depressing consumer demand, thereby also increasing profits, retained earnings, and expanding productive capacity.
- The result is the ever-present tendency for supply to outrun demand – a typical case of subprime lending and housing markets during 2002–2008. The more this happens, the more giant corporations will emerge, smaller corporations will weaken, and mergers or leverage buyouts will be the order of the day.
- Industrial concentration will result in monopolies and serious income inequalities (Mascarenhas et al., 2005a, 2005b). Poverty and marginalization will coexist amid affluence and luxury (Galbraith, 1956, 1958, 1967).
- Corporate monopolistic power can control expansions, create, or depress labor demand, convert labor-intensive to capital-intensive productivities, create artificial shortages in essential commodities; in short, re-enact the Great Depression of 1929/1933 and Great Recession of 2008. Actually, we may not be too far from another depression if monopolistic capitalism is allowed to rule national economies and fuel a possible Third World War.
- A well-disciplined capital system or FECS is worth saving as long as increasing income inequalities and other social inequities of capitalism in general, and of any FECS in particular, can be gradually eliminated.
- The choice is not between pure competition and government socialism, nor between "more competition" and "more socialism," but between *monopolistic capitalism* and *social capitalism*.
- The former is industrial concentration, a few manufacturers and sellers controlling prices and wages and avoiding taxes, which quickly results in distressing income inequalities. Social capitalism is politically monitored private competition.
- Given the current track record of overcomplicated and opaque financial instruments (e.g., derivatives, derivatives of derivatives, hedge funds, and private equity funds), massive corporate fraud and collapsing gigantic investment markets, serious moral questions arise.

We have finally passed out of the Industrial Age and truly entered the Information Age. Now the information itself fuels the predominant business model. It is not the manufactured good, even if that manufactured good happens to be a really sophisticated electronic device, a mobile phone, a software platform, or a chemical compound. Business models will no longer be predicated on the manufacturing of a thing but on the value and understanding of the data that each of these things create. This represents the most fundamental change in the business model of capitalism since the rise of manufacturing and the Industrial Age. An objective understanding of data needs critical thinking. We welcome critical thinking research and applications in data analysis such that data scandals of Facebook (arguably in complicity with Cambridge Data Analytics) could be pre-empted.

Critical Thinking Exercise 1.4

Apply critical thinking in responding to the following problems associated with FECS:

- With the recent fall or near fall of the Command economies (e.g., the Union of Soviet Socialist Republics , Russia, China, North Korea), American and West European capitalism have emerged as the apparent winners. *A prevailing efficient system or theory goes under attack only when it cannot cope with its own products* (see Senge, 2006). Its variant constellation becomes so extended and complicated that it verges on the self-contradictory. Every effort to account for its aberrations causes ever-increasing complications with even more anomalies that eventually reach crisis proportions.
- The fact is that the market was unable to resuscitate itself after the Great Recession. What was obvious for all in the depths of the 2008 global financial crisis was that the economy was in disarray – stock markets had crashed, export markets were grinding to a halt, cross-border flows had virtually stopped, the banking system was in collapse, thousands of companies were failing and laying off labor, and unemployment had reached unprecedented levels – in a word, FECS had failed, and the public began to lose confidence in its resuscitation capacity (Rajan & Zingales, 2014, p. x).
- There are and were unmanaged risks inherent in the FECS. The sheer number of the distressed – the unemployed, the retirees who lost their savings, the small business owners and households who saw their home foreclosed and repossessed by creditors – all this precipitated the October 2008 crisis. Apart from their governments, the public had no buffers to cushion them from the blows inflicted by the market. With the collapse of the financial system, political intervention shifted toward the financial markets as an attempt to bring stability into the system.

(Continued)

(*Continued*)

- Trout (2004) argues that neither capitalism nor socialism is inherently immoral, yet capitalism offers more goods than socialism.
- Feminists charge that capitalism inevitably leads to inequality, from which women suffer more than men. Socialist feminists offer a vision of economic democracy that they say will improve life for almost everyone, and particularly for women.

Despite these debacles, we assume the legality, viability, and validity of FECS. We presume that FECS is the best economic system we currently have as it has been working in most developed world markets for over two centuries. It has its flaws and problems, and so does every economic system of the world today. Critical thinking affirms faith in FECS and its strengths, while, in the spirit of critical thinking points out its obvious weaknesses and current shortcomings.

Curbing Boardroom Capitalism

Parker and Pearson (2005) offer some rules for controlling boardroom capitalism. They argue for the ethicality, morality, viability, and economic effectiveness of rules in terms of Parker–Pearson justice.

Critical Thinking Exercise 1.5

Applying critical thinking to unravel the assumptions, presumptions, suppositions, and presuppositions and related social constructions of the following 12 rules and assess their feasibility, viability, and practicality in boardroom governance:

(1) Employees of any target company should have a vote equivalent to 25% of the voting equity on any merger or takeover proposition.

(2) Shareholder voting rights should only accrue three months after share purchase.

(3) No individual can be an executive director of more than one listed company, or two nonlisted companies.

(4) Independent nonexecutive directors must be appointed by shareholders.

(5) Independent directors must be genuinely independent with no professional, consultancy, or supply relationships with the company.

(6) No individual can be a nonexecutive director of more than two listed companies or four nonlisted companies.

> (*Continued*)
>
> (7) No individual can be a director of any listed company that already has a director who holds a directorship of any other listed company of which he or she is a director.
> (8) Shares acquired through an executive stock option scheme should not be salable until a minimum of five years after the option is exercised.
> (9) Shareholders with more than 2.5% of a company's shares must vote on all shareholder voting issues.
> (10) A company's auditors must not have any relationship with the company other than auditing.
> (11) A company's auditors can only serve for a maximum of five years.
> (12) If any shareholder fails to register a vote on executive pay three years running, then those shares lose their voting rights.
>
> *Note:* The 1992 Cadbury report sought to establish rules of good governance, e.g., requiring independent nonexecutive directors to set the pay of executive directors.[7] But most nonexecutive directors actually have multiple directorships. Rules 3–7 (above) are intended to break this particular cartel. Rules 9 and 12 are intended to revitalize shareholders' responsibilities, while Rule 8 reinforces the ownership role of managers in relation to shareholders rather than allowing shares to become merely a source of added income. Rules 10 and 11 are intended to reinforce the independence of audit firms, while Rules 1 and 2 are intended to limit the opportunity of dawn raid type abuses. These regulations protect the capitalist system from anticompetitive behavior. They are not driven by personal preferences or a particular vision of a brave new world.

Currently, discontent is not being heard in the places where it matters most. Our arguments against corporate capitalism should not imply hostility to competition per se. One must judge who benefits from particular forms of competition, and by utilitarian judgment consider that competition as good that brings greatest good of the greatest number (Michalos, 1982; Warnock, 1962). Currently, benefits from competition are spread most unevenly, both within and between nations, and corporate dominance seems to be one of the causes of this inequality.

Marxian Response to Capitalism

Karl Marx (1818–1883) critiqued capitalism by analyzing the division of labor in Europe from a historical perspective. He argued that people's human nature, more specifically their ideas "were largely a product of class, economic structures

---

[7]See *The Financial Aspects of Corporate Governance* dated December 1, 1992. Retrieved from https://www.icaew.com/-/media/corporate/files/library/subjects/corporate-governance/financial-aspects-of-corporate-governance.ashx?la=en

and social positions. Ideas justified or rationalized the economic structure at any one time – they did not cause that structure" (Wilk & Cliggett, 2007, p. 97). Marx concluded that the division of labor contributes to perpetual inequality between the masses of low-income workers (proletariat) whose numbers are far greater and wealth far less than the minority and more powerful upper class (bourgeoisie) who are often politicians and business owners (Marx & Engels, 1970). Marx's historical perspective focused on the role of politics in contributing toward and legitimizing modes of production that created separate socioeconomic classes.

"The division of labor inside a nation leads at first to the separation of industrial and commercial from agricultural labor, and hence to the separation of town and country and to conflict of their interests" (Marx & Engels, 1970, p. 43). The term "town" in this sense can be understood as the centers of political power and economic decision-making and the people who live in towns possess comparatively more power than those working in the countryside. According to Marx, those with the most power enjoy the benefits of capitalism, while those with less power are excluded from such benefits.

"Capitalism" is an 18th-century *economic* concept and theory (see Adam Smith's *Wealth of Nations*, published in 1776) but a 19th-century *ideological* concept popularized by Karl Marx and other socialists. The term "capitalism" was coined in the 19th century, and it is often attributed to Karl Marx. Etymologically, capitalism means the "condition of having capital," and "capital" was previously used to designate "the principal sum of a money loan." Capitalists presumably are the people who control the source and use of capital – whether or not they personally own the capital. In the late 19th century, the word "capitalist" acquired the meaning of a "political or economic system which encourages capitalists."

Critical Thinking Exercise 1.6

Apply critical thinking in responding to the following objections and problems raised by Marxists regarding FECS:

- Capitalism, as Marx defined it is "an economic system characterized by private or corporate ownership of capital goods, by investments that are determined by private decision, and by prices, production, and the distribution of goods that are determined mainly by competition in a free market." This is a very broad definition of capitalism that admits different variants.[8]

---

[8]In *Das Kapital*, Marx analyzed the "capitalist mode of production." Marx himself, however, rarely used the term "capitalism," although it was used twice in the more political interpretations of his work, primarily authored by his collaborator Friedrich Engels (Williams, 1983, p. 51).

(*Continued*)

- The first contradiction of capitalism may be stated simply. The rate of exploitation is both a sociological and economic category. It expresses the social and political power of capital over labor, and capitalism's inherent tendency toward a realization crisis, or crisis of capital overproduction.
- Marx predicted that a speedy decay of the "capitalist system" was inevitable; else, the rich would grow steadily richer, the poor poorer, and capitalistic imperialism would loot and oppress the world; the working classes would be ground underfoot; and the ownership of property would be concentrated in the hands of a few unscrupulous men with enormous capital holdings.

In its modern sense, "capitalism" includes the meaning of an economic system based on competitive markets, capital accumulation, and labor for a wage, with prices determined by the market without any further consideration.

In his seminal textbook, *Business Ethics* (1999), Richard De George questions whether the capitalist system as a whole is morally acceptable. Given his prior interest in Karl Marx and Marxism, he frames his inquiry into the morality of capitalism from the viewpoint of justice, especially distributive justice. According to De George, capitalism not only offers the great goods of freedom and efficiency but also brings with it moral dangers, namely inequality and indifference to those who cannot compete in the market well enough to provide for themselves, which must be kept in check through government programs.

Capitalism According to Adam Smith

Adam Smith (1723–1790), a Scottish philosopher and economist, founder of modern political economy, said, "Man's principal concern was with subsistence and material improvement, generally as ends in themselves, and at best as proxies for the achievement of respect and admiration. Hence, either man had no passions or his passions could be satisfied through the pursuit of his interests."[9]

Adam Smith was regarded as the Newton of economics, i.e., its founder as science. Modern economics is considered to have been started with Smith's *Wealth of Nations*. American capitalism has basically fulfilled its fivefold mission (stated earlier) since its founding years. Hence, today, the United States is the best surviving model of free enterprise capitalism and the largest industrial capital base in the world. However, with the US market embroiled in recession or stagflation, some timely government interventions in terms of appropriate monetary and fiscal policies are needed.

---

[9]See Hirschman (1976, p. 112).

Opposition to Capitalism

Critical Thinking Exercise 1.7

Apply critical thinking in responding to the following objections and problems raised by the opponents of capitalism:

- In his book, *The Cultural Contradictions of Capitalism*, Daniel Bell (1973) states his central thesis that capitalism has some inherent cultural contradictions. For instance, capitalism emphasizes and glorifies accumulation of wealth or capital as an end in itself and not as a means for higher ends, such as civilization and virtue.
- Capitalism fosters individualism, since much of capitalist accumulation is for individualist ends, with very little geared for social and collective betterment. Hence, the very culture that capitalism creates can sometimes backfire, leading to its eventual destruction (Bell 1973, 1976).
- Galbraith (1976) agrees with Bell's (1973) thesis and further expands it. Others feel that capitalist business, which is the groundwork for American business, seems to be inherently immoral – this is because its task presupposes the legitimacy of the private pursuit of at least economic self-interest, and this pursuit may be immoral or may lead to immorality (Machan & Uyl, 1987).
- If business ethics is understood as a science of socioeconomic values, and a science for identifying what business executives ought to do and ought not to do in promoting common socioeconomic good, then capitalism that is *ex professo* fueled by private self-interest may be geared to do the opposite (Bell, 1973; Galbraith, 1956, 1958).
- Obviously, capitalism-fed corporate greed can also dominate executive thinking. Several theories explaining or justifying market inequities and injustices have been suggested. For instance, *Machiavellianism* believes that "might is right," and thus, one grabs the largest share one can get regardless of inputs and efforts (Christie & Geis, 1970).[10] *Darwinian justice* or Spencer's *Social Darwinism* (Hofstadter, 1955) advocates natural selection by "survival of the fittest" corporations.
- The philosophy of *justified self-interest* distributes goods proportional to what the distributor wants – *self before others*; particularly, distributor's needs come first when goods are scarce.

---

[10]Niccolò Machiavelli (1469–1527) was an Italian (Florentine) statesman and political theorist. Based on his writings, Calhoon (1969, p. 211) defined a Machiavellian executive as one who "employs aggressive, manipulative, exploiting and devious moves in order to achieve personal and organizational objectives."

(*Continued*)

- The theory of "the bigger the better" control proclaims that larger sales and revenues yield larger market shares and profits, which in turn generate better scale economies, optimal size, expansion opportunities, increased market power, and control (Schumacher, 1973).
- Capitalist business can be a corrupting influence on social life and values. By commercializing everything from Christmas to the professions, businesses can have immoral influence (Jung et al., 1983).
- The three most profitable businesses in the world are – unfortunately and shamefully – not companies producing food or clothes, medicines, or educational tools. They are three businesses earning the most and involved in the production and sale of arms; production and sale of drugs; and – worse still – trafficking of human beings. This third "trade" was less profitable than the first two. Now, especially since the escalation of domestic and international forced asylum migration, it has begun to occupy the second rung, since criminal gangs have found that, unlike drugs, a human being can be sold again and again.
- Advertising and marketing creates trivial, frivolous, and extravagant needs in peoples that would never have arisen without media influences; allegedly, media advertising siphons off scarce consumer resources that could have been better spent on other real needs (Galbraith, 1976).
- Thus, if a capitalist system by its very nature institutionalizes selfishness as a virtue (Rand, 1964) and exploits opportunities to advance corporate goals and personal wealth, then the business executive who works within that capitalist system could get unwittingly caught up in this race, be fired by and committed to its ideology, and propelled to work hard, especially when rewards are ultimately conditioned on and determined by higher levels of profitability (Molander, 1980).
- In particular, big business corporations controlled by a self-perpetuating, irresponsible power elite are charged with the exercise of concentrated economic and political power contrary to the public interest (Jacoby, 1973).
- Often, under the guise of obtaining welfare and security for the marginalized, the bureaucrats and incumbent politicians also obtain security and kickbacks for themselves by regulating and repressing the free markets. The final victim is the free market and the poor who look for better opportunity (Rajan & Zingales, 2014, p. 293).
- Smith's philosophy of human nature and ethics provided the foundations for a socioeconomic system that has enabled nations to accumulate great wealth and power. However, the shallow ethical foundations of Smith's system (e.g., see Table 1.1) also hold the seeds of its own destruction. The aspects of human nature ignored in Smith's system may be, in fact, real and their neglect is the reason for the existence of persistent socioeconomic problems that seem beyond the scope of prevailing paradigms.

(*Continued*)

(*Continued*)

- Norman Podhoretz (1981, p. 106) asserts that "capitalism is a necessary, if not a sufficient, condition of freedom; that it is both a necessary and a sufficient condition of wealth; and that it provides a better chance than any known alternative for the most widespread sharing in the wealth it produces."
- Eugene Rostow (1963, p. 20) believes that the case for competition as a social force and a cultural influence is a good deal like the case for democracy in the sphere of politics; its theoretical footing is not altogether convincing, but all its alternatives are even worse.
- According to Milton Friedman (1962), economic activity is only limited by laws and other legislation and perhaps on occasion by some local ethical customs. Thus, respect for people and for the environment depends exclusively on regulation, and managers have no social responsibility other than loyally serving shareholder interests.
- If and when property needed to be widely distributed, then representative government arises. But even in most democratic governments there was no guarantee that policies would reflect the needs of the people. Such a scenario might well invite blatant exploitation of workers and poor working conditions, massive layoffs only for the sake of increasing profits (not to survive or to maintain a competitive position), selling financial products with the aid of misleading information – as in the subprime crisis, lack of concern for long-term sustainability, and so on.
- Economic prosperity does not necessarily mean a good society. Furthermore, economic activity cannot solve all social problems through the simple application of commercial logic.

Critical Thinking Exercise 1.8

Apply critical thinking in responding to the following positive hopes about capitalism.

- In a competitive free market economy, the presence of myriad financial institutions and the decisions of thousands of small or big business participants create free markets, determine prices, determine revenue sharing, market sharing, profit sharing, and wealth sharing. The "invisible hand" of the markets and the visible hand of the governments can both shape capitalism, and if done well, can save the world from chronic indebtedness that perpetuates poverty and can save the world from depressions, recessions, and wars.

(*Continued*)

- For Smith, "value cannot be measured by money, because sometimes money is artificially scarce [...] because all labor is of equal value to the worker, labor is the best measure of value" (Wilk & Cliggett, 2007, pp. 51–52). Thus, the concept of capitalism is rooted in an idea of human nature being inherently self-interested and the value of goods and services are derived from labor.
- Government's respect of property rights is the first step toward the development and stabilization of financial markets (Rajan & Zingales, 2014, p. 201).
- Based on market and business skills, this respect of property has been mostly realized when property was owned by the most competent and specialized.
- If capitalism is based on the reality of private property, healthy competition, freedom of economic choice, and the right of every person to be oneself, then it will thrive, not just survive.

Inclusive Capitalism

Inclusive capitalism, which explicitly includes all, especially the poor and the marginalized, into the benefits of capitalism, is a more recent hope to revive and invest in capitalism. Two contemporary scholars popularized the term "inclusive capitalism," individually and through collaborative publications, C. K. Prahalad and Allen Hammond.[11]

Prahalad opens his 2005 book, *The Fortune at the Bottom of the Pyramid: Eradicating Poverty Through Profits* by asking "why can't we create inclusive capitalism" (Prahalad, 2005, p. xv). He uses the term "inclusive capitalism" to invite readers to commence talking about underserved consumers and markets. The process must start with bottom-of-the-pyramid consumers as individuals. New and creative approaches are needed to convert poverty into an opportunity for all concerned. That is the challenge (Prahalad, 2005, p. xvii). The inside cover of the book asserts that in the term "bottom of the pyramid" coined by Prahalad, the pyramid represents capitalism and those benefiting from it are the majority of people at the bottom, who are all poor.

In an article, Hammond (2001) describes how technology in the 1990s has led many people to experience greater wealth and allowed for their overall quality of life to improve. He also notes that billions of people continue to live in poverty in countries developing their capitalistic society. In order to address this exclusiveness of capitalism,

---

[11]C. K. Prahalad was the Paul and Ruth McCracken Distinguished University Professor of Corporate Strategy at the Ross School of Business in the University of Michigan. Allen Hammond is senior entrepreneur and a member of the Leadership Group at Ashoka, as well as cofounder and Chairman of a start-up company, Healthpoint Services. Prior to joining Ashoka, he was vice president of Innovation at the World Resources Institute.

a new capitalistic model should be used, argues Hammond. "What is needed instead is a bottom-up model that makes credit, communications, information, energy sources, and other self-help tools available to all, especially the marginalized."

In 2002, Prahalad and Hammond copublished an article in the *Harvard Business Review* that advanced their ideas of using market-based solutions for poverty allevi-ation through a hypothetical case study of development in India. In 2004, they advanced their ideas in another coauthored publication, this time highlighting three misconceptions of poor people commonly held by companies: (a) that poor people have little buying power when in fact "low-income households collectively possess most of the buying power in many developing countries" (Hammond & Prahalad, 2004, p. 32), (b) that low-income people do not like change when in fact they often receive little opportunity to choose among a variety of products and services, and (c) that little money can be made by selling to the poor. The "world's poor – families with an annual household income of less than US\$ 6,000 – is enormous. The 18 largest emerging and transition countries include 680 million such households, with a total annual income of US\$ 1.7 trillion-roughly equal to Germany's annual gross domestic product" (Hammond & Prahalad, 2004, p. 32).

In a speech at Davos on January 24, 2008, Bill Gates called for a more inclusive capitalism that "would have a twin mission: making profits and also improving lives for those who don't fully benefit from market forces." Mr Gates was arguing that capi-talism, appropriately pursued, is in fact the best hope to bring services and improve productivity and create opportunity for the world's four billion poor people – and that, accordingly, the world needs to invest much more heavily in the micro-, small-, and medium-sized enterprises that are close to the poor (Hammond, 2001).

Critical Thinking Exercise 1.9

Apply critical thinking in accepting and incorporating the following challenges of inclusive capitalism:

- The idea behind this new development model is that "basic services should generally be provided by businesses – sometimes directly, some-times in partnership with governments or networks of non-governmental organizations (NGOs)" (Hammond, 2001, p. 98).
- Privatizing public services is a central idea of inclusive capitalism, suggesting government policies have largely failed poor people, and businesses and nongovernmental organizations should assume a greater role in poverty alleviation.

Various Causes Attributed to the Success/Failure of Capitalism

---

Critical Thinking Exercise 1.10

Apply critical thinking in responding to the following models of neocapitalism:

- It is generally agreed that capitalism works. At least, it has worked better in the United States and the developed world than any of the alternatives that have been tried so far. The question is how to make it work (more) equitably. Any commitment to any one political philosophy (e.g., Nozick, 1974) that claims rights to freedom from state interference, may not work.
- We do not need any form of aggressive state regulation, howsoever defined, e.g., the state setting a defined limit on the acceptable ratio of profit to turnover, or a maximum size on corporations.
- What is needed is a legal framework, preferably with international standing, within which enterprises are free to be creative, risk-taking, even to maximize profits, if that is what drives them (Parker & Pearson, 2005, p. 97).
- We cannot, however, let unbridled competition carry on unwittingly looting and impoverishing the poor. The problem is that the "market" is not in any sense a level playing field, and is actually dominated by large corporations and the lobbying institutions that speak on their behalf (a form of crony capitalism).
- This is causing wealth to be further concentrated with certain classes of people and certain parts of the globe. How do we stop this?
- We all agree that some self-interested capitalists would abuse the system if they could and exploit the weak. So, the market has to be regulated. But regulation should seek to prevent abusing the poor, not undermine or replace the market itself. A regulation that does not work will not have the resources to clean up its act. Nor could unsuccessful economies afford to dispense social justice to the third world.

Putative Models for Supporting Capitalism

Critical Thinking Exercise 1.11

Apply critical thinking in responding to the following putative models of sustaining capitalism:

- Soon after the Depression, in the mid-1930s, John Maynard Keynes suggested that to avoid depressions in the future the government should employ strong fiscal and monetary policies (e.g., deficit government spending by increased government expenditures or reduced taxes, coupled with increased money supply via reduced interest rates, reduced capital gain taxes, and liberalized credit terms).
- If current government spending is very large and if the money credit system is sufficiently flexible and federally controlled, then Keynesian remedies may work. Nevertheless, with deregulation and continued privatization of hitherto government-controlled industries, and with gigantic banks controlling credit and money supply, even the federal government of the United States is incapable of fighting the evils of monopolistic capitalism.
- If FECS cooperates (e.g., via business expansions, more employment, price decreases, and the like) with federal liberating fiscal and monetary policies, then recession or depression may be controlled. Otherwise, federal deficit spending and easy credit may generate inflation followed by recession, or stagflation. Keynesian optimism works with competitive capitalism but not with monopolistic capitalism (Eckstein et al., 1974; see also Kahn et al., 1976; Palusek, 1977).
- *Scientifically* viewed, the free market system is a natural phenomenon, with an internal self-regulatory mechanism that enables it to function as though it were a physical system independent of all human interference. The prevailing belief was that economics followed mechanistic laws like those of classical physics. (Modern economics is considered to have been started with Adam Smith, especially with his *Wealth of Nations*.)
- *Sociologically* viewed, Smith believed that the intrinsic laws of the free market system could lead to the prosperity of all nations, provided one allowed them to work without outside intervention of the state. When each strives for riches via absolute competition, selfish agents in the market systems would hold one another in check and advance developments in a way that would be favorable to all.

Table 1.2. Critical Analysis of Free Enterprise Capitalist System (FECS): Values Versus Disvalues.

Adam Smith's Qualities of FECS	FECS Values	Typical FECS Disvalues
Management of productive skills	Labor productivity Labor specialization Labor enrichment Labor remuneration Skills development	Employee alienation, exploitation, maquiladora Forced unemployment or under employment Child labor, sweatshops, hiring illegal immigrant labor Under-waged, underinsured, forced part-timers Planned skills obsolescence via outsourcing and Downsizing
Diffusion of technology and innovations	Product innovation Service innovation Innovations diffusion Technology transfers Enriched lifestyles	Planned product obsolescence Planned service obsolescence Diffusion not reaching developing countries Diffusion of outmoded ineffective technologies Enslaving consumptive lifestyles; jeopardizing family stability
Human and financial capital accumulation	Strong skills and human base Strong equity base Strong infrastructure Strong capital base Strong money base	Cheap insourcing and outsourcing Undue executive compensation that causes income inequality and inequities Social destructure and destruction; ghost towns Liquidity crisis; low interest rates; inflation Weakened dollar; reduced fixed income among the elderly
Large market base	High growth, gross national product High buying power Consumption multipliers Investment multipliers Market-based pricing	Uneven distribution of growth and opportunity Uneven distribution of consumer buying power Forced consumer overspending Corporate frauds and scams Profiteering and predatory pricing

(Continued)

Table 1.2. *(Continued)*

Adam Smith's Qualities of FECS	FECS Values	Typical FECS Disvalues
Raising general living standards	Higher incomes Improved life quality Happier/longer life expectancy High consumer comfort and convenience Adequate healthcare for all	Income inequality and marginalization Ghettos, slums, ghost towns, pollution, AIDS, COVID-19 High infant mortality; poor neonatal care Created needs and desires beyond comfort and convenience Large numbers of uninsured and underinsured in terms of healthcare; life-saving drugs and hospitalization Mismanaged Medicare, Medicaid and disability programs in the United States; Lack of a national health care insurance scheme in India

Source: Compiled by the authors.

FECS is based on the first three assumptions in Table 1.1. Assumption 4 seeks to justify the advertisement–promotion communication system which is an integral part of the capitalist system. Assumptions 5–8 justify the free market system. They were not proposed by Adam Smith. But several moral philosophers, such as John Locke et al. (1907), and Kurt Baier (1965), have proposed similar or equivalent defense systems of FECS.

But conditionally granting assumptions in Table 1.1, has capitalism fulfilled its FECS mission evenly, equitably, and distributively? FECS does fail when corporate power gets abused along the same five dimensions of FECS for which capitalism was instituted in the United States. Corporate power is the ability of executives, corporations, and other economic institutions to manipulate the market or business environment (Steiner & Steiner, 1991). Several values and disvalues emerge from wielding this manipulative power.

Table 1.2 lists some basic values and disvalues of the putative models of FECS that currently emerge and affect our society under FECS. Most entries are suggestive or provocative but worth examining through the critical thinking lens.

Conscious Capitalism

Recent initiatives present new ways of understanding capitalism, such as conscious capitalism, benefit corporation, and inclusive capitalism. *Conscious capitalism* (Mackey & Sisodia, 2014) considers the effects of business actions that benefit both human beings and the environment. A *benefit corporation* is a new legal business entity that is obligated to pursue public benefit in addition to the responsibility to return profits to shareholders (Hiller, 2013). *Inclusive capitalism* (Lagarde, 2014; Robinson, 2013) entails economic growth with fewer inequalities and more integrity in the financial system. This is capitalism based on trust, opportunity, rewards for all within a market economy – allowing everyone's talents to flourish (Melé, 2016, p. 302).

John Mackey, Co-CEO of Whole Foods, wrote: "The world urgently needs a richer, more holistic, and more humanistic philosophy and narrative about business than the one we have encountered in economic textbooks, in business school teachings, and even from the mouths and pens of many prominent business leaders" (see Mackey & Sisodia, 2014, pp. 7–8).

Currently, the business world is still not 100% eco-friendly or environment friendly. In many countries, especially the rural areas, environmental degradation goes on unabated. Students of business and related studies, the corporate leaders of tomorrow, have therefore an extremely important role to play in building a more sustainable society (Robinson, 2014). Hence, almost all courses in the business curriculum must train students to understand and be sensitive to the environmental lens of sustainability, not only in terms of sustainability knowledge but also in terms of skills and models for formulating, designing, and implementing sustainability solutions throughout the company (e.g., see Molthan-Hill, 2014).[12]

---

[12]The Earth Charter proclaims:

> Humanity is part of a vast evolving universe. Earth, our home, is alive with a unique community of life. The forces of nature make existence a demanding and uncertain adventure, but Earth has provided the conditions essential to life's evolution. The resilience of the community of life and the well-being of humanity depends upon preserving a healthy biosphere with all its ecological systems, a rich variety of plants and animals, fertile soils, pure waters, and clean air. The global environment with its finite resources is a common concern of all peoples. The protection of Earth's vitality, diversity, and beauty is a sacred trust.

See The Earth Charter. Retrieved from https://earthcharter.org/read-the-earth-charter/?doing_wp_cron=1690654329.0914580821990966796875

Presumed Supremacy of US-Based FECS and Primacy of Technology

The capitalist world is making advances every day in its research and technology capabilities. It can technically produce almost anything. The moral and ethical questions now are: *Is it permissible to make everything we are capable of making? Is it permissible to market everything we are capable of marketing?* These two questions are very similar, and yet, they have different practical implications. Currently, several theories listed under Exhibit 1.1 influence our attitudes toward these questions:

Exhibit 1.1. Presumptuous Theories Defending Our Technological Supremacy.

- *Breakthrough theory*: Mankind will always achieve a technical breakthrough into all the problems that arise in its technical environment.
- *Balance-of-nature theory*: Human life and the life of our environment will always adjust to each other.
- *Neutrality theory*: Science and technology in themselves are ethics-neutral (or, amoral or trans-ethical) and must be freed from any ethical and moral impositions of a few, lest humanity's progress be impeded.
- *Self-limitation theory*: Our commitment to quality life and moral values imposes limits on human inquiry on the one hand and on technological progress on the other.
- *Creation theory*: Our universe and the world of humankind are created realities. The world and its nature should be left as God created it. Nature has been given a fixed form, and man and woman have their place in it. Humankind should not play God, nor displace or dispense God, nor try to take control of nature and thus author or alter its own destiny. We ought not to create a new humanity that intends to solve all the problems of nature.
- *Anthropocentric theory*: Humankind is the center of the universe; it has been given the task of shaping the world to its own ends. Manipulation of the world and its resources (which includes man himself) for the betterment and survival of mankind is not only a human right and duty but is essential for a better understanding and realization of human destiny.

Source: Compiled by the authors.

The first four theories are primarily philosophical; the last two are theological. The best way to approach these problems is through a holistic approach such as "integral humanism." Integral humanism stands to better the whole human system, body and spirit, mind and matter, individual and society, present and future, all ecosystems, all human beings, and the cosmos we live in. Integral humanism as applied to capitalist business implies a basic shift in values such as in Exhibit 1.2.

Exhibit 1.2. Attitudinal Changes to Defend Our Technological Supremacy.

- From "big is better" to "small is beautiful"
- From unscrupulous profiteering to equitable profit sharing
- From limitless possessions of a few to prosperity of the most
- From industrial concentration to wholesome competition to unraveling new markets
- From uncontrolled free trade to harmonizing global trade
- From total mastery over nature to sustainability of Mother Nature
- From the primacy of productivity to the primacy of human dignity
- From individual claim of rights to mutual duties toward human dignity and justice
- From work as bondage and duty to work as freedom and privilege
- From authoritarianism and dogmatism to participative "open society" management
- From centralization and uniformity to decentralization and diversity
- From individual aggrandizement to social betterment
- From unbridled individualism to a generous form of community
- From anthropocentrism to Nature-centrism or nonanthropocentrism
- From limitless production, distribution, and consumption (LPDC) to resourceful conservation and regeneration
- From total independence to healthy interdependence

Source: Compiled by the authors.

Critical Thinking Exercise 1.12

Apply critical thinking in assessing the presumptuous theories defending our technological supremacy listed in Exhibit 1.1 and the attitudinal changes required to defend our technological supremacy listed in Exhibit 1.2.

Concluding Remarks

The United States has favored FECS since its early beginnings. Adam Smith's seminal treatise, *Wealth of Nations* (1776), could have influenced this choice, and also John Locke's "Property" (1697). The list of conditions that constitute an ideal free market system has been given different forms (Buchanan, 1985; Hunt & Morgan, 1995). But among other things, it provides that:

- There shall be many sellers and buyers, none of whom has a dominant share of the market.
- All the sellers and buyers are in a position to enter or exit the market freely.
- All have complete information about the prices, quantities, and quality of goods placed in the market.
- The costs and benefits of production and the use of goods exchanged should fall entirely on those who buy or sell the goods, and not on outside third parties.

The first two conditions define "perfect competition" and the latter two define the "perfect market." All four combined constitute the free market method of organizing productive and distributive economic activity. It prescribes that the quantity of goods offered, and the prices attached to them will spontaneously tend toward a "point of market equilibrium" at which prices reflect: (a) the value that the consumers attach to goods they purchase and (b) the costs that sellers sustain in producing and marketing them. The above four conditions are the "positive" aspect of FECS. Critical thinking should search for the "normative." Are these four conditions verified in our market systems? If not verified, why not?

Given such ideal conditions, critical thinking should verify if various desirable outcomes and conditions of FECS or its ethical imperatives are realizable. Some of these imperatives are:

- *Teleological justice*: Each buyer or seller can maximize their own interest, thereby automatically producing an economic and social asset conducive to the common good of all and national prosperity.
- *Deontological justice*: The free market system (especially via conditions one and two) can safeguard as well as realize the rights of the individual freedom of all entrepreneurs involved.
- *Distributive justice*: In this way, the moral demand of equity and justice is also realized, more precisely as *commutative justice*, which prescribes that each participant in the exchange receives the exact equivalent, other things being equal, of what they give (Rawls, 1971).
- *Ecological justice*: Perfect competition strives on optimal efficiency of the productive system understood as the elimination of waste, and that producers will produce only those goods and services for which there is adequate and real market demand such that market gluts are avoided, superfluous needs are not created or fulfilled, and scarce resources are never wasted.

When these or similar ideal conditions of the ideal free market system are realized, critical thinking could pose even further concerns, such as, is FECS too ideological in that it systematically leaves the fundamental reality of our earth and society out of account? That is, the market mechanistic growth that the FECS presumes, abstracts from the physical conditions of our existence, the finitude of our natural resources, and from our real needs. Said differently, the market reacts to (often created) market demand, but not necessarily real needs. The natural conditions of human existence, namely, the consumption of energy and other resources, are external to the logic of the free market. That is, natural resources that are not produced by the free market are treated as though they are unlimited. In the current FECS, market economies that keep the classical promise of rationality of all actors and prosperity and freedom for all are almost nonexistent. FECS naïvely presupposes LPDC goals which are currently challenging ecological sustainability.

Operationally defined, the free market is seen as a privileged place for costless information access so that meaningful and informed economic decisions and exchanges may be brought about. While Adam Smith (1976) advocated a free market system, self-regulated by the "invisible hand," he also followed the administrative tradition in dealing with fiscal problems. Hence, Smith saw the economics of the free market system as a branch of moral philosophy and jurisprudence. (In fact, the original title of the *Wealth of Nations* was *An Inquiry into the Nature and Causes of the Wealth of Nations*.)

Corporate sustainability should consider every dimension of business operation, from supply chain to marketing in environmental, ethical, economic, social, and cultural spheres. It creates long-term values for all the involved stakeholders of that business activity, such as employees, clients, owners, community, consumers, and so on. It helps in developing strategies to build a company which adopts ethical and sustainable practices to create a positive impact on the environment and society. Meanwhile, the Paris Summit Agreement may inspire leaders of cities and companies to redouble their ecology and sustainability efforts. Firms such as Apple, Google, and Unilever are taking steps toward cutting their emissions by large amounts, as are some cities such as Hong Kong, London, and Rio de Janeiro.

Today, many people feel that a deep sense of ecological commitment has been awakened by observing how our planet is fragile and threatened. The effect of this observation of planetary fragility is not only a sentiment of responsibility but a call to act in a responsible way. In this transition from inner feeling to concrete ecological action, we need our rationality. We must conceptualize our intuition, make a trade-off between different aims, and allocate time and scarce means. What is clear is that a spiritual sense of responsibility must precede the stage of rational conceptualization and implementation.

Chapter 2

Critical Thinking Applied to Profit Maximization and Its Presumptive Capitalist Models

Executive Summary

In Chapter 1, we critically reviewed the foundations of the free enterprise capital system (FECS), which has been successful primarily because of its wealth and asset accumulation potentiality and actuality. In this chapter, we critically argue that this capacity has been grounded upon the profit maximization (PM) theories, models, and paradigms of FECS. The intent of this chapter is not anti-PM. The PM models of FECS have worked and performed well for more than 200 years of the economic history of the United States and other developed countries, and this phenomenon is celebrated and featured as "market performativity." However, market performativity has not truly benefitted the poor and the marginalized; on the contrary, market performativity has wittingly or unwittingly created gaping inequalities of wealth, income, opportunity, and prosperity. Critical thinking does not combat PM but challenges it with alternative models of profit sharing that promote social wealth, social welfare, social progress, and opportunity for all, which we explore here. Economic development without social progress breeds economic inequality and social injustice. Economic development alone is not enough; we should create a new paradigm in which economic development is the servant of social progress, not vice versa. Such a paradigm shift involves integrating the creativity and innovativity of market performativity and the goals and drives of social performativity together with PM, that is, from market performativity to social performativity.

Introduction

One of the world's leading business thinkers, Professor Michael Porter of the Harvard Business School, in a dialogue with social entrepreneurs and government innovators of the world, recently confessed (*Skoll World Forum*, 2015):

A Primer on Critical Thinking and Business Ethics, 31–64

Copyright © 2024 Oswald A. J. Mascarenhas, Munish Thakur and Payal Kumar

Published under exclusive licence by Emerald Publishing Limited

doi:10.1108/978-1-83753-312-120231002

> The last 50 years have been dominated by the idea that economic growth is the most direct route to better our lives for the world's expanding population. But the signs are everywhere – environmental destruction, inequality, injustice – that is, economic development alone is not enough. What is the framework for the next 50 years? We must create a new paradigm in which economic development is the servant of social progress, not vice versa.

Students, teachers, readers, and practitioners of business management should note this paradigm shift: economic development alone is not enough; it should be the *servant of social progress*. Economic development without social progress breeds economic inequality, social injustice, and popular unrest and hence regional and global unsustainability. This chapter explores this paradigm shift and strives to formulate some of its basic imperatives in conjunction with modified profit maximization (PM).

Many scholars have lamented lack of attention to social growth and social progress in management theory, research, and curriculum (e.g., Walsh et al., 2003). They lament an "eerie silence" in the management literature with respect to issues of human welfare and social progress and urge management scholars to "bring social welfare back in" to their research agenda, most importantly by integrating social and economic objectives (Walsh et al., 2003, pp. 860, 875). Two years later, the *Academy of Management Journal* (Shapiro & Rynes, 2005) published a special forum on organizational research in the public interest, again calling for more consideration of social welfare in organizational research. Some 10 years thereafter, a similar forum was held by the *Academy of Management Review* (AMR, 2016) presenting reasons why social welfare issues are so difficult to address in the context of current management theory (Jones et al., 2016), which summarized and concluded: "The assessment and measurement of social welfare and, by extension, the relationship of social welfare to management theory are not problems for which easy solutions are apparent" (p. 225).

Critical Thinking Exercise 2.1

Apply critical thinking (see footnote 3 in Chapter 1) to appreciate the following arguments that question profit or wealth maximization.

- The recent Rio Declaration (2012) claimed that for more than 100 years, management education has sought to support organizational leaders with the insight and know-how to create wealth through helping people improve their quality of life. This claim confounds ends and means. Rather than the end goal being improved quality of life with the means of wealth creation, the priority is on creating wealth through improving quality of life. The former may not necessarily ensure the latter.

(Continued)

- This subjugation of societal welfare to individual business profits jettisons social and environmental considerations when they conflict with the financial interest of business organizations (Brooks, 2010). For instance, prioritization of shareholder wealth maximization imposes costs upon society, such as global warming and pollution, which are felt by all.
- Similarly, maximizing shareholder benefits that cut costs also engages in manufacturers cutting corners on safety, with factories polluting rivers and oceans, and banks making large profits with high-risk investments that negatively affect the world's poor.
- Agency theory (Jensen & Meckling, 1976; Williamson, 1975) assumes that managers are self-interested, and unless richly incentivized, will put their needs before those of the shareholders. Such beliefs about human nature soon become enshrined in theories and institutions, which then perpetuate themselves through the double hermeneutic to become self-fulfilling (Ghoshal, 2005).
- Not only do such beliefs help normalize self-interest as acceptable or even desirable (Miller, 1999), they help justify unethical behavior through the common rationalization that "everybody does it" (Green, 1991).
- Businesses are seen as stewards of society's economic resources or as self-interested organizations with a legal duty to maximize profits. Ghoshal (2005) argues that these contextual assumptions are self-fulfilling and self-serving and play a crucial role in unethical management behavior.
- Research also indicates that teaching a utility-maximizing model of human behavior draws students to behave according to this model and reinforces such behaviors (Frank et al., 1993; Frey & Meier, 2005).
- Management scholars consider the field of management itself irrelevant (Cabantous & Gond, 2011; Ferraro et al., 2005; Kieser et al., 2015; Marti & Scherer, 2016). Its overemphasis on PM to the utter neglect of social relevance and social development is counterproductive and creates social inequalities.
- It has contributed significantly to corporate scandals, fraud, corruption, and money laundering in all forms, thus increasing the gap between the rich and the poor (e.g., Abrahamson et al., 2016; Callon, 2007; Garcia-Parpet, 2007; Inman, 2013, 2014; Jones et al., 2016; MacKenzie, 2007; Marti & Scherer, 2016; Walsh et al., 2003).
- Seemingly, traditional management theory and business curriculum, if unexamined critically and not redesigned in time, may continue to produce "bad" leadership while training management graduates who will continue to get embroiled in global scandals, similar to what occurred over the last two to three decades (Orr, 1990).
- Indeed, many of the scandals and corporate collapses associated with the 2008 financial crisis has been traced to "bad" leadership (Furnham, 2010; Orr, 1990). One aspect of this bad leadership relates to the way we train

(Continued)

(*Continued*)

and develop leaders and the role that business schools play in this process (Higgs, 2012; Mintzberg, 2004).

• The apparent focus on data and knowledge as opposed to wisdom and social development is suggested by several scholars to account for the poor performance of several knowledge information intensive management initiatives (Ackoff, 1988; Bierly et al., 2000; Ghoshal, 2005; Ghoshal & Moran, 1996; Jashapara, 2005; Sternberg, 1998, 2001, 2003). Rowley (2006) highlights the benefits of wisdom in terms of enhancing management theory and practice.

Major Criticism Against Management Theory and Research

Summarizing major criticisms against the current management concept – theory and paradigm – driven by PM, we note the following critical observations.

Critical Thinking Exercise 2.2

Apply critical thinking (see footnote 3 in Chapter 1) to incorporate the following major criticisms against prevalent business management theory advocated in business school curricula. Check also which criticisms support or denounce PM.

• Traditional management theory is based on a flawed methodology: management theory applies a scientific method designed for use with physical sciences to a social science (Hayek, 1989).
• Hence, economists have tended to focus on factors that are amenable to measurement and disregard as irrelevant factors that are by their nature difficult to quantify; we should be skeptical of assertions that appear to be scientific simply because they have been based on mathematical models and scientific methods, as they are false knowledge based on unsound foundations (Hayek, 1989).
• Inappropriate adoption of objective, quantitative "scientific" modes of explanation take a deterministic perspective that ignores subjective mental phenomena such as deliberation, intentionality, and commitment; the preference for scientific explanations and quantifiable criteria also accounts for the excessive focus on shareholder rights over those of other competing stakeholders (Ghoshal, 2005).
• Further, such causal modes of explanation self-servingly adopt pessimistic assumptions about human nature that assert all behavior is based on self-interest (Ghoshal, 2005), and management science and discipline

(*Continued*)

assume and rationalize self-interest as the business "norm" and ignore as irrelevant values and behavior that do not conform to these assumptions (Ghoshal, 2005; Ghoshal & Moran, 1996).

- These "norms" perpetuate as theories (e.g., agency theory) as they easily become self-serving and self-fulfilling (Ferraro et al., 2005).
- The use of management devices (e.g., net present value (NPV), internal rate of return (IRR), return on investment (ROI), return on assets (ROA), and its subsets, return on invested capital (ROIC), return on capital employed (ROCE), or return on market value of equity (ROMA)) have not been useful for the world of social development; instead, they have served as a self-fulfilling prophecy benefitting the privileged few trained and educated in those finance models (Ferraro et al., 2005).
- This culture of self-interest in finance or financial economics has been a key factor in the spate of economic collapses over the last century (Baden & Higgs, 2015, p. 546; Rajan, 2010; Rajan & Zingales, 2003; Werner, 2012).
- We need to distinguish "objective" data from useful knowledge (Hayek, 1989). It is wiser to pursue incomplete, messy, contextualized, uncertain knowledge that enriches our understanding of how to promote social and cosmic sustainability than to amass lots of clean data that is easy to manipulate and present, and yet is based on false assumptions (Baden & Higgs, 2015, p. 541).
- Both financial and nonfinancial firms contribute to rising top incomes by paying ever larger compensations to their executives (Atkinson et al., 2011; Cobb, 2016). Management theory, under the formality of "executive compensation" has rationalized, theorized, and justified this process. As Piketty (2014) noted, as these increase, they cause rising income inequality.
- The growing use of rational management techniques would enact a world in which employees' intrinsic motivation decreased and extrinsic motivation increased (Abrahamson, 1997; Abrahamson & Eisenman, 2008).
- As a result of all these factors, management theory has steadily over-emphasized PM, to the utter neglect of social relevance and social development; accordingly, it has contributed significantly to corporate scandals, fraud, corruption, and money-laundering in all forms, thus increasing the gap between the rich and the poor (e.g., Abrahamson et al., 2016; Callon, 2007; Jones et al., 2016).

In this context, we must ask: Does our current management theory, research, and practice – which emphasize PM – ensure human dignity, assure social progress and development, sustain planetary ecology, and support cosmic sustainability, and the like which they should be concerned about? Does the management discipline produce the type of wise, ethical, moral, and spiritual leadership that our world needs? We address these questions in the following sections, and explore the potential of wisdom that transcends data, devices, theories, and models in reorientating management theory to go beyond profit and shareholder wealth maximization to focus also on social progress and development, leading to planetary ecology and cosmic sustainability.

Inclusive capitalism, which we touched upon in Chapter 1, maintains that political accountability in contributing to poverty is limited to not doing enough to encourage private enterprise (a) to create more jobs for low-income people; (b) to allow poor people access to financial capital for entrepreneurialism, (c) to enable poor people the opportunity to purchase a variety of goods and services. No consideration, however, is given to governments and companies that benefit from having low-income and poorly educated populations who provide necessary underpaid labor.

The major refocus of the existing management thought, theory, and research should minimally include considerations of ensuring human dignity, currently deprived to over a quarter of the global population living in extreme poverty, redefine our current gross domestic product (GDP) to include, besides economic progress, factors and areas that will empower social progress and development, and above all, enable currently badly jeopardized planetary ecology and global sustainability.

Our critical thinking challenge is to address these criticisms and move forward. What do we carry forward into the new business management science and curriculum, and what do we leave behind, and at what at cost or benefit to all stakeholders?

Narrow Self-Interest (NSI)

NSI is a decision-making style in corporations conditioned on a single-value objective, such as PM. Jensen (2002, p. 237) argues that "any organization *must have a single-valued objective as a precursor to purposeful or rational behavior*" [emphasis added]. Accordingly, Jensen (2002, p. 237) maintains that a multiple-objective view, "while not totally without content, is fundamentally flawed because it violates the proposition that any organization must have a single-valued objective as a precursor to purposeful or rational behavior" (Jensen, 2002, p. 237). Jones and Felps (2013b, p. 352) also hold that corporate action requires a "singled-valued objective . . . that allows managers to make principled choices among policy alternatives." Sundaram and Inkpen (2004) also affirm the single-valued objective as necessary for effective corporate decision-making.

However, analyzed from a critical thinking point of view, single-objective views are close in form to monistic views of value. A value monist claims that there is one basic value, good, or principle to be sought or followed, while the value pluralist argues for multiple basic and irreducible values. The pluralist (in contrast to the monist) argues that multiple moral considerations (as in multitasking) might be independently (i.e., nonderivatively, *see* Arnold et al., 2010) relevant to the moral status of an action or state of affairs. That is, multiple considerations might be relevant, apart from whether they serve as instrumental means toward the fulfillment of some single end and instead merit consideration on their own terms. That is, these views treat shareholder wealth maximization (SWM) as fundamentally unitary (e.g., as preference satisfaction or as happiness) and similarly treat corporations as having a single objective that either directly (e.g., stakeholder happiness) or indirectly (e.g., preference satisfaction by means of SWM) contributes to that social outcome.

Seemingly, the argument over monistic versus pluralist values is over foundational matters; there is no dispute between value monists and value pluralists that a variety of different human practices might contribute to the same foundational value outcome. For example, if happiness is the fundamental human value, there can be many actions and social systems that contribute to happiness. However, Mitchell et al. (2016) argue the tenability of the single-objective idea as the basis for circumscribing the foundational goals to which a corporation might be committed, with the aim of legitimating the possibility of a multi-objective corporation. Critical thinking agrees that a happy blend of monist and pluralist value strategies can achieve a composite outcome. Moreover, PM even as a monist value can be combined with profit-sharing pluralist values. That is, there is no a fortiori or intrinsic necessity that the single monist value objective be PM. It smacks of self-serving bias of self-interest or self-aggrandizement.

Management theory in general and each subdiscipline in particular (e.g., human resources management, marketing, finance, production, or strategy) are thus designed and developed to enhance the (self-interested) financial bottom line of organizations. However, there is limited understanding of how implementation or overuse of certain business practices may have sustainable and unsustainable impacts on organizational outcomes and stakeholders (e.g., employees, their families, and communities; on suppliers and distributors; on customers and their families) and the environment. Recently, an emerging research trend, sustainable human resources management, explores business practices about enhancing both PM for the organization and simultaneously minimizing the unsustainable impacts on human/social and environment sustainability based on a paradox perspective (e.g., Chiva & Alegre, 2005; Kramar, 2014; Mariappanadar, 2003, 2012, 2014; Mariappanadar & Aust, 2018; Mariappanadar & Kramar, 2014).

Critical Thinking Exercise 2.3

Apply critical thinking (see footnote 3 in Chapter 1) to the monist theory that seemingly sustains PM, allowing no competing alternative single values.

- "Any organization *must have a single-valued objective as a precursor to purposeful or rational behavior*" [emphasis added] (Jensen, 2002, p. 237). This assertion is not proved either theoretically or empirically, nor that is it a necessary or sufficient condition for maximization of revenues or minimization of costs.
- Corporate action requires a "singled-valued objective … that allows managers to make principled choices among policy alternatives" (Jones & Felps, 2013b, p. 352).
- The pluralist (in contrast to the monist) argues that multiple moral considerations might be independently (i.e., nonderivatively; Arnold et al., 2010) pursued relevant to the moral status of an action or state of affairs. That is, multiple considerations might be relevant, apart from whether they serve as instrumental means toward fulfilling some single end and instead merit consideration on their own terms.
- There is no dispute between value monists and value pluralists that a variety of different human practices might contribute to the same foundational value outcome. For example, as observed earlier, if happiness is the fundamental human value, there can be many actions and social systems that contribute to happiness.
- The single-objective idea as the basis for circumscribing the foundational goals to which a corporation might be committed, with the aim of legitimating the possibility of a multi-objective corporation, is tenable (Mitchell et al., 2016).
- Corporations could simultaneously seek PM with promotion of social progress and betterment of social welfare under a generalized monist objective.
- Management scholars and students can "bring social welfare back in" to their research agendas by integrating social and economic objectives (Walsh et al., 2003, pp. 860, 875).

Transactional Economics Versus Relational Economics

PM is conditioned by and thrives on transactional economics that maximizes margins on each transaction. Margin economics operates by: (a) increasing price (making goods less affordable, more elitist, and more exclusive of the greater numbers of the marginalized) and (b) decreasing costs (e.g., downsizing, relocation, domestic and offshore outsourcing, massive layoffs), thus (c) creating and impoverishing the unemployed or underemployed classes, who are not necessarily contributing to social progress, social wealth creation, and social development (Bosse & Phillips, 2016; Bosse et al., 2009; Bridoux & Stoelhorst, 2014; Freeman et al., 2010).

Bridoux and Stoelhorst (2016) suggest relational economics in the place of pure transactional economics. They suggest four models of relational economics in this regard: (a) *market pricing* (a relationship where people compute cost–benefit ratios and pursue their self-interest), which is the presumed primary focus of economic theory, (b) *communal sharing* (people can also frame relationships of unity, community, and collective identity), (c) *authority ranking* (a relationship of hierarchical differences accompanied by the exercise of command and complementary display of deference and respect), or (d) *equality matching* (a relationship among equals manifested in balanced reciprocity) (Fiske, 1991; Sawhney & Zabin, 2002).

Accordingly, Bridoux and Stoelhorst (2016) share two predictive hypotheses on relational economics. First, contributions to joint value creation depend on how individual stakeholders frame their relationships with other participants in the value creation process and in relation to the four relational models from market pricing to authority ranking, equality matching, and communal sharing. Second, depending on their social dispositions (such as trait-like differences in preferences for distributions of outcomes to self and others in interdependent situations), individuals will be differently predisposed toward adopting one of the four relational models, yet regardless of their dispositions, all individuals are capable of framing relationships in terms of any of the four models if situational cues are strong enough.

Together, these predictions point to an important role for managers in contributing to social welfare by fostering cooperative stakeholder relationships that are not based on market pricing. In line with stakeholder theorists' emphasis on building cooperative relationships (Freeman, 1984; Freeman et al., 2010; Jones & Wicks, 1999; Phillips, 2003; Post et al., 2002), this theory of relational economics suggests that social welfare is better served by stakeholder relations based on authority ranking, equality matching, and, especially, communal sharing.

PM Within Relational Economics

Since PM is basically a strategy (with no normative content other than mono-valued pursuit) and an algorithmic procedure, it can be framed within the four relational economics models of market pricing, communal sharing, authority ranking, and equality matching proposed by Bridoux and Stoelhorst (2016), we propose to include all four relational models together with their two predictive hypotheses stated above that seem to include the best from both transactional and relational economics. Further, going beyond instrumental stakeholder theory that is built on the traditional dichotomy of a "transactional" approach that emphasizes self-interest and financial incentives, Bridoux and Stoelhorst (2016) propose a broadly defined, stakeholder-oriented "relational" approach based on compassion, honesty, integrity, and kindness (e.g., Bosse et al., 2009; Harrison et al., 2010; Jones, 1995; Jones & Felps, 2013a, 2013b; Mahoney et al., 1994).

According to the theory of relational models (Fiske, 1991, 1992, 2004, 2012; Fiske & Haslam, 2005; Haslam, 2004), communal sharing is characterized by a fusion of the self with the community, which means that the community identity is psychologically salient, while the personal identity is pushed to the background. All four relational models of Bridoux and Stoelhorst (2016) that invite broader social interest also propose a broadly defined, stakeholder-oriented "relational" approach based on compassion, honesty, integrity, and kindness (e.g., Bosse et al., 2009; Harrison et al., 2010; Jones, 1995; Jones & Felps, 2013a, 2013b; Mahoney et al., 1994). Consequently, actors adopting a community sharing frame see themselves and their relational partners as community members who are equivalent and undifferentiated and who share motivations and goals. Actors are motivated to contribute altruistically (i.e., regardless of personal rewards) to the achievement of these common goals.

The four relational models uphold profitability that leads to prosperity for all (Griffin, 2004; Griffin & Mahon, 1997). They are "building blocks from which very rich and complex relationships are formed" (Sheppard & Tuchinsky, 1996a, p. 365), and they operate at all levels of social interactions, from dyadic interactions among individuals to organization of linkages between groups to formulation of public policies at the societal level (Fiske & Haslam, 2005). The theory of relational models holds that these four models suffice to generate very high diversity in social relationships observed in practice since (a) actors may relate in different ways when interacting in different domains of their relationship, which generates variety across relationships (Fiske, 1991, 2004, 2012; Fiske & Haslam, 2005), and (b) the cultural context (i.e., ethnic, national, organizational, etc.) determines the exact implementation rules of the relational models, i.e., when, how, and with whom to implement, and an actor in each relational model must have a shared understanding of what is the proper interval between receiving and giving in return (Fiske, 1991, 2004).

Critical Thinking Exercise 2.4

Apply critical thinking (see footnote 3 in Chapter 1) to *transactional economics* versus *relational economics* as alternatives justifications of PM allowing and enabling FECS.

- Assess the merits of each theory in terms of corporate and welfare trade-offs.
- Is margin economics worse than PM in terms of their effects on people, welfare, and poverty? Why? What can critical thinking do about it?
- Discuss the potential and feasibility of the relations model to tame PM or challenge it with a more humanizing and egalitarian alternative.

Other More Promising Alternatives to PM

In general, PM implies two supplementary strategies: cost containment and revenue enhancement. The former may directly impact society and social welfare if cost cutting involves divestitures, factory closings, domestic or offshore outsourcing, automation, mechanization, and hence, massive labor layoffs or displacement or early retirement. The latter could be socially harmful if it implies aggressive strategies such as exorbitant pricing, excessive margins, price collusions, drug cartels, killing competition, creating artificial shortages, ghetto over-pricing (e.g., Andreasen, 1975, 1982), and other market entry barriers, such as domestic or international dumping. On the other hand, if revenue generation is achieved by introducing and designing creative and innovative new products and services that serve customer needs, wants, and desires, then it may enable wealth maximization for the firm and its shareholders, and indirectly, larger groups of stakeholders (such as employees, customers, suppliers, distributors, local communities) may also benefit.

If both cost containment and revenue generation strategies occur while ignoring the competition by creating new markets (Kim & Mauborgne, 2004), then the prospect of social progress and development may be even better. There are exemplary companies today that focus on social progress and national development while seeking profits (e.g., the Tata Group, Levi Strauss, and Whole Foods, as described in Bollier, 1997; Casey, 2014; Mackey & Sisodia, 2014). If both strategies, cost containment and revenue generation, on the other hand, ignore critical social issues created such as increasing the income gap between the rich and the poor (top management and blue-collar workers), and eventually contributing to poverty, social instability, and structures of social injustice, then PM is deleterious to society, as the current market experience confirms.

However, even if this causal sequence is true and dangerous, it does not necessarily convince (or convert) corporate executives as to why they should be implicated in these issues or be involved in social progress and social development. Moreover, the latter social issues are too equivocal and ambiguous to be included among the productive and normative goals of the corporation. For instance, management literature has studied some means of PM and shareholder wealth creation that led to negative social externalities such as forced product obsolescence and consumer lifestyles (e.g., Abrahamson & Eisenman, 2008; Abrahamson & Fairchild, 1999), disadvantaging the poor (e.g., Andreasen, 1975, 1982), high frequency trading (e.g., Angel & McCabe, 2013; Gomber et al., 2011; MacKenzie, 2015), underpaying employees or structuring employee relationships (e.g., Cobb, 2016), and monopolistic competition (Dixit & Stiglitz, 1977). Hence, corporations feel morally obliged to maximize profits for shareholders, while legitimately focusing on cost containment and revenue enhancement and wealth creation – these may indirectly contain and alleviate poverty and increase social welfare.

In this context, alternatives to PM are "honest profits" (Baumhart, 1968), profit seeking (Drèze, 2019), profit redistribution to weaker economies (Sen, 1992, 1997, 2009), profit sharing to uplift societies totally ignored by profit maximizers

(Stiglitz, 2015), communal sharing and social wealth creation (Bridoux & Stoel-horst, 2016), or profitability that leads to prosperity for all (Griffin, 2004; Griffin & Mahon, 1997). During the past 50 years or more, we have unwittingly developed management theory, research, and practice primarily in relation to PM and shareholder wealth creation. We must now focus on other alternative goals that also ensure human dignity, social progress and development, planetary ecology and cosmic sustainability – all of which have been grossly neglected by typical management theory and business school PM-driven curricula.

Critical Thinking Exercise 2.5

Apply critical thinking (see footnote 3 in Chapter 1) to assess the following more promising alternatives to PM: honest profits, profit seeking, profit redistribution to weaker economies, profit sharing to uplift societies totally ignored by profit maximizers, communal sharing and social wealth creation, or profitability that leads to prosperity for all.

Management scholars and critics have also suggested several means we can use to voluntarily restrain PM. We can interpret and classify them using the concept of "justice." Critical thinking can establish their urgent need and relevance. All or any of these alternate models to PM should be accorded serious management attention.

Critical Thinking Exercise 2.6

Apply critical thinking (see footnote 3 in Chapter 1) to assess the following alternatives to PM proposed by academic scholars.

Distributive justice–related alternatives to PM:

• Striving for honest profits (Baumhart, 1968);
• Seeking social stability and social justice (Habermas, 1971);
• Seeking justice (Habermas, 1998, 2003; Miller, 1999; Nussbaum, 1992; Rawls, 1971; Sen, 2009);
• Being more thoughtful and conscious about others (Barrell, 1995; Mackey & Sisodia, 2014).

Social justice–related alternatives to PM:

• Controlling exaggerated individualism (Bellah et al., 1985, 1991);

(*Continued*)

- Seeking fairness and reciprocity (Fehr & Gächter, 2000; Kahneman et al., 1986);
- Humanizing consumption (Mascarenhas, 1988a, 1988b);
- Being creative and innovative to serve the bottom of the pyramid (Chandy & Tellis, 1998, 2000; Christensen et al., 2006, 2009; Deming, 1994; Hamel & Prahalad, 1994; Neumeier, 2009; Prahalad, 2004).

Responsible justice–related alternatives to PM:

- Responsible capitalism (Rajan, 2010; Rajan & Zingales, 1998, 2003; Scherer & Palazzo, 2007, 2011; Sonenshein, 2014; Sonenshein et al., 2014);
- Responsible marketing (Mascarenhas, 1995, 2008, 2018; Mascarenhas et al., 2004, 2005c; Vann & Kumcu, 1995);
- Seeking profits and prosperity (Griffin, 2004, 2016; Griffin & Mahon, 1997);
- Seeking sense and solidarity (Drèze, 2019);
- Learning from our inevitable "mistakes" on the journey to developing the management discipline (Schoemaker & Gunther, 2006).

Sustainability justice-related alternatives to PM:

- Greening GDP and seeking sustainability (e.g., Boyd, 2007; Gladwin et al., 1995; Jones & Freeman, 2013; Lourenço, 2013; Shrivastava, 2010);
- Seeking sustainable human resources development (Mariappanadar, 2003, 2012, 2014, 2016; Mariappanadar & Aust, 2018; Mariappanadar & Kramar, 2014).

Stakeholder justice–related alternatives to PM:

- Responsible stewardship (e.g., Davis et al., 1997);
- Responsible stakeholdership (Freeman, 1984; Jones, 1995; Jones et al., 2007; Jones & Wicks, 1999);
- Seeking stakeholder happiness (e.g., Jones & Felps, 2013b).

Welfare justice–related alternatives to PM:

- Developing and exercising authentic servant leadership (e.g., Greenleaf, 2002; Luthans & Avolio, 2003);
- Seeking social welfare (e.g., Jones et al., 2016; Marti & Scherer, 2016; Mitchell et al., 2016; Sonenshein et al., 2014);
- Value sharing and sharing wealth creation (Porter & Kramer, 2011; Prahalad, 2004; Priem, 2007).

Happiness justice–related alternatives to PM:

- Seeking better meaning (e.g., Frankel, 1968; Sedlacek, 2011; Seidman, 2012; Selnes & Sallis, 2003);

(*Continued*)

(Continued)

- Seeking wisdom (e.g., Ackoff, 1988; Schoemaker & Gunther, 2006; Sternberg, 1998, 2001, 2003);
- Seeking change and strategic change management (e.g., Kotter, 1996, 2007; Porter, 1996; Sonenshein, 2005, 2006, 2007, 2009);
- Aiming higher and seeking greatness (Bollier, 1997; Collins, 1998; Covey, 2004);
- Striving for happiness (e.g., Graham & Pettinato, 2001; Layard, 2011);
- Seeking spiritual intelligence (Zohar & Marshall, 2000, 2004);
- Seeking spirituality and sustainability (e.g., Bouckaert, 2015; Bouckaert & Zsolnai, 2007, 2011; Dhiman & Marques, 2016; Karakas, 2010; Mitroff, 2016; Pruzan, 2011, 2014, 2015a, 2015b; Zsolnai, 2015).

Modelling PM

In the simplest, one variable, linear profit growth model, we assume that:

$$\text{Profit } \pi = V(p - c) - FC \qquad\qquad 2.0$$

(where "c" is unit variable cost and "p" is unit variable price at which market clears with "V" units sold in a given period, given that V units were produced with total fixed costs "FC" and total variable costs "pc" and profit margin "$(p - c)$."

If we assume that at breakeven point all profits are just about absorbed by costs, that is, profit $\pi = 0$ or Eq. (2.0) is $= 0$, then solving Eq. (2.0) $= 0$ for c, p, V, and FC, we have:

$$\text{Breakeven price (BEP) is } [(FC/V) + c] \qquad\qquad 2.1$$

$$\text{Breakeven cost (BEC) is } [p - (FC/V)] \qquad\qquad 2.2$$

$$\text{Breakeven volume (BEV) is } [(FC/(p - c)] \qquad\qquad 2.3$$

$$\text{Breakeven fixed costs (BEFC) is } [V(p - c)] \qquad\qquad 2.4$$

Each breakeven point serves as a PM model. However, Eqs. (2.1–2.4) are profit-maximizing models with questionable moral inputs or outputs. That is, any means of increasing p, reducing c, increasing V, and reducing FC (all PM models) is economically or morally not *ipso facto* justified.

Any revenue beyond BEP, BEV, or BEFC, or below BEC, is profit that can be maximized. For instance, reducing breakeven points, especially BEC or BEV or BEFC is an efficient (if not effective and moral) PM tool that can eventually lead to wealth maximization. Much would depend upon a corporation's capacity to manipulate c, p, FC, or V. For instance, reducing FC, e.g., via government's socialist public policy of owning production property and charging no or low rent or fee for its use, a phenomenon quite common in socialist countries such as

China and North Korea, which gives them undue advantage for competing in the free-market zones of World Trading Organization (WTO) markets.[1] Reducing BEP is a double-edge strategy: it hastens profits by anticipating and exploiting bottom lines and lowers breakeven price points, providing strategic leverage to reduce price further to win more customers and market shares.

Traditional basic models of PM include (a) revenue maximization, (b) cost minimization, and (c) margin maximization. Each model has developed several versions, as sketched in Table 2.1.

Performativity of Markets

Does management theory influence and shape social reality as much as it does market and financial reality? In recent years, management researchers (e.g., Ferraro et al., 2005) and sociologists (e.g., Callon, 2007) have analyzed how management theories in general, and economic theories and financial economics theories in particular, have shaped or "performed" the markets in the right direction.

In particular, MacKenzie et al. (2007) published a volume of influential articles in their edited book, *Do Economists Make Markets? On the Performativity of Economics*, which has provoked and re-evoked the question of relevance of economics, financial economics in particular, and indirectly, that of management theory. Some critics affirm the market "performativity" thesis that economics, financial economics, and management theory as advocated by top business schools have indeed performed the markets (e.g., Ferraro et al., 2005; MacKenzie, 2006). Other scholars propose the "counter-performativity" thesis (e.g., Porter & McKibbin, 1988, p. 173), while others have stood neutral. Researchers have also pointed out that performativity theories can have a positive impact on social welfare (Ghoshal, 2005; Ghoshal & Moran, 1996; Porter & McKibbin, 1988).

For example, Ferraro et al. (2005) described three mechanisms through which theories shape social reality: (a) theories influence institutional designs, (b) theories transform social norms of individual behavior, and (c) theories offer a language that influences how individuals see the world. Similarly, Callon's (2007) thesis is that the theories, devices, techniques, and models of management science have been useful for interpreting and predicting and even transforming empirical regularities, in a way that confirms these devices and the predictions of this science. In particular, Callon (2007) argues that the widespread diffusion of the use of Black and Scholes (option-pricing) model (BSM) has transformed the price of options. Social science theories contribute to the social construction of reality.

---

[1]This strategy is especially used currently in government subsidizing of steel and agricultural commodity markets, as in China. It is a form of government strategy for public subsidy for entering, staying, and thriving in international markets. Such subsidies can lower FC to such an extent that countries can offer unit prices well below international breakeven points, enabling a phenomenon also called *international dumping* (which is illegal in the United States). The current United States–China trade war might be fueled by such subsidies.

Table 2.1. Critical Analysis of Profit Maximization (PM) Models.

Basic PM Models	PM Applied to:			Critical Thinking Mandates
	Input Operations	Process Operations	Output Operations	
Revenue maximization	Price increasing for PM must be tempered by customer affordability and loyalty. Exorbitant pricing of luxury products is morally permissible when exclusive markets bear them without creating exclusive signature markets that reinforce income or talent or market inequality. Similarly, wage decreasing for PM, when imposed, should compensate victims for the social harm created. Revenue increasing via increased rental fees, lease rates, high-interest rates, high counseling fees, charging high maintenance fees (e.g.,	Inducing high market capitalization (via hyping IPOs or collusive oversubscribing or undersubscribing shares) should be executed without excessive frequency trading or undue sharking, or undue speculation. Minimizing cutting costs via corporate tax evasion, tax dodging, or claiming high tax exemptions are dubious morally, even if not illegal, as these disaffect infrastructure and nation-building. Avoid risks and costs of fraud, bribery, deception, and money-laundering, howsoever, gainful or aiding in wealth accumulation.	Decreasing labor costs via divestitures or mergers and acquisitions, or via factory closings, labor displacement, labor relocation, downsizing and right-sizing, and the like should proportionately enrich worker climate, worker development and welfare, and reduce worker malaise, and labor union apathy. PM through improving labor bonding, forming labor communities, worker creativity, and intrapreneurship should be encouraged as win–win strategies.	All means of PM must be ethically justified by distributive and proportionality justice conditions, not vice versa. When market abuses result, corrective justice should be invoked to remediate immediately. Any PM strategy adopted should be justified by social justice (informed by social progress and development, peace, harmony, labor solidarity), and by social externalities. Any means that promote PM should not only avoid anthropocentrism, but positively be equalizing, leveling, sustainable, and humanizing.

energy and supply logistics costs, insurance costs, parking fees, waiting costs, storage fees, high equipment costs, and the like), is justified if properly balanced by enhancing welfare.

| Cost minimization (CM) | CM via reducing workers' rest and leisure, vacation and bonuses; promotion and awards, especially when workers are entitled to them, is a serious violation of employee justice. CM via reducing FC for lower maintenance costs, reducing worker-safety costs, and worker healthcare costs compromises worker safety by preventing and protecting from work-related diseases, and reduces worker welfare. | CM realized via reducing labor through outsourcing, off-shoring, automating (mechanizing) labor; reducing wages via downsizing, right-sizing, labor relocation to low-wage zones (see Maquiladora auto-parts companies along cities in the United States–Mexico border), i.e., reducing labor costs via globalization and massive layoffs are unjust (see last column). | Cost cutting via increasing unemployment or underemployment, reducing wages via forced early retirement, increasing contractual labor while reducing permanent labor, reducing medical and health insurance coverage, reducing worker satisfaction and fulfillment – all these are questionable means, which hurt labor. | All these means are instrumentally unjust, they serve only management with no compensation to labor or welfare, and such practices widen income and social inequality gaps, eventually leading to poverty and social violence, structured social injustice, and even totalitarianism. |

(Continued)

Table 2.1. (*Continued*)

Basic PM Models	PM Applied to: Input Operations	Process Operations	Output Operations	Critical Thinking Mandates
Margin $(p - c)$ Optimization	Net margin boosters should enhance long-term worker development, enrichment, and worker cooperation strategies.[2] Increasing margins while lowering (FC/V) is a margin-boosting strategy; moreover, if V increases faster than FC, it becomes a market-booster strategy if margin $(p - c)$ increases. Margin boosters as increasing FC alone are good if they result in promoting development for all via developing infrastructure that increases the quality of life for all, e.g., creating	Net margin increases can be brought about via negotiations, arbitrations, mediations, collective bargaining, labor unionization with capacities for higher worker training, skill update, and efficiency, worker–team transformation, and the like. Such transformations are regular features among labor in the United States and other Western or developed EU countries.	Net margin increases via pollution-free, environmental sustainability and cosmic regeneration, restoration, and cradle-to-cradle product development. These should be explored by creative environmental entrepreneurship. Margin boosting streamlined for better developmental outputs for all should be a requirement for all production and labor policies such that they ensure planet-wise development that lifts all.	All net margin boosters should *ipso facto* promote general development directly and not only indirectly via welfare. General development should boost the environment via greening, nature regeneration via reforestation, species preservation, biodiversity conservation, zero pollution, and other sustainability measures. It is a win-win strategy for all stakeholders.

newer and better
industries that radically
improve job markets that
increase incomes for all
rich and poor alike.

Thus, margin boosting
eventually reduces income
inequalities and enhances
democracy and quality
life for all.

Source: Compiled by the authors.

[2]Given Eq. (2.0) and solving for margin $(p − c)$ at breakeven point (i.e., profit = 0), net margin boosters are: (a) when FC increase, (b) when V decreases, or (c) when (FC/V) increases. All three are feasible, especially alternative (c), when [FC/V] decreases, which is challenging and is followed in the last row of Table 2.1.

Evaluating the "performativity" of each of these financial techniques, Callon (2007) concluded that the use of these techniques by financial or business practitioners did not change financial markets (e.g., in making better choices), but possibly made them more opaque and nontransparent, and later, fraudulent and corruption prone.

The "performativity" thesis is that business economics and management theory have indeed developed and performed the markets (Ferraro et al., 2005; MacKenzie, 2006), and the "counter-performativity" thesis that they have not performed nor developed the markets evenly (e.g., Ghoshal, 2005; Ghoshal & Moran, 1996; Porter & McKibbin, 1988, p. 173). We propose a *golden mean* between these extreme positions which we call "social performativity" of the markets, and that all business stakeholders should emphasize human dignity, social progress, social development, planetary ecology, and cosmic sustainability – as equally worthy and desirable bottom lines (as profits and growth) for market performativity, management theory, research, pedagogy, and practice.

Capitalism, or more precisely, FECS, is arguably the most effective way that human beings have found to organize production, distribution, and consumption. While free markets, particularly free financial markets, expand peoples' cash holdings, they have made surprisingly little inroads into their hearts and minds. Financial markets are among the most highly criticized and least understood parts of the capitalist system. The behavior of those involved in scandals like the collapse of Enron and the creation of October 2008 financial crisis only solidifies the public conviction that these markets are simply tools of the rich to get richer at the expense of the general public.

Critical Thinking Exercise 2.7

Apply critical thinking (see footnote 3 in Chapter 1) to assess the thesis of market performativity as arguably justifying PM.

- The market "performativity" thesis maintains that economics, especially financial economics and management theory as advocated by top business schools, have indeed performed the markets (e.g., Ferraro et al., 2005; MacKenzie, 2006). Other scholars, however, propose the "counter-performativity" thesis (e.g., Porter & McKibbin, 1988, p. 173), while others have stood neutral.
- Researchers have also pointed out the negative consequences that performative theories can have on social welfare (Ghoshal, 2005; Ghoshal & Moran, 1996; Porter & McKibbin, 1988).
- Yet, one could argue, that just, healthy, and competitive financial markets are an extraordinarily effective tool in spreading opportunity and fighting poverty. Because of their role in creatively developing and financing new ideas, concepts, products and brands, financial markets keep alive the process of "creative destruction" – whereby old ideas and organizations are constantly challenged and replaced by new and better ones. Without vibrant, innovative financial markets, economies would invariably ossify and decline (Rajan & Zingales, 2003/2014, p. 3).

(*Continued*)

- Porter and Kramer (2011) also point out that a dominant focus on shareholder value creation is not only bad for society but also that it ignores important factors that have a negative impact on long-term success. They propose an alternative view around the concept of shared value as a paradigm that "involves creating value in a way that also creates value for society by addressing its needs and challenges" and companies must refocus on building shared value, and "take the lead in bringing business and society back together."
- Baden and Higgs (2015) argue that the Cuban social developmental approach demonstrates greater wisdom in that it teaches how to develop profitable enterprise as a means to achieve greater social welfare; profits should be a tool to achieve social goals not the end goal in itself.
- "Whereas in capitalist nations, responsible marketing focuses on issues such as avoiding deception to customers or exploiting vulnerable consumers such as children, in Cuba it means ensuring that the right products are produced to meet the real needs of all citizens, and encompasses concepts of social inclusion" (Baden & Higgs, 2015, p. 545).
- Davis (2015) argues that the purpose of management research and teaching has gone beyond serving just managers to serving society more broadly.
- Marti and Scherer (2016) suggest that management research and teaching should go beyond a conception of human actors only as efficiency maximizers to include conceptions of human actors as seeking social stability and social justice (Habermas, 1971).
- Hence, Abrahamson et al. (2016, p. 374) suggest that it would be interesting for management professors to study whether classes that reinforce students' receptiveness to management techniques and devices serve not only business organizations but also society more generally, in terms of both economic efficiency, social stability, and social justice.
- The major strengths of the FECS have been open access to, and mobility of, major resources like capital, property, law and order, manpower and machines, technology and patents, markets and buying power.
- The major strategies of FECS were old and new, product/service development in changing economies such as agriculture to manufacturing, from the service economy to its subsets such as transportation, knowledge, education, health care, insurance, information and software, sports and entertainment, energy and alternative energies, and currently, planetary ecology and cosmic sustainability concerns.
- Ferraro et al. (2005) agree and present evidence that behavior which is altruistic or self-interested is strongly influenced by our education and culture. They go on to show how the description and assumption of behavior as self-interested, as perpetuated by such theories, develop into norms of behavior and thus become self-fulfilling.
- However, rather than totally discard these management theory and research practice theories, social performativity theory seeks to refine and

(*Continued*)

(Continued)

purify them and use their best potential to serve social progress, social development, and cosmic sustainability.

- Faulhaber and Baumol (1988) selected nine important, scientifically derived techniques or devices taken from financial economics (marginal analysis, net present value for capital budgeting, peak load pricing, econometric forecasting, the portfolio selection model and the associated beta coefficient, duration analysis, BSM, Ramsey pricing, and the stand-alone cost test) and studied their impact historically – from their emergence stage, to their development stage, to their adoption stage, and to their diffusion stage.[3] They found that financial economists, for each of the nine techniques, played a role during at least one of these four stages.

Paradigm Shift From Market Performativity to Social Performativity

Critical Thinking Exercise 2.8

Apply critical thinking (see footnote 3 in Chapter 1) to assess the thesis of social performativity as justifying modified versions of PM.

- How can management research, theory, techniques, and devices help business students, business practitioners, and specifically, the disadvantaged and marginalized world of today via social performativity?
- How can a refocus to existing management research theory and practice ensure human dignity to all, human development and social progress of all, while enhancing planetary ecology and cosmic sustainability?

In responding to these key questions, we must first examine the implicit assumptions and suppositions of the existing management theory, research, and practice.

- Profit is not only not bad, but also good for the economy. Especially, profits as earnings before interest and taxes (EBIT) or as earnings before interest, taxes, depreciation, and amortization (EBITDA) is the necessary condition of survival, revival, growth, and moving forward. In this sense, profits are the only engine of growth and prosperity in FECS.

---

[3]Peak or peak load pricing is a form of congestion pricing where customers pay an additional fee during periods of high demand. Peak pricing is most frequently implemented by utility companies (such as airlines, railroad, movies, business travel, and the like) which charge higher rates during times when demand is the highest. The purpose of peak pricing is to regulate demand so that it stays within a manageable level of what can be supplied. Peak pricing is also used among ride-sharing services and other transportation providers, and food service aggregators, and is known as "surge pricing."

(*Continued*)

- PM, however, is a different concept and domain altogether. As an end in itself, it can be harmful because it disrupts the balance of an equilibrium economy. It can be argued that "PM as an end" can make markets less efficient in reaching natural, social, political, and economic harmony. Profits are, to a large extent, required for the survival and growth of enterprises that contribute to social welfare or broad social interest.
- Nevertheless, PM can be ruthless when it is achieved by doing whatever it takes (i.e., any means), such as cheating, deception, obfuscation, opacity, fraud, bribery, avarice, greed, collusion, cartelization, overextraction, overmining, species extinction, deforestation, industrial pollution, and ocean acidity, as we have unwittingly done these all along.
- PM unexamined by critical thinking can be very divisive between the rich and the poor, the naturally advantaged and naturally disadvantaged, and thus very disruptive for humankind, resulting in gaping inequities and inequalities among different levels of poverty and prosperity, talent, and opportunity as our current civilization evidence everywhere in the globe.
- In general, we have uncritically assumed *anthropocentrism*: a convenient self-serving philosophy affirming that the planet and its scarce resources and the cosmos are solely for humankind. Hence, we have freely used the earth and its scarce resources: elements such as water, air, earth, and sky; minerals and metals from mines and mountains, vegetation such as plants and fruits, fields and forests, and life such as fish from lakes, rivers, and oceans, birds and animals from all over, and even cheap labor from local natives and tribes, slaves and employees, particularly from the less developed countries and emerging nations.
- In the process, we have used them for production, distribution, and consumption, even overused and abused them, often usurped them through wars and conquests, invasions, and colonization, and now dispose them with a wanton throwaway culture of forced migration, emigration, and asylum immigration.
- Another major supposition and presumption was that FECS is good for society, the planet, and the cosmos: that is, FECS that involves free market entry and exit of producers, distributors, and consumers as buyers and sellers, suppliers and labor, creditors and debtors, shareholders and stakeholders, governments and regulators, local and global communities, is eventually "performing" well for society.
- The worst effects of FECS were the unforeseen and presumably unwilled consequences of consequences – the gaping divide between kings and subjects, feudal lords and slaves, master and servants, baron owners and owned, and currently, employer and employees, rich and poor, naturally skilled and advantaged and undeservedly unskilled and disadvantaged.
- We are left with a polluted and globally polarized world, vexed with domestic and international trade war and WTO violations, a divided world of inequalities (of income, social, gender, cultural, resource, and

(*Continued*)

(Continued)

opportunity); racial and religious conflicts, tensions, and terrorism; and teeming millions seeking asylum migration.

- Some suggest that to make management education more prosocial requires discarding old economic theories such as transaction cost economics which "norm" self-interest as they equate rationality with self-interest and ignore behavior that does not conform to these assumptions (Ghoshal, 2005; Ghoshal & Moran, 1996).
- This is the world that business management theory, research, and development, among all other disciplines, can best understand, explain, predict, and control, and above all, can heal and harmonize, humanize, and socialize with renewed human dignity, energized social progress and development, and restored planetary ecology and cosmic sustainability.
- An alternative understanding of capitalism and how to make it more inclusive is offered by anthropologists, historians, medical doctors, and sociologists (Davis, 2006; Farmer, 2003; Goode & Maskovsky, 2001; O'Connor, 2001; Yelvington, 1995).
- These social and medical scientists use ethnography, economic data, and political history to document intentional public policies supported by business interests to maintain the status quo of low-income populations. Governments and businesses collude to prevent access to affordable housing, health care, education, and nutrition to low-income populations because they divert resources to maximizing profits from middle- and upper-income populations.
- Making capitalism more inclusive certainly includes suggestions of encouraging companies to sell goods to poor people at affordable prices. But inclusive capitalism must also address political considerations that maintain structural inequalities within any economy.

Poverty Eradication Through Inclusive Capitalism

Critical Thinking Exercise 2.9

Apply critical thinking (see footnote 3 in Chapter 1) to assess the theory of inclusive capitalism as justifying modified versions of PM.

- Prahalad (2005) opens his book, *The Fortune at the Bottom of the Pyramid: Eradicating Poverty Through Profits* by asking, "Why can't we create inclusive capitalism?" (p. xv). He uses the term "inclusive capitalism" to invite readers to "commence talking about underserved consumers and markets. The process must start with Bottom of the Pyramid consumers as individuals [. . .]. New and creative approaches are needed to convert poverty into an opportunity for all concerned. That is the challenge" (Prahalad, 2005, p. xvii).
- Hammond (2001, p. 98) wrote: "What is needed instead is a bottom-up model that makes credit, communications, information, energy sources,

> *(Continued)*
>
> and other self-help tools available to all, especially the marginalized. The idea behind this new development model of Inclusive Capitalism is that basic services should generally be provided by businesses – sometimes directly, sometimes in partnership with governments or networks of non-governmental organizations (NGOs)."
>
> - Privatizing public services is a central idea of inclusive capitalism, suggesting government policies have largely failed poor people and businesses, and NGOs should assume a greater role in poverty alleviation.
> - "The poor can be profitable," wrote Prahalad and Hammond. Poor people have little buying power when in fact "low-income households collectively possess most of the buying power in many developing countries" (Hammond & Prahalad, 2004, p. 32).
> - The "world's poor – families with an annual household income of less than $6,000 – is enormous. The 18 largest emerging and transition countries include 680 million such households, with a total annual income of $1.7 trillion-roughly equal to Germany's annual gross domestic product" (Hammond & Prahalad, 2004, p. 32).

Morality of Profits and Losses

Our current markets of hyper capitalists have unnecessary excesses: conspicuous and extravagant consumption, creation of new wanton needs, wants and desires, exorbitant pricing, aggressive pricing, cartelization, price collusions, corporate giants that exploit more than they "employ" people, and the current epidemic of fraud, deception, obfuscation, corruption, bribery, and money laundering. The latter have delegitimized the markets and "alienated" us from them.

Critical Thinking Exercise 2.10

Apply critical thinking (see footnote 3 in Chapter 1) to assess the theory of morality of profits and losses as justifying modified versions of PM.

- Can we prefer not to have profits and losses?
- But then who would create, design, and innovate new products and services?
- Who would create new markets, malls and supermarkets, new brands, more competition, and lesser prices?
- Above all, who would design new "convenient" products and services, which we have today, which save us money, time, effort, anxiety, routinized work, boredom, retirement worries – all of which we call improvement of civilization?
- Moreover, who would create jobs for those who do not own "capital" to start on their own – such as cottage industries, entrepreneurs, start-ups, and small and big businesses?

(Continued)

(Continued)

- Nobody stops us from being owners. Capitalism provides all the opportunity for social upward mobility of "rags to riches." Even though some gigantic capitalists are powerful, it can be argued that the consumers are still their masters; *see* McRae (2003), Whitley (1992); Wray-Bliss and Parker (1998); Monbiot (2000, 2004); Parker (1998); Pearson (1995); Pearson and Parker (2001).
- It is by responding to us, to our needs and wants for cheaper prices, and better conveniences that some free markets have become so successful and improved the quality of our lives.[4]
- Even Thomas Aquinas affirmed the supreme dominion of God over everything, adding that "man has a natural dominion over external things, because, by his reason and will, he is able to use them for his own profit" (1981, II–II, 66, 1).[5] Aquinas added that it is lawful for man to possess property because this is a necessary element in human life for three reasons. First, because every man is more motivated to procure what is for himself alone than that which is common to many or to all. Second, because human affairs are conducted in a more orderly fashion if each man is charged with taking care of some particular thing himself. Third, because a more peaceful state is ensured for man if each is content with his own. However, Aquinas stated that man ought to possess external things, not as his own but as common, so that he is ready to communicate them to others in their need.
- Aquinas' view entails, therefore, a natural right to property, but regarding its use, he stresses the responsibility of property owners to pay attention to other people's economic needs.

---

[4]William Morrison first set up a shop in Keighley in the aftermath of the Second World War; through hard work and attention to his customers' needs, Morrison's became a supermarket chain in the United Kingdom, winning over 40 million online customers. So did Sam Walton with his largest retailing chain in the world Walmart, and so did Bill Gates with his global software Microsoft, and Michael Dell with his worldwide distribution of personal computers.

[5]Italian Dominican theologian St. Thomas Aquinas was one of the most influential medieval thinkers of Scholasticism and the father of the Thomistic school of theology. He was born in 1225 in Roccasecca, Kingdom of Sicily, Italy. Combining the theological principles of faith with the philosophical principles of reason, he ranked among the most influential thinkers of medieval Scholasticism. An authority of the Roman Catholic Church, Aquinas, died on March 7, 1274, at the Cistercian monastery of Fossanova, Italy. A prolific writer, St. Thomas Aquinas, wrote or dictated close to 60 known works ranging in length from short to tome-like compositions. Handwritten copies of his works were distributed to libraries across Europe. His philosophical and theological writings spanned a wide spectrum of topics, including commentaries on the Bible and discussions of Aristotle's writings on natural philosophy. His major work called *Summa Theologica* has been preserved in several volumes. For citations presented here, see Aquinas (1981).

Profit Sharing and Socialist Firms

Explicit in the explanation of the capitalist firm is the assumption that the cost of managing the team's inputs by a central monitor, who disciplines himself because he is a residual claimant, is low relative to the cost of metering the marginal outputs of team members. If we look within a firm to see who monitors – hires, fires, changes, promotes, and renegotiates – we should find him being a residual claimant or, at least, one whose pay or reward is more than any others', correlated with fluctuations in the residual value of the firm. They more likely will have options or rights or bonuses than will inputs with other tasks (Alchian & Demsetz, 1972, pp. 785–786).

An implicit "auxiliary" assumption of this explanation of the firm is that the cost of team production is increased if the residual claim is not held entirely by the central monitor. Part of the residual claim includes rights to profits earned, dividends declared, and so on. That is, if profit sharing had to be relied upon for all team members, losses from the resulting increase in central monitor shirking would exceed the output gains from the increased incentives of other team members not to shirk. If the optimal team size is only two owners of inputs, then an equal division of profits and losses between them will leave each with stronger incentives to reduce shirking than if the optimal team size is large, for in the latter case only a smaller percentage of the losses occasioned by the shirker will be borne by him. Incentives to shirk are positively related to the optimal size of the team under an equal profit-sharing scheme.

Profit sharing is more viable if small team size is associated with situations where the cost of specialized management of inputs is large relative to the increased productivity potential in team effort. The cost of managing team inputs increases if the productivity of a team member is difficult to correlate with his behavior. In "artistic" or "professional" work, watching a man's activities is not a good clue to what he is actually thinking or doing with his mind (Alchian & Demsetz, 1972, p. 786). As a result, artistic or professional inputs, such as lawyers, advertising specialists, doctors, and speculative and proprietary traders, will be given relatively freer rein with regard to individual behavior. To the extent CEOs and top management deploy specialized inputs which are artistic and unique, a certain portion of the profits accruable to them may belong to the top management.

If the management of inputs is relatively costly, or ineffective, as it would seem to be in these cases, but, nonetheless if team effort is more productive than separable production with exchange across markets, then there will develop a tendency to use profit-sharing schemes to provide incentives to avoid shirking (Alchian & Demsetz, 1972, p. 786).

On the other hand, socialist firms need not be the most viable when political constraints limit the forms of organization that can be chosen. It is one thing to have profit sharing when professional or artistic talents are used by small teams. But if political or tax or subsidy considerations induce profit-sharing techniques when these are not otherwise economically justified, then additional management techniques will be developed to help reduce the degree of shirking (Alchian &

Demsetz, 1972, p. 787). For example, most, if not all, firms in former Yugoslavia were owned by the employees in the restricted sense that all share in the residual claims. This is true for large firms and for firms which employ nonartistic, or nonprofessional, workers as well. With a decay of political constraints, most of these firms could be expected to rely on paid wages rather than shares in the residual.

This rests on the auxiliary assumption that general sharing in the residual results in losses from enhanced shirking by the monitor that exceed the gains from reduced shirking by residual-sharing employees. If this were not so, profit sharing with employees should have occurred more frequently in Western societies where such organizations are neither banned nor preferred politically. Where residual sharing by employees is politically imposed, as it was in former Yugoslavia, some management technique will arise to reduce shirking by the central monitor, a technique not found frequently in Western societies since the monitor retains all (or much) of the residual and profit sharing is largely confined to small, professional artistic team production situations.

In the larger scale residual-sharing firms in former Yugoslavia, for example, there were workers' committees that could recommend (to the state) the termination of a manager's contract (veto his continuance with the enterprise). The workers' committee was given the right to recommend the termination of the manager's contract precisely because the general sharing of the residual increases "excessively" the manager's incentive to shirk (Alchian & Demsetz, 1972, p. 787).

Critical Thinking Exercise 2.11

Apply critical thinking (see footnote 3 in Chapter 1) to assess the theory of profit-sharing firms and socialist firms, as proposed by Alchian and Demsetz (1972), as justifying disciplined PM.

Concluding Remarks

From these long discussions, we should be able to summarize and synthesize alternatives to PM that are viable, feasible, and desirable models of management theory, research, and practice, and resultant business school curriculum. A paradigm shift from PM to social welfare and social development is a long journey that may, at the minimum, need a change of mental models along one or more of these lines:

- From NSI that justifies PM, to broad self-interest that accepts modified forms of PM. NSI is not bounded by social norms of fairness, reciprocity, and justice, while broad self-interest is open to such social values and norms (Bosse & Phillips, 2016, pp. 276–277).
- Traditional agency theory that delegates business by principals (e.g., owners and board of governors) to agents (e.g., top management and executives such

as chief experience officers [CXOs]) with divergent self-interests (e.g., NSI), can promote shareholder wealth creation. The latter is safeguarded by motivating the agents with high monetary incentives and substantial executive compensation that, in turn, are financed by business transactions driven by PM. This traditional agency theory needs to be refined to include broader social and moral norms of fairness, reciprocity, and social justice (Habermas, 1991), such that PM and shareholder wealth maximization are tempered by broader goals of human dignity, social progress, social development, and cosmic sustainability (Ghoshal, 2005; Ghoshal & Moran, 2005).

- Both management scholars as well as business practitioners must identify, interpret, legitimize, and prioritize social issues (e.g., social welfare, social development, equality matching, profit sharing, social wealth creation, and social wealth distribution) such that they could be incorporated in business management thinking, research, and practice, especially as substitutes or alternatives to current preoccupation with PM and shareholder wealth maximization. If these social issues are currently considered as vague, equivocal, and hence, illegitimate and not worthy of management attention or resource diversion from PM and growth-oriented strategies (Sonenshein, 2006, 2016), then the paradigm shift of management theory, research, and practice must clarify, legitimize, and justify these social issues as socially viable, feasible, and desirable.
- As discussed earlier, Bridoux and Stoelhorst (2016) suggest relational economics in the place of pure transactional economics. Besides market pricing, which is the primary focus of traditional economic theory, people can also frame relationships as communal sharing (a relationship of unity, community, and collective identity) and authority ranking (a relationship of hierarchical differences accompanied by a relationship among equals manifested in balanced reciprocity).
- We submit that PM and wealth maximization, the long championed and claimed goals of traditional business models and schools, might have been then warranted under assumptions of transaction economics that, in turn, justified high-residual claims or higher executive compensation or incentives for voluntarily reducing shirking via metering. Similarly, one could assume that PM was itself a residual claim of anthropocentrism, a convenient self-serving philosophy that (among others) affirms that this planet and its scarce resources and the cosmos are solely for humankind. Hence, we can freely use, extract, and exploit the earth and its scarce resources for infrastructure of cities and towns that pave the way to PM, unwittingly through industrial concentration, monopolistic competition, or feudal ownership.
- At the same time, if we assume that the four relational models of Bridoux and Stoelhorst (2016) (i.e., market pricing, authority ranking, equality matching, and communal sharing) are interpreted as broader social interest of profitability, it could also lead to prosperity for all (Griffin, 2004; Griffin & Mahon, 1997). According to relational models' theory (Fiske, 1991, 1992, 2004, 2012; Fiske & Haslam, 2005; Haslam, 2004), communal sharing is characterized by a fusion of the self with the community, which means that the community

identity is psychologically salient, while the personal identity is pushed to the background.

- All four relational models of Bridoux and Stoelhorst (2016) imply that broader social interest based on compassion, honesty, integrity, and kindness (e.g., Bosse et al., 2009; Harrison et al., 2010; Jones, 1995; Jones & Felps, 2013a, 2013b).
- In consequence, actors adopting a community-sharing frame see themselves and their relational partners as community members who are equivalent and undifferentiated and who share motivations and goals. Actors are motivated to contribute altruistically (regardless of personal rewards) to the achievement of these common goals.
- In conclusion, we submit that major enabling conditions for taming over-commitment to PM are: responsible profits (Baumhart, 1968), profit sharing (Drèze, 2019), inclusive capitalism (Prahalad & Hamel, 1994), sharing resources and opportunities among the hitherto excluded (Mackey & Sisodia, 2014), and seeking progressive independence from the restraining assumptions of: (a) transactional economics as opposed to relational value economics, (b) inordinate adherence to self-serving value monism, (c) intolerance of value pluralism that upholds value egalitarianism, common good, community opportunity sharing, and social progress. All the latter objectives directly or indirectly support nonanthropocentrism with embracing relational economics and a willing adoption of environmental ethics that saves and regenerates our common home via sustainability.

Current models of profit sharing or responsible profits minimally mandate relational economics that invoke the four relational models (i.e., market pricing, authority ranking, equality matching, and communal sharing) and profitability that under perfect markets and perfect competition leads to prosperity for all (Griffin, 2004; Griffin & Mahon, 1997). Self-interested agents (SIAs) deeply specialized in and committed to transactional economics as opposed to relational economics, will "shirk" (Alchian & Demsetz, 1972) from relational or team production that leads to social wealth creation and choose to "underinvest" in it (Blair & Stout, 1999). But some SIAs will still cooperate and show concern for the collective interest of communal sharing and social welfare (Fehr & Gintis, 2007; Van Lange et al., 2013).

Hence, in proposing an alternative or complimentary social issue such as human dignity, social progress, and social development to PM, it is important that one establishes the legitimacy and unequivocality of the social issues involved (such as social progress, social development, social welfare) before they are embraced as a change agent in a corporation or management theory or in a business school curriculum. That is, management theory and business school curriculum should incorporate broadened corporate self-interest to include social and moral norms of social progress, social development, planetary ecology and cosmic sustainability. Thus, mere PM and shareholder wealth maximization should be broadened to include other alternatives such as profit sharing, community sharing, market pricing, equality matching, equality ranking, opportunity sharing, social affordability, social fairness, social stability and harmony, peace and social solidarity via distributive justice, corrective justice, and beneficent justice.

This will enable issues of PM to be understood not as inherently objective issues but rather as subjective social issues through meaning-making (Spector & Kitsuse, 1977). By the time top managers realize they have a decision to make regarding a social issue, a rich interpretive process could already strongly influence them to make that decision in a particular way. Often, a social change agent (e.g., a corporate social responsibility [CSR] regulation, an NGO, a social progress advocate) shapes how a firm's top managers make decisions about social issues by advancing an interpretation of a set of cues bundled into an "issue." Once top managers interpret that they have a decision to make about a social issue, the social change agent has already done significant interpretive work that subtly shapes how these managers ultimately make decisions about the issue.

Table 2.2 strives to understand traditional PM biases, with value imperatives to counteract them.

Critical Thinking Exercise 2.12

Apply critical thinking (see footnote 3 in Chapter 1) to assess the contents of Table 2.2 and separate which biases, prejudices, and presumptions could contribute the most to rationalizing PM, from those which are neutral, and those that are negatively disposed to PM.

Table 2.2. A Set of Profit Maximization (PM) Biases, Prejudices, and Presumptions With Value Imperatives.

Thinking Base	Biases	Prejudices	Presumptions	Value Imperatives
Wealth	Wealth is the limitless possession of a few. Wealth is individual aggrandizement.	We are the world. We are the superpower. The world is for the United States.	The United States is or should be the wealthiest and most powerful nation in the world. Wealth is power.	The wealth of the nations is the prosperity of all people. The primacy of human dignity is the condition of all progress.
Profits	Profitability is the necessary condition for growth.	Profits of one corporation are the losses of its competitor (the win-lose prejudice).	Profit is the bottom line of all business. High buying power and high market demand assure profitability.	Shared profitability is the engine of growth. The poor can be profitable too (Prahalad, 2004, 2005).
Productivity	The primacy of productivity is a supreme principle. Humans are mere factors of production.	Productivity is the increased efficiency of all resources.	Industrial concentration spurs productivity.	All human beings are ends in themselves and cannot be used for the ends of others.
Scale	Bigger is better. The larger a corporation becomes, the more productive it is.	Limitless growth is corporate prosperity.	Larger corporations have been the engine of growth in the United States.	Small is beautiful.
Control	Mastery over nature is critical. Technology is conquest of nature.	Mankind will always achieve a technical breakthrough into all the problems that arise in its current environment.	Human life and the life of our environment will always adjust to each other.	Harmony with nature is growth. Respect for nature is civilization.

Research and experimentation	We ought not to create a new humanity that intends to solve all the problems of nature.	Manipulation of the world and its resources (which includes humans) for the betterment and survival of mankind is not only a human right and duty but is essential for a better understanding and realization of human destiny.	Science and technology in themselves are neutral (amoral or trans-ethical) and must be freed from any ethical or moral impositions of a few, lest humanity's progress be impeded.	Our commitment to quality life and moral values should impose limits on human inquiry on the one hand and on technological progress on the other.
Globalization	The mobility of employment, capital, products and technology across countries and trade regions is critical for globalization.	Respect for the dignity and interests of all its stakeholders are fundamental to globalization.	Current international laws and market forces are necessary but insufficient guides for global business conduct.	Shared values, including a commitment to shared prosperity are as important for a global community as for communities of smaller scale.
Responsibility	Our responsibility is for ourselves. Our corporate social responsibility is for our stockholders.	Compensating peoples and nations for the harm that our global greed and actions cause is global justice.	The only responsibility of corporations is to make profits.	Accepting global responsibility for the politics and actions of business is imperative.

(Continued)

Table 2.2. (*Continued*)

Thinking Base	Biases	Prejudices	Presumptions	Value Imperatives
Rights and duties	Limitless consumption is our birthright.	Individual claims of rights are more important than claims of duties toward others.	Global social and economic betterment is the duty of all.	Human dignity enhancement and scarce resource conservation are our primary global duties.
Happiness	Limitless possession is supreme human happiness.	Happiness is the fulfillment of all our wants and desires.	Money is the source of all happiness.	Happiness doubles when shared.

Source: Compiled by the authors.

Chapter 3

Critical Thinking for Owning Moral Responsibility for Turbulent Markets

Executive Summary

This chapter addresses one of the most crucial areas for critical thinking: the morality of turbulent markets around the world. All of us are overwhelmed by such turbulent markets. Following Nassim Nicholas Taleb (2004, 2010), we distinguish between nonscalable industries (ordinary professions where income grows linearly, piecemeal or by marginal jumps) and scalable industries (extraordinary risk-prone professions where income grows in a nonlinear fashion, and by exponential jumps and fractures). Nonscalable industries generate tame and predictable markets of goods and services, while scalable industries regularly explode into behemoth virulent markets where rewards are disproportionately large compared to effort, and they are the major causes of turbulent financial markets that rock our world causing ever-widening inequities and inequalities. Part I describes both scalable and nonscalable markets in sufficient detail, including propensity of scalable industries to randomness, and the turbulent markets they create. Part II seeks understanding of moral responsibility of turbulent markets and discusses who should appropriate moral responsibility for turbulent markets and under what conditions. Part III synthesizes various theories of necessary and sufficient conditions for accepting or assigning moral responsibility. We also analyze the necessary and sufficient conditions for attribution of moral responsibility such as rationality, intentionality, autonomy or freedom, causality, accountability, and avoidability of various actors as moral agents or as moral persons. By grouping these conditions, we then derive some useful models for assigning moral responsibility to various entities such as individual executives, corporations, or joint bodies. We discuss the challenges and limitations of such models.

Each of us has the capacity to make business not only a source of economic wealth, but also a force for economic and social justice. Each of us needs to recognize and use the power we have to define

A Primer on Critical Thinking and Business Ethics, 65–109
Copyright © 2024 Oswald A. J. Mascarenhas, Munish Thakur and Payal Kumar
Published under exclusive licence by Emerald Publishing Limited
doi:10.1108/978-1-83753-312-120231003

the character of our enterprise, so they nurture values important to our society. Only then will each of us know full rewards that a career in business can yield. Only then will business achieve the true potential of its leadership. Only then will business fulfill its obligation to help build an economy worthy of a free society and a civilization worth celebrating.

– Walter Haas, Jr., ex-CEO of Levi Strauss & Co.

Introduction

Moral values and turbulent markets are not always social constructions; they constitute "the beliefs held by individuals or groups regarding means and ends organizations 'ought to' or 'should' identify in the running of an enterprise" (Enz, 1988, p. 287). Moral values are important in the determination of strategic choices that agents of an organization make and influence how organizations are designed and run (Amis et al., 2002). Major ideological changes in an organization in terms of structure, vision, or design are accompanied by an emphasis of certain moral values (Ranson et al., 1980). "By creative visualization, through responses to art ... through contemplation ... people sense values which seem to emanate from 'beyond' us" and obligate us to respond (Woods, 2001, p. 695). Without a strong tie to stated values, organizational change is less likely to be successful (Locke, 1991). On the other hand, moral disvalues or weakly held values together with moral weakness can cause moral turbulence, which if unexamined periodically by critical thinking can generate fraudulence, greed, envy, and moral decadence, all of which give rise to turbulent markets that quickly escalate into moral market crises that we seek to address in this chapter.

As Mary Barra, CEO of General Motors, put it after the company agreed to pay a hefty US$ 900 million fine for hiding a deadly ignition switch defect for more than a decade, "apologies and accountability don't amount to much if you don't change your behavior" (Vlasic, 2016). The global managing director of McKinsey and Company, Dominic Barton, went a step further, stating, "business leaders face a stark choice: Either they reform capitalism, 'the greatest engine of prosperity ever devised', or stand by and watch as government takes control" (quoted in Bridgman et al., 2016, p. 736).

When and why should a corporation as a group of top executives (e.g., the board of directors or governors, or its CXOs) take responsibility (legal, ethical, moral) for its actions, both individually and/or collectively, especially when the actions, given market and industry turbulence, result in unforeseen or unforeseeable physical and/or social harm to many of its stakeholders, customers, and clients? That is, under what necessary and/or sufficient conditions is a corporation morally bound to or exonerated from accepting moral responsibility for its individual or corporate plans and strategies, decisions and activities that result in foreseen or unforeseen malfeasance?

Corporate executives immersed in the chaotic and turbulent markets of today face a world not just of certainties or clear-cut moral dichotomous dilemmas looking for answers such as right or wrong, good or bad, fair or unfair, but instead must confront large corporate gray areas of lesser good, lesser evil, lesser truth, less unfair, and less unjust situations (Mascarenhas, 1995). Not much attention has been paid to this challenging area and that may be for obvious reasons: for instance, most business ethicists may not feel comfortable to look for the locus of corporate moral responsibility in such chaotic ever-changing markets. Nevertheless, it is these chaotic markets that cause untold economic and psychological damage to millions of innocent bystanding shareholders and market-dependent customers, creditors, suppliers, clients, and consumers.

Additionally, markets are too large and diffused, and it is difficult to point a finger at any one individual person or corporation or even industry for wrong-doing. Further, business ethicists often adopt a retributive mood of assigning corporate moral responsibility as punishment or guilt (Hasnas, 2012, 2017) and do not find definite culprits in the wide-open chaotic markets. As Constantinescu and Kaptein (2015, p. 326) observe, the debate has overlooked an important practical issue: is there any point in discussing the morality of organizations when they are already regulated by law? Nevertheless, the law does not cover all aspects of corporate behavior; often it prescribes just the minimum, and corporations and their members display (un)ethical behavior that is not fully condemnable by regulations.

As chaotic and random as world events seem today, they seem as chaotic in organizations, too. Yet for decades, managers have acted on the basis that organizational events can always be controlled. A new theory (or some say "science"), chaos theory, recognizes that events indeed are rarely controlled. Many chaos theorists (as do systems theorists) refer to biological systems when explaining their theory. They suggest that systems naturally go toward more complexity, and as they do so, these systems become more volatile (or susceptible to cataclysmic events) and must expend more energy to maintain that complexity. As they expend more energy, they seek more structure to maintain stability. This trend continues until the system splits, combines with another complex system, or falls apart entirely. This trend is what many see as the trend in life, in organizations and the world in general.

Net Moral Goodness Triumphs Over Moral Failure

Thus, in encouraging sustainable behaviors and markets, the importance of moral values is paramount. An individual's value set is a major factor for influencing (or motivating) behavior. Good moral values (linked to aesthetics) are likely to affect a person's motivation to act toward sustainable initiatives. Moral values are "the emotive mechanisms needed to create positive, sustained ethical action in human organizational systems" (Bagozzi et al., 2013, p. 70). As guiding principles

(Schwartz et al., 2001), moral values can be emotional predispositions toward empathy, caring, and concern for others (Bagozzi et al., 2013). The stronger the moral values are felt emotionally, the more likely the person's intention to act in a moral manner is assured. Values "can be understood as human emotional responses to sources of importance" (Woods, 2001, p. 694). This magnifies the fact that moral values are linked to individuals' natural human drives (Frederick, 1995; Shrivastava et al., 2017, p. 373). Good moral virtue, cultivated and lived together in communities, creates good markets that counteract the evil of immorally turbulent markets. By and large, human nature is intrinsically good and reliable and often overpowers evil in this world, thus explaining and predicting the subtle predominance of good over evil, good markets over morally decadent turbulent markets. It is Adam Smith's "invisible hand" that empowers net moral goodness to triumph over moral failure.

Part I
Turbulent Markets Stirred by Scalable Industries

According to Nassim Nicholas Taleb (2004, 2010), our markets could safely be partitioned into scalable and nonscalable industries.[1] In general, "scalable" jobs and scalable industries are those where income, wealth, fame, and recognition grow nonlinearly in jumps and fractures or amidst Black Swan events where luck, serendipity, and randomness offer huge rewards disproportionate to executive efforts. With scalable businesses, output (revenue) is not directly related to input (resources). Thus, as an author, you can sell 100 or 100,000 books. Your input remains the same, but your output (book sales) can differ enormously. Your output does not face headwind in scalable business. But with nonscalable businesses, output (revenue) is directly related to input (resources), i.e., as a dentist or an engineer, you cannot sell your services beyond a certain point because you simply cannot be present at multiple clients at the same time. As your output (revenue) increases, your input (cost, time) will increase as well.

Before and after the financial crisis of 2008, there have been recurrent and widespread multibillion-dollar frauds and other corporate crimes that have implicated executives and directors at firms ranging from Wells Fargo Bank to Lehman Brothers, Volkswagen to Purdue Pharma. Obviously, scalable industries are vulnerable to risk, uncertainty, unpredictability, ambiguity, and market chaos and are often plagued by Black Swans where disproportionately large rewards are granted to corporate executives for partially taming market turbulence and for

---

[1]The exact meaning and definition of scalable versus nonscalable is not fully established yet. Both are buzzwords associated with each one's careers and activities. The term "unscalable" implies not capable of being climbed or scaled: as in not scalable or unscalable peaks, or unscalable barriers; "scalable" is often misused to describe a company's potential to grow in market share, revenue, profit, etc. Similarly, the term "nonscalable" is often misused for companies that have exhausted their growth. We follow the meaning as used by Nassim Nicholas Taleb, in his books *Fooled by Randomness* (2004) and *The Black Swan* (2010).

confronting risk, uncertainty, ambiguity, and market chaos. There are no physical constraints on what or who can be a number one – the scalable markets are often dominated by intense competition with extreme winners taking all, leaving inequities and inequalities behind.

The Silicon Valley billionaires offer some examples. Despite, or because of, lesser knowledge about these turbulent markets of the world, it often takes a long time to know what's going on. For example, Enron, the dot.com bubble of 2002, the October 2008 global financial crisis, Uber, the Facebook Cambridge Analytica scandals. Silicon Valley corporates have sought to explain, understand, predict, and control market turbulence, and to the extent their predictions have been partly right and reliable, they have exploited such predictions, and accordingly, been successful in generating and hoarding wealth and power, meanwhile contributing to socially harmful externalities (e.g., inflation, poverty, pollution, extraction, and deforestation) that affect innocent bystanders, society, and stakeholders.[2]

Scalable and Nonscalable Industries

In general, "scalable" jobs and industries are those where luck, serendipity, and randomness offer huge rewards disproportionate to efforts. Examples of non-scalable industries are investment banking, proprietary trading, stock market trading, derivatives trading, commodities trading, big bet casino gambling, private equity companies, hedge funds markets, large portfolio management, asset/wealth management companies, giant arts auction houses, big commercial banks, oil- and gas-based energy companies, precious metals mining companies, hydrocarbon companies, Bollywood industries, major opera houses, major sports stardom, best-selling authors, best-selling music albums, and Silicon Valley industries. That is, these scalable industries constitute a significant percentage of modern turbulent markets and industries. It is nonlinear luck of market perceptions and buyer mania. For instance, "there is more money in designing a shoe than in actually making it: Nike, Dell, and Boeing get paid for just thinking, organizing, and leveraging their know-how ideas while sub-contracted blue-collar factories in developing countries do the grunt work" (Taleb, 2010, p. 31).

Matters that belong to scalable industries and jobs are: fast accumulation of wealth, strategies for income and profit maximization, book sales per author, citations per author, celebrities and name recognition, revenue sizes of companies, top ranked companies on *Fortune* or *Forbes* magazines, managers-of-the-year industry awards, *Time* magazine's front cover personalities, explosive market capitalization of corporations, financial markets, commodity prices, oil cartel prices, inflation rates, money supply rates, federal monetary and fiscal policies, terrorists, Mafia, corporate aircrafts and yachts, exotic cruises and vacation cities, and the like. It is the world of the extraordinary, what Taleb calls the Extremistan (of extremely lucky or fortuitous celebrities!). It is the Type II randomness (Taleb, 2010, pp. 34–37). It is the world made also possible by our lack of or resistance to critical thinking.

---

[2]Here, this term is used to indicate members of corporations, as owners or shareholders.

> **Critical Thinking Exercise 3.1**
>
> Apply critical thinking (see footnote 3 in Chapter 1) to the theory of scalable versus nonscalable industries. Is this distinction valid and objective or self-serving, allowing different parties to shirk moral or business responsibility? What are the basic biases, stereotypes, assumptions, presumptions, suppositions, and presuppositions of this distinction? Is this distinction a social construction, or does it really reflect today's reality of market turbulence?

Randomness and Black Swan Events

A Black Swan event has three properties (Taleb, 2010, p. xxii): (a) it is an outlier, lying outside the realm of normal knowledge and expectations at the time it happened, as nothing in the past was anything like it; (b) it carries an extreme impact; (c) despite its rarity or outlier status, we have many *post-factum* explanations for it, making it retrospectively explainable and predictable. We formulate theories leading to their projections and forecasts without focusing on the robustness of these theories and the consequences of their errors. It is much easier to deal with the Black Swan problem if we focus on robustness of errors rather than on improving our predictions. What is surprising is not the magnitude of our forecast errors but our ignorance of it. According to Taleb (2004), there are so many things we can do if we focus on antiknowledge, or on what we do not know. Contrary to social science wisdom, almost no discovery, no technological breakthrough, no marketing breakthrough, and no radical innovation, came from design and planning – they were just (positive) Black Swan events.

Arguably, the most successful companies in any industry today are the Silicon Valley titans Amazon, Alphabet (Google), and Meta (Facebook), and their fellow Chinese titans, Baidu, Alibaba, and Tencent. Although each of the Silicon Valley giants is nominally in a different business – e-commerce, data search, or social networking – they all are unified by a common business model. All are in the business of collecting as much data as possible, by every means possible, and making money off that data. This is all they do. This is what might be known as the "Amazoogle" business model. It is the world made possible by our lack of critical thinking.

History has known many Black Swan events. Obvious examples are: World Wars I and II, the Black Friday of 1929, Adolf Hitler, the Holocaust, the crumbling of the Berlin Wall in 1989, and the demise of the Soviet bloc in 1990, the stock market crash of October 1987, the Japan meltdown of 1990, the internet bubble of 1993, the bond market debacle of 1994, the Fall of Russia in 1998, the Enron scandal of 1999–2001, the Dot.com Bubble of 2002, the global financial crisis and the fall of Lehman Brothers in October 2008, Brexit in 2017 and its current impasse, some pandemic diseases, the current US–China trade war, and the Facebook scandal and the alleged Cambridge Analytica complicity.

These were turbulent markets of our times. These were outliers of our history; nobody suspected or expected them, nobody took responsibility for them, but most suffered from them. Those who claimed to explain these events said: "There were different times," "the market forces were different," or "we just took bad risks," and so on. There was no courage in taking such risks, just ignorance (Taleb, 2004, p. 54). "The inability to predict outliers implies the inability to predict the course of history" (Taleb, 2010, p. xxiv).

Periodic Dominance of Black Swan Turbulence

Most turbulent markets of corporate scandals of late have taken place in scalable industries where "Black Swan" (Taleb, 2010) events and opportunities abound and where people can be easily "fooled by randomness" (Taleb, 2004) in the markets. In these industries, if you are at "the right time and in the right place" (i.e., encounter luck, serendipity, and survival advantage) and with the right type of asset management skills, you can make (or lose) millions of dollars overnight, move from rags to riches, or from luxury and extravagant living to solitary confinement in prisons. "A scalable profession is good only if you are successful; they are more competitive, produce monstrous inequalities, with huge disparities between efforts and rewards where a few can take a large share of the pie, wiping out others entirely at no fault of their own" (Taleb, 2010, pp. 28–29). It is the winner-takes-all morality and ecology. "The inequity comes when someone perceived as being marginally better gets the whole pie" (Taleb, 2010, p. 30).

On the other hand, in nonscalable steady growth industries (paid mostly piecemeal or by the hour) like dentistry, hairdressing, teaching, clerking, nursing, retailing, cab or truck driving, farming, cottage industries, cooking, baking, processed foods industries and the like, where income grows linearly and in marginal jumps, and it may take a lifetime to realize a small percentage of scalable incomes. Matters that belong to nonscalable industries are ordinary, such as height, weight, calorie consumption, mass transportation, economy cars, daily lottery, regular housing, economy class airfares, fast food restaurants, small bars and taverns, daily newspapers, and social media. It is the world of the ordinary what Taleb (2010) calls "mediocristan" or the *Type I randomness*. It is the world made possible by our critical thinking and considered choices.

Critical Thinking Exercise 3.2

Apply critical thinking (see footnote 3 in Chapter 1) to the concept and paradigm of randomness. To what extent are we fooled by randomness, as Taleb (2004) claims? Is randomness a valid and objective concept, or just another social construction to objectify and institutionalize or legitimize manmade chaos to shirk moral responsibility? What are the basic biases, stereotypes, assumptions, presumptions, suppositions, and presuppositions of this concept and why?

Randomness-Prone Industries

The degree of randomness, however, differs from industry to industry. In general, the behavioral financial economics industry involving stocks and bonds, mutual funds and insurances, derivatives and hedge funds, venture capital and private equity, investment banks and wealth management companies, Wall Street analysts and debt rating agencies, asset trading and proprietary trading, and any such branch that needs high speculation, conjectures, estimation, and predictions, Monte Carlo simulations and random walk game theories and the like, are wrought with Black Swans and randomness, uncertainties and unpredictabilities, humungous risks and ambiguities. The data mining, data analytic, data snooping, and data selling professionals in these industries are well-known for their corroboration bias, sunk-cost bias, survivor bias, over-reliance on past data bias, over-fitting regression to the mean, and the like, where their performance is exaggerated by the observer owing to misconceived importance of randomness. Why is financial economics so rich a field for these aberrations? Taleb (2004, p. 151) opines: "Because it is one of the rare areas of investigation where we have plenty of information (in the form of abundant price series and time series data) but no ability to conduct experiments as in, say, physics. The dependence on past data brings about its salient defects." However, nobody accepts randomness in their own success, only in their failure (Taleb, 2004, p. 156). We tend to blame adverse selection, ergodicity, and occasionally, moral hazard to our failures. All these are instances of lack of critical thinking.

Randomness-Free Industries

On the other hand, nonscalable industries are low in luck, like small bet casinos that manage to tame randomness. Even in finance, not all traders are speculative traders, especially those who make their income by each transaction they make. Other things being equal, in the world of the scalable industries, there is not much scope for greed to make windfall profits or maximize wealth in the shortest time, and accordingly, they are "immune to randomness" (Taleb, 2004, p. 86) while also not "operating in the most random of environments" (Taleb, 2004, p. 91). Hence, they do not face that many challenges of legal and moral responsibility, especially in terms of attributional or appropriational moral responsibility. On the other hand, moral responsibility in scalable industries is getting to be more and more problematic, as these industries are either fooled by randomness or exploit randomness or Black Swan events, luck and serendipity, and such behaviors can increase the scale and scope and involvement of moral responsibility.

Part II
Understanding Moral Responsibility of Turbulent Markets

The debate whether corporate individuals as executives of scalable industries, or as corporation collectives of such industries, should be held morally responsible for turbulent markets, and their harmful consequences has been raging for more than seven decades in theoretical and applied ethics. We follow this debate with critical thinking, not so much for blaming corporates but from the point of understanding and spreading responsibility for the harmful consequences on third party innocent bystanders negatively affected by turbulent markets.

Critical Thinking Exercise 3.3

Apply critical thinking (see footnote 3 in Chapter 1) to the concept and paradigm of randomness-prone versus randomness-free industries. To what extent is our economy determined or influenced by randomness? Is this randomness that bifurcates industries as indicated ultimately man-made and a convenient social construction to justify inequalities? If not, to what extent does randomness explain turbulence as determining our markets? Are we fooled by randomness, as Taleb (2004) claims? Or is randomness fooled by us and is caused by our fraud and avarice? What are the basic biases, stereotypes, assumptions, presumptions, suppositions, and presuppositions of randomness in industries and why?

The Problem of Moral Responsibility

Apparently, the moral responsibility debate has been fueled by three schools of thought with differentiating arguments, as noted in Exhibit 3.1.

Neat and tidy as these schools are, the endless and inconclusive debate (that follows) between moral agents, moral actors, and moral persons stems from these schools and their differentiating traditions.

What is Responsibility?

Goodpaster (1983) distinguishes three uses of the term "responsible" when used without the modifier "moral," referring to them as *causal, rule-following*, and *decision-making*, respectively. In the causal sense, a certain action or event was brought about by the individual in question, wholly or in part; for example, we might ask who was responsible for a broken window, we speak of "holding" persons responsible, and we are concerned with determining such matters as intent, free will, degree of participation, as well as reward and/or punishment.

We also speak of an individual's "responsibilities" as a parent or as a citizen or in other roles. This use of the term reflects the rule-following sense, not the causal sense. Here the focus is not on determining who or what brought about a certain action or event but on the socially expected behavior associated with certain roles. Parents have responsibilities for their children, doctors for their patients, lawyers for their clients, producers to customers, executives for business markets, and citizens for their country. To speak of a person as responsible in such contexts is essentially to commend him or her for following the rules of the profession or meeting the expectations of their station.

Exhibit 3.1. Locus of Corporate Moral Responsibility in Business Corporations.

Locus of Moral Responsibility	Major School and Argument	Authors (Chronologically Listed)
Individual corporate executives and not corporate collectives	*Individual Responsibility School:* Only individual executives are moral persons or moral agents who can originate actions and their consequences and are hence held morally responsible.	Held (1970), Searle (1980), May (1983), Velasquez (1983, 1985, 2003), Goodpaster and Matthews (1982), Goodpaster (1983), Ladd (1984), Danley (1990), McMahon (1995), Hasnas (2010, 2012, 2017), Rönnegard (2013), Rönnegard and Velasquez (2017), and Sepinwall and Orts (2017)
Corporate collectives and not individual executives	*Corporate responsibility school:* Executive collective choices and strategies are freely and deliberately chosen even though constrained by market uncertainty and ambiguity, government regulation, corporate governance boards, major promoters and influential stakeholders, government regulation, corporate governance boards, major promoters, and influential stakeholders, and hence held morally responsible.	Ladd (1970), Bates (1971), French (1975, 1982, 1984), Keeley (1979), Ozar (1979), De George (1981), Donaldson (1980, 1982), May (1987), Werhane (1985), Rafalko (1989), May and Hoffman (1991), Walt and Laufer (1991), Nesteruk (1992), Phillips (1992, 1995), McMahon (1995), Seabright and Kurke (1997), and Williams (1999)
Both individual and corporate collectives	*Joint Responsibility School:* They mostly work in teams and face market, competitive, and	Frankena (1980), Goodpaster and Matthews (1982), Goodpaster (1983), Surber and French (1983), Thompson (1986), Werhane

Exhibit 3.1. *(Continued)*

Locus of Moral Responsibility	Major School and Argument	Authors (Chronologically Listed)
	regulatory constraints together, and are hence held morally responsible.	(1989), McKenna (2006), Wyma (1997), Otsuka (1998), Soares (2003), Arnold (2006), Mellema (2006), Pettit (2007), Braham and Van Hees (2012), and French (2016)

Source: Compiled by the authors.

Critical Thinking Exercise 3.4

Apply critical thinking (see footnote 3 in Chapter 1) in responding to the following questions:

- How do we assess and assign moral responsibility to various actors fooled by randomness, plagued by Black Swan events, and particularly operating in scalable industries?
- Further, if individual executives, corporations, singly or jointly, had to deal with high levels of risk, uncertainty, and ambiguity of scalable executive jobs and industries, to what extent can we critically factor those variables in assessing and/or exonerating moral responsibility?
- Moreover, if "the great strength of the free market system is the fact that company executives do not need to know what is going on" (Taleb, 2010, p. 17, footnote), does market ignorance exonerate corporate moral responsibility? If so, when and why?
- Further, if so, then to what extent does executive or corporate ignorance of harmful consequences define and exonerate executive crime or malpractice or malfeasance?

The third use of the word "responsible" relates to the way in which individuals think about and respond to situations. Goodpaster (1983) calls it the decision-making sense of the word. Thus, when we say that John Doe is a responsible person, we convey that he is reliable and trustworthy, that he can be depended upon to interpret situations and take actions that manifest both integrity and concern for those affected by them. The emphasis is not on John Doe as the agent who brought about a certain result (the causal sense), or on his following rules or role expectations (the rule-following sense) but on his independent judgment and the ingredients that go into that judgment. This third sense of "responsibility" will be our primary concern in critical thinking.

What is Moral Responsibility?

This distinction relates not to the senses or uses of "responsibility" but to the function of the modifier "moral." When we speak of an individual as "morally responsible," we contrast moral responsibility with other possible interpretations of responsibility. Most frequently, the contrast is with "legal responsibility." We acknowledge a difference in the causal sense when we distinguish between individuals being legally responsible ("liable," "blamable," or "imputable") for an event and being morally responsible for it. Similarly, we understand the difference (rule-following sense) between a person's legal responsibilities and their moral responsibilities in a certain role. The latter are often said to include but go "beyond" the former. For example, the legal responsibilities of parents to their children are part of their moral responsibilities, but their moral responsibilities do not stop at the boundary of the law. Thus, it is not illegal for a parent to criticize a child to the point where the child loses any sense of self-worth, but a parent who did this would be acting in a morally irresponsible manner.

In general, the modifier "moral" is used to signal a broad context in which the notion of responsibility is to be situated, a context that validates attributions of responsibility to individuals according to criteria distinct from law, religion, etiquette, and custom, for example. This distinction has to do with the force of attributions, such as "she is morally responsible in her decision-making."

Critical Thinking Exercise 3.5

Apply critical thinking (see footnote 3 in Chapter 1) to the *causal, rule-following*, and *decision-making* definition types of responsibility by Goodpaster (1983). Do all these definitions exclude or necessarily include considerations of morality? For instance, can legal responsibility as willful compliance be amoral? Can liability, imputability, or blamability be amoral? Similarly, can obligation, mandate, rule, or injunction, even though imposed by governments, be truly amoral in our obedient acceptance of it and adoption?

Manuel Velasquez (1983, 2003) also distinguishes three meanings of responsibility. First, the term is used sometimes to describe a person as having the character trait of dependability or integrity as in "he is a very responsible person," or "she acted with great responsibility." He calls this the *virtue sense* of responsibility (this is equivalent to the third *decision-making* sense of Goodpaster (1983). Second, the term can be used to mean "obligation" or "duty" as in "the social responsibility of business is to serve its stakeholders," or "business is responsible for serving its stakeholders." We may call this the *deontic sense* of responsibility. In its deontic sense, responsibility is about what ought to be done but might not yet have been done. Third, the term can be used to denote who or what is to blame for something that happened, as in "the storm is responsible for the damage," or "the ultimate responsibility for World War II belongs to Hitler." We can call this the *causal sense* of responsibility.

The notion of responsibility that Velasquez (2003, p. 533) discusses is a form of this third or causal sense of responsibility. In this causal sense, responsibility is retrospective, and looks toward the past, toward some act or event that someone or something has already caused. The responsible party in this sense is the party (or parties) that is identified as one of the primary, or most salient or significant, cause of the past act or event.

Velasquez (2003) discusses two kinds of causal responsibility. The first is what he calls natural responsibility. Natural causal responsibility is the kind of responsibility that we attribute to natural or nonintentional agents. Hurricanes, avalanches, tornadoes, and earthquakes are examples of natural agents, and obviously they can be responsible for inflicting damage on the world. The actions of natural agents, however, are not intentional. The second kind of causal responsibility is what we ordinarily speak of as moral responsibility. Moral responsibility is causal responsibility that we attribute to an agent when the agent acts intentionally. We call such actors as intentional agents. While natural agents, like hurricanes and avalanches cannot be morally responsible for the injuries they cause, intentional agents like human beings often are. Moral responsibility, then, is the kind of causal responsibility that we attribute to intentional agents like human beings when they cause (or helped to cause) some past event and did so intentionally.

Critical Thinking Exercise 3.6

Apply critical thinking (see footnote 3 in Chapter 1) to the definitions of moral responsibility proposed by Velasquez (1983, 2003) and compare them to those of Goodpaster (1983). For instance, is "causal" in Goodpaster same as "natural" in Velasquez? Is "virtue sense" in Velasquez same as "decision-making" in Goodpaster, and why? Is Velasquez's *deontic* responsibility (as obligation) not explicitly covered by Goodpaster? Where is the common denominator between Goodpaster and Velasquez that we can adopt for our use of moral responsibility? Do all these definitions exclude or necessarily include considerations of morality? Thus, to what extent can we describe natural causes (such as avalanches, tsunami, and so on) as *nonintentional?* Nature has a mind and heart of her own that we still do not fathom or accept because we naturally usurp intentionality, mind, consciousness, and purpose as solely belonging to humans!

Further, how do you respond to the following concerns regarding moral responsibility?

(Continued)

(*Continued*)

- Despite scholarly debate and contributions on moral responsibility for more than five or six decades, the "concept and cognates of moral responsibility are still ambiguous and there exists no standard terminology" (Braham & Van Hees, 2012, p. 604).
- Much of the literature speaks about moral responsibility as blameworthiness for bad outcomes; it is retrospective and predominantly retributive, and hardly prospective and nonjudgmental (Hasnas, 2010).
- That is, moral responsibility is primarily for harmful social outcomes that have already happened. Taking blame or responsibility for prevention of harm or violation of one's duties toward others is prospective responsibility, also called "substantive responsibility" or "accountability" (Watson, 2004) or "attributive responsibility" (Scanlon, 1998); this type of responsibility does not get the attention it deserves.
- Moreover, moral responsibility is mostly defined in terms of past actions as commissions. There is hardly any moral responsibility taken for omissions! For instance, think of our deliberate omissions to counteract conditions that precipitated World Wars I and II, the Holocaust, the 9/11 tragedy, and numerous other terrorist impositions.

Organizations Do Not Enjoy Moral Immunity

Once we are clear about which sense of "responsible" is at issue, and once we recognize that it is moral responsibility rather than, say, legal responsibility that is meant, the question arises: *In saying that an individual is morally responsible, are we merely describing some of their cognitive, emotional, or decision-making characteristics or are we instead (or also) commending and recommending them?* Put another way, is the concept of moral responsibility, as we are pursuing it, a normative concept or a descriptive concept or some mix of the two? The last seems more promising.

In any case, we may distinguish attributing moral responsibility to the *person* who acts (in the causal or rule-following or decision-making senses) from the action of the person (in the same three senses). To say that individuals are morally responsible, e.g., in the decision-making sense, is to say something about them, about the cognitive and emotional processes that precede and accompany their actions; it is descriptive and not normative. That is, we do not issue a verdict about the rightness and wrongness of their actions in every case.

Some philosophers characterize this feature of the concept of moral responsibility by saying that it refers to "subjective" rightness (or in the case of irresponsibility, wrongness), while "objective" rightness and wrongness are the central concerns of ethics. But this would be too hasty. Though moral responsibility may be a virtue insufficient to ensure complete moral rectitude in what one does, it is clearly to be thought of as an essential, even dominant, component. Actions that are taken without it might in some cases be "objectively" right, but more frequently they will not be. And actions that are taken with it might in some cases be "objectively" wrong, but more frequently they will not be.

Critical Thinking Exercise 3.7

Apply critical thinking (see footnote 3 in Chapter 1) to the following query of Frankena (1980) and subsequent responses of moralists, such as Goodpaster (1983):

- William K. Frankena, a leading American moral philosopher, poses this question: whom should a moral spectator rank higher, a person who does the right thing from bad motives or one who acts from good motives but does the wrong thing? Which person should we regard as morally better? (1980, p. 5)
- The first observation, writes Goodpaster (1983, p. 7), is that the concept of moral responsibility is normative with respect to the virtues of individual decision-making more than with respect to the rightness or wrongness of specific actions or behavior. It is what we might call a process concept.
- The second observation supplements the first. Attributions of moral responsibility are not only process-oriented rather than aimed directly at the content of behavior, they are also generic. That is, the cognitive and emotional processes associated with moral responsibility are less specific than those associated with the principles usually discussed in normative ethics.
- To attribute the normative-cum-descriptive concept of moral responsibility to an individual, then, is to allude to certain generic decision-making traits (cognitive and emotional dispositions) of the individual. It is not to pass judgment directly on the rightness or wrongness of the individual's acts, nor is it to impute a specific normative ethical principle to the individual's reasoning.
- That is, ethics of moral responsibility is more descriptive than judgmental, more descriptive than normative, more commending and recommending than condemning, more retributive than prescriptive.
- The modern challenge for the professional manager lies not with the growing number of tasks associated with the growing complexity of the role. Though formidable, the quantitative dimensions of the challenge can be met by more sophisticated approaches to control, production, and organizational structure. The most dramatic challenge lies in the qualitative domain, the domain in which management must exercise judgment and self-understanding (Goodpaster, 1983, p. 19).

(Continued)

(Continued)

- Issues of corporate responsibility, therefore, are of larger scope and context than the issues at stake in personal executive choices. Individuals make corporate policy decisions, of course, but these decisions are not merely personal; they are choices made for and in the name of the corporation. The notion of corporate responsibility finds its home in this larger context (Goodpaster, 1983).
- Issues of corporate responsibility are of smaller scope than the ethical foundations of capitalism since they presuppose to a great extent the fundamental legitimacy of capitalism, private property, for example, and free enterprise (Goodpaster, 1983, p. 3).

The Broader Context of Corporate Moral Responsibility

Corporate moral responsibility must be assessed against the broader context of the outcomes of responsible corporate decisions and choices that underlie them. Arguably, Kenneth Goodpaster (1983, p. 3) started the discussion of corporate moral responsibility in the context of the then famous Ford Pinto case, and said that Ford Motor Company confronted a long series of difficult policy questions, starting with competitive response to foreign imports, including engineering safety, product liability, and public relations.

Corporate moral responsibility, like its analogue in the individual, argues Goodpaster (1983, p. 19), "requires management of people and resources," but most importantly what we might call self-management. The competitive and strategic rationality that has for so long been the hallmark of managerial competence must be joined to a more "disinterested," community-centered rationality. Gamesmanship must be supplemented with moral leadership.

Critical Thinking Exercise 3.8

Apply critical thinking (see footnote 3 in Chapter 1) to the armchair philosophy context of business ethics among some scholars who, instead of focusing on broader and more relevant aspects of corporate behavior, are indulging on micro aspects and decisions and contexts, missing the woods for the trees. Thus, consider the following observations from this critical thinking viewpoint:

- Issues of corporate responsibility are of larger scope and context than the issues at stake in personal executive choices.
- Individuals make corporate policy decisions, of course, but these decisions are not merely personal; they are choices made for and in the name of the corporation. The notion of corporate responsibility finds its home in this larger context.

(*Continued*)

- Following Goodpaster (1983), we could conceive moral responsibility as a function of several sequential stages such as moral perception, moral reasoning, moral coordination, moral projection, and moral implementation (see also Table 3.1).
- Consequently, whether considered a fictional legal entity or a real organization, corporations do not originate acts in a manner required by attributions of moral responsibility – namely, by directly moving one's own body (Velasquez, 1983).
- In the real world of today, corporations "perform" by making certain (often risky) choices backed by appropriate strategies (e.g., new product design and development, purchases, mergers and acquisitions, strategic alliances, divestitures, joint ventures, outsourcing, etc.). Can corporations "perform" such serious decisions without intrinsic rationality, protracted research, and long strategic planning?

Necessary and Sufficient Conditions for Moral Responsibility

In a seminal article, Peter French (1979) identified what he believed to be two necessary and sufficient conditions for moral responsibility: (a) *causation* – that a potential subject of moral responsibility be capable of acting so as to be the cause of an event, and (b) *intentionality* – that the action in question was intended by the subject or that the event was the direct result of an intentional act of the subject. Since all corporations have institutional decision-making procedures such as corporate internal decision structures, French (1979, p. 211) concluded that corporations can both cause events and act intentionally. Because of these internal structures and the level of involvement they commit, French claimed that this was sufficient to show not only that corporations are proper subjects of moral responsibility but also that they are "full-fledged moral persons and have whatever privileges, rights and duties as are, in the normal course of affairs, accorded to moral persons" (French, 1979, p. 207).

Critical Thinking Exercise 3.9

Apply critical thinking (see footnote 3 in Chapter 1) to the necessary and sufficient conditions for individual or corporate moral responsibility as prescribed by Velasquez (1983, 2003), French (1979), and others.

- Velasquez (1983, 2003) considers moral responsibility as a function of several components such as rationality and intentionality, and therefore

(*Continued*)

(*Continued*)

causality and accountability; he argues that corporations as a group do not have "intrinsic" rationality and intentionality, other than those of its corporates, and hence no causality or moral responsibility can be attributed to them, other than metaphorically. Do you agree, why or why not?

- Intrinsic intentionality is the necessary condition of moral responsibility, and since corporations do not exhibit intrinsic intentionality, they cannot be held morally responsible. When or under what circumstances is intrinsic intentionality neither the necessary nor a sufficient condition of moral responsibility? That is, does this condition overdetermine moral responsibility, thus letting corporates that overwhelmingly (although arguably under competitive pressures) indulge in fraud, greed, and money laundering off the hook?
- Velasquez (1983, p. 7) argues that a corporation cannot act intentionally unless through its executives, who alone can be attributed with moral responsibility for their decisions and actions: moral responsibility for an act can be "attributed only to that agent who originated the act in his own body, that is, in the movements of a body over which he has direct control."
- In corporate agency, action does not originate in a body belonging to the corporation to whom the act is attributed, but in bodies belonging to those human beings whose direct movements constituted or brought about the act that is then attributed to the corporation.

Michael Keeley (1979, p. 149) also argued that corporations cannot be moral persons because "organizations have no intentions or goals at all." Keeley contended that although an organization's corporate internal decision structure "may serve to identify organizational behavior, it does not ordinarily establish the organizational intent of that behavior or that it has any real organizational intent at all" (Keeley, 1979, p. 151). That is, organizations may act such that actions produce effects (good or bad), but it does not follow that organizations intended that effect. Only corporate executives do, and hence can incur moral responsibility (Keeley, 1979, p. 152). Similarly, John Ladd argued that formal organizations such as corporations are capable of only means-end rationality; that is, given a predetermined goal, corporations can make empirical judgments about the best means to achieve it but contended that corporations have no mechanism by which they can process or evaluate normative propositions. Consequently, corporations cannot produce intentions to act rightly or wrongly in a moral sense (Ladd, 1970).

Critical Thinking Exercise 3.10

Apply critical thinking (see footnote 3 in Chapter 1) to the responses of Donaldson (1982) to Peter French's (1979) necessary and sufficient conditions for moral responsibility as moral persons. That is, consider the following observations from a critical thinking viewpoint:

- Corporations lack the autonomy necessary to perform primary actions, one of the conditions necessary to be ascribed full personhood (Donaldson, 1982).
- Donaldson (1982) also argued that being an intentional causal agent is not sufficient for moral personhood.
- French's (1979, p. 207) argument implied that corporations "have whatever privileges, rights and duties as are, in the normal course of affairs, accorded to moral persons." But Donaldson (1982, pp. 22–23) claimed this to be undesirable – do we really want to consider corporations as "moral persons," with the right to vote, worship, be sentenced to prison, or denied the right to pursue happiness, thus overdetermining corporate moral responsibility?

Critical Thinking Exercise 3.11

Apply critical thinking (see footnote 3 in Chapter 1) to the necessary or sufficient conditions for *moral agency* as argued by Donaldson (1982) and Werhane (1985).

- How are they different from French's (1979) necessary and sufficient conditions for *moral responsibility*?
- In this connection, what is the real difference between moral responsibility and moral agency, when the subject for both are real corporations that act, deliberate, and decide, and can create socially harmful consequences?
- The real object of corporate moral responsibility is corporate actions and their harmful consequences on innocent society as bystanders, as also on the poor and the marginalized affected by these actions. Whether these actions originate from corporates as moral agents, or moral actors, or moral persons is irrelevant, and sidelines the real issue of corporate moral responsibility, thus depriving victims of proper justice.
- By the doctrine of *strict liability*, that dates back to 1966 in the United States, it matters little from whom (as moral agents, moral causes, or moral persons, as primary or secondary actors or actions) the liability

(Continued)

(*Continued*)

originates, as long as the affected victims of liability are adequately compensated for harm done to them.

- Despite their criticism of French, both Donaldson (1982) and Werhane (1985) argued that corporations can bear moral responsibility. This is because *full moral personhood is not necessary for moral responsibility* – although all moral persons are morally responsible, subjects that do not satisfy all the requirements of moral personhood can nevertheless be morally responsible agents.

- To demonstrate this, both Donaldson (1982) and Werhane (1985) argued their own set of conditions for moral agency. According to Donaldson, to qualify as a moral agent, a corporation needs only "embody a process of moral decision-making" (Donaldson, 1982, p. 30). This requires (a) the capacity "to use moral reasons in decision-making," and (b) "the capacity of the decision-making process to control not only overt corporate acts, but also the structure of policies and rules" (Donaldson, 1982, p. 30).

- Donaldson claimed that many, if not most, corporations meet these two requirements. While admitting that corporations "are unable to think as humans," he argued that corporations can be morally accountable in the sense that "with the proper internal structure, corporations, like humans, can be liable to give an account of their behavior where the account stipulates which moral reasons prompted their behavior" (Donaldson, 1982, p. 30).

- Further, there is no reason why a corporation's internal decisions procedures cannot be applied *self-referentially* so that it is the corporation itself that controls the creation and "maintenance of the corporation's decision-making machinery" (Donaldson, 1982, p. 30).

- Hence, *although not moral persons, corporations can nevertheless be morally responsible agents.*

Critical Thinking Exercise 3.12

Apply critical thinking (see footnote 3 in Chapter 1) to the necessary or sufficient conditions for moral personhood, as argued by Werhane (1985), Danley (1990), and Velasquez (1983).

- *Is "moral personhood" a convenient social or philosophical construction that we often invoke to morally blame corporations, as well as to exonerate them from justice to the disadvantaged affected from corporate actions?*
- Patricia Werhane's conditions for moral agency were essentially the same as French's conditions for moral personhood: (a) the capacity to act, and (b) the ability to form intentions (1985, pp. 57–59).

(*Continued*)

- Werhane (1985, pp. 52–56) contended that corporations have the capacity to act because they can undertake secondary actions – actions taken by individual corporate agents who are authorized to act on behalf of the corporation by the corporate charter and bylaws as interpreted and amended by the board of directors, corporate management, and market forces.
- These are true corporate actions because they "cannot be re-described in terms of the actions of constituents" (Werhane, 1985, p. 56). Further, Werhane agreed with French that *corporate structure incorporates the intentions of individual human executives.*
- Werhane also argued that a corporate intentional system combines the sum of the decision-making procedures carried out by boards of directors, stockholders at Annual General Body Meetings (AGBM), management, foremen, and other employees, with the advice of outside agents such as lawyers, accountants, and public relations persons, which together form collective "corporate" "intentions" that exhibit "corporate decision-making," corporate "action," and organizational goals (1985, p. 56).
- Thus, although corporations are not moral persons, they "like persons, are and should be, held morally responsible for actions within their control" (Werhane, 1985, p. 59).
- However, all these considerations still do not prove that corporations have intentions or do intend to act with full rationality and intentionality (Danley, 1990, p. 204). While individuals within the corporation can intend, combat with malice and greed, the corporation on its own cannot (Danley, 1990, p. 203).
- In the same vein, Velasquez (1983) argued that corporations do not possess the integration of body and mind required for intentional action because an act is intentional only if it is the carrying out of an intention formed in the mind of the agent whose bodily movements bring about the act.
- The underlying reason for corporate policies and procedures being unable to generate intentional action is that the concept of intentional action is rooted in the concept of an agent with a certain mental and bodily unity that corporations do not have (Velasquez, 1983, p. 8).

Critical Thinking Exercise 3.13

Apply critical thinking (see footnote 3 in Chapter 1) to the distinction between moral persons, moral agents, and moral actors, primary versus secondary actors and actions, in relation to moral responsibility as postulated by scholars of business ethics. What are the postulated necessary and/or sufficient conditions for primary versus secondary actors and actions in relation to moral

(*Continued*)

(*Continued*)

responsibility? To what extent are these distinctions really valid, reflecting reality, objectivity, and necessity? Do they explain and judge moral behavior as much as they do to confuse, obfuscate, and exonerate it? Do they "over-determine" corporate moral responsibility as much as they undermine it?

Hence apply critical thinking to the following developments.

- Peter French (1995, p. 10), possibly influenced by Thomas Donaldson (1982) and Patricia Werhane (1985), revised his position: corporations are not full moral persons, but to be morally responsible, one need only be a moral "actor" or moral agent and not a moral person.
- Accordingly, French's new necessary and sufficient conditions to be a moral actor are: (a) the ability to act intentionally, that is, having "purposes, plans, goals, and interests" that motivate behavior, (b) the ability to make rational decisions and consider rational arguments regarding their intentions, and (c) "the facility to respond to events and ethical criticism by altering intentions and patterns of behavior that are harmful to others or detrimental to their own interests" (1995, pp. 10–12).
- However, French (1995, p. 12) contended that because corporations possessed corporate internal decision-making structures, they satisfy each of these conditions for moral agency.
- Velasquez (2003), however, rejects French's (1995) argument about corporate intentions. French's corporate internal decision-making structures simply could not do the work required to transform individual intentions into corporate intentions. "The fact that we attribute intentional qualities to groups – including corporations and organizations – that are not attributable to their members, then, does not imply that those groups have real intentions. The intentions that we attribute to groups are metaphorical, based on analogies to the literal intentions we attribute to humans" (Velasquez, 2003, pp. 545–546).
- Pettit (2007, p. 175) introduced his own version of necessary and sufficient conditions for moral responsibility: (a) *value relevance* – the subject "is an autonomous agent and faces a value relevant choice involving the possibility of doing something good or bad or right or wrong," (b) *value judgment* – the subject "has the understanding and access to evidence required for being able to make judgments about the relative value of such options," and (c) *value sensitivity* – the subject "has the control necessary for being able to choose between options on the basis of judgments about their value."
- Pettit argued that corporations satisfy the first condition because they can (a) qualify as agents and (b) act autonomously. Corporations qualify as agents "when members act on the shared intention that together they should realize the conditions that ensure agency," which they do by acting in accordance with a constitution "whereby the members of a

(*Continued*)

group might each be assigned roles in the generation of an action-suited body of desire and belief and in the performance of the actions that it supports" (2007, p. 179).

- Pettit claimed that corporations satisfy the second and third conditions as well. They can form value judgments "over a certain proposition when the proposition is presented for consideration and the group takes whatever steps are prescribed in the constitution for endorsing it" (2007, p. 186).

Critical Thinking Exercise 3.14

Apply critical thinking (see footnote 3 in Chapter 1) to the necessary and sufficient conditions for moral responsibility as proposed by Braham and Van Hees (2012).

- According to Braham & Van Hees (2012), at least three conditions should be fulfilled for moral responsibility: (a) agency condition (AC): the person is an autonomous agent performing action intentionally; (b) causal relevancy condition (CRC): there should be a causal relation between the action of the agent and the resultant state of affairs; and (c) avoidance opportunity condition (AOC): the agent should have had a reasonable opportunity to have done otherwise.
- Is the first, AC, tautological – is by definition a morally responsible person always an autonomous agent who acts intentionally?
- Regarding CRC, how can you establish a *causal* relation between the action of the agent and the resultant state of affairs? Even courts shy away from demanding causality, as it is very difficult and complex to establish causality between any two events; moreover, by the time you collect enough evidence to establish causality, conditions may change that make causality unimportant.
- Regarding AOC, what if the agent did not have a reasonable opportunity to avoid the action; does moral responsibility cease even when harmful effects follow? By strict liability law, you may not be charged for wrongdoing, but be liable for adequate compensation for harmed parties.
- Hence, Braham and Van Hees (2012) add that AC is a necessary condition for moral responsibility because we may do many things that affect outcomes but do not bear the mark of "authorship," where such authorship is a requirement for blame or praise to be justified or appropriated.
- Similarly, CRC is a necessary condition for moral responsibility because we cannot say that a person is the author of an action if the person played

(*Continued*)

(Continued)

no causal role in bringing it about. Does lack of proven "authorship" reduce liability or guilt? Further, how is authorship established? What is needed for authorship? The problem is diverted but not resolved.

- Although the two conditions are necessary, Braham and Van Hees (2012) add that they are not yet sufficient for a judgment about a person's praise – or blameworthiness. A common line of thought is that some form of control other than being a causal factor is required. In Watson's (2004, p. 280) view, because blaming responses potentially affects the interests of those blamed, moral responsibility is closely related to the issue of avoidability. Hence, AOC is needed as a necessary or a sufficient condition. But, when and how long and by whom should an action be avoidable before it can be legally declared as avoidable by a given agent?

- Even with full knowledge, one may not have the freedom to avoid it (Benn & Weinstein, 1971; Sugden, 1998), or is the avoidable opportunity "eligible" for affecting executive freedom (Braham & Van Hees, 2012, p. 618)? What is eligibility and to what extent can it be fully ascertained before the action?

- Despite these problems, in general, Braham and Van Hees' (2012) conditions for moral responsibility seem to be realistic and relevant.

Part III
Synthesizing Necessary and Sufficient Conditions for Accepting or Assigning Moral Responsibility for Turbulent Market Conditions

In the narrative of the tragedy of the commons, it is difficult to assign moral responsibility for a common outcome arising from several agents such as corporates, corporations, and industries, e.g., global climate change, depletion of common resources such as forests, flooding, tsunami, deep sea mining, deep sea fishing and the like, where no individual or corporation has direct control over the outcome in the form of actions that are necessary or sufficient for such an outcome to occur. In such cases, it is not obvious who is to be assigned responsibility for the outcome. But we can all take joint responsibility to prevent further damage to the commons.

Further, even though a corporation is a fluid institution with changing CXOs and boards of directors, with shifting visions, missions, and identities, is that stable enough to accept and appropriate moral responsibility? Or, regardless of the three conditions – agency relevance, agency causality, and avoidability (Braham & Van Hees, 2012) – verified or not verified in the corporation, can we be satisfied that the corporation is legally held liable for its harmful effects, while its corporates might be held additionally moral responsible for the harmful effects of the corporation they belong to? Or can we consider both attributions to corporation and to corporates just as metaphorical or "as-if" propositions without necessarily reifying them or vilifying them?

Table 3.1 summarizes individual and corporate moral responsibility from thought to action (i.e., moral perception to moral reasoning to moral coordination to moral projection to moral implementation). Collective intentionality, rationality, causality, and hence collective accountability, are complex organizational realities that entail several discrete, sequential, and connected strategies such as group intention, group market scanning, group industry response, group planning, group understanding of goals and objectives, group action projects, group discernment, dialogue and deliberation, group prediction of outcomes, group willing of outcomes, and group culpability and blame for bad outcomes, and group achievement and praise for good outcomes. Lack of active and willed participation in some of these group activities may reduce guilt and culpability, individual or collective.

Critical Thinking Exercise 3.15

Apply critical thinking (see footnote 3 in Chapter 1) to Table 3.1 that summarizes individual and corporate moral responsibility from thought to action. Does corporate moral responsibility increase from moral perception to moral reasoning to moral coordination to moral projection to moral implementation – if so, why? Are these distinct and necessarily discrete stages of corporate moral responsibility as input preparation? Or are these stages of continuous corporate moral responsibility processes in action?

Being descriptive, Table 3.1 *does not prescribe mandates.*

Table 3.2 combines the necessary and sufficient conditions set forth by French (1995), Velasquez (2003), and others in modeling individual or corporate moral responsibilities.

Critical Thinking Exercise 3.16

Apply critical thinking (see footnote 3 in chapter 1) to Table 3.2, which summarizes individual and corporate moral responsibility based on necessary and sufficient conditions composed of rationality (R), intentionality (I), causality (C), freedom or autonomy (F), and accountability (A), at both the individual and collective levels of an organization. Are these necessary and sufficient conditions discrete and descriptive (and not normative) stages of corporate moral responsibility as input processes? Or are these stages of continuous corporate moral responsibility processes in action?

(Continued)

(*Continued*)

Apply critical thinking also to the following concerns regarding Table 3.2.

- To be necessary and sufficient, each condition has to *preoccur* in all forms of moral responsibility as with moral actors, moral agents, moral persons, and moral organizations. Is this assumption realistic and defensible? Do these conditions indicate sufficient – individual or corporate – reflection, interaction, deliberation, and control?
- Are all these determinants (i.e., R, I, F, C, and A) significantly distinct from or supplementing or complementing each other? Of these, which are necessary or sufficient preconditions of corporate moral responsibility and why?
- Do the individual-versus-corporate responsibility models (see bottom rows of Table 3.2) make sense; to what extent do they capture the business market turbulent reality?
- Do these models adequately represent moral responsibility as suggested? How could you improve upon these models, both at the individual and corporate levels?
- Most of these moral responsibility models could really be nonlinear and nonadditive as suggested in the note under Table 3.2. How would you respond?
- Are R, I, C, F, and A realistic constituents or determinants of moral responsibility at both individual and corporate levels?
- Are these necessary and sufficient conditions mutually exclusive and collectively exhaustive (MECE) categories? Can there ever be an MECE categorization of corporate moral responsibility, the latter being context-driven and subjectively complex?
- The attribution of R, I, F, C, and A states can serve as either rewarding (merit, credit, recognition) or inculpating (guilt, liability, punishment) conditions for collective action. Hence, instead of over-stressing individual responsibilities, should we focus on joint (legal, ethical, and moral) responsibility that the corporation would collectively more easily appropriate and own, and accordingly change behavior for the greater good of the society?

Assigning Legal and Moral Responsibilities to Various Actors

If we still (retributively) seek to assign moral responsibility to corporate individuals, and to corporations as a business entity, then Exhibit 3.2 is one such characterization that might help in assigning moral responsibility. It can be calibrated and perfected further by advanced critical thinking. However, apportioning moral responsibility to individuals in "corporate groups" or "organizations" can be problematic. For instance, Miller (2001, pp. 174–176) argues that

Table 3.1. Individual and Corporate Moral Responsibility From Thought to Action.

Moral Responsibility Components	Corporate Individual	Corporate Collective
Moral perception	*Perception stemming from scanning the environment:*	*Moral perception arising from scanning the corporate environment:*
	Election and selection in scanning specific markets (lucrative or profit-maximizing, ghetto inner-city underserved markets, or urban high buying power niches) testing (feasibility, viability, desirability), research and analysis (objective, abductive, honest, verifiable, replicable), inference, consumer satisfaction, consumer welfare, worker safety and welfare, product and production safety, ecologically friendly operations, green procedures, etc.	Selectivity of data: test data, test procedures, worker safety, worker rights and duties, consumer health, consumer rights and duties, consumer ecology, cosmic sustainability consumer feedback, local or neighborhood community health, education.
		Corporate sensitivity to stakeholder issues, concerns, and moral/legal responsibilities, ecology, sustainability, recycling, regeneration, restoration, and greening of ghost cities and dilapidated neighborhoods.
Moral reasoning	Individual rationality and intelligence of selecting, storing, analyzing relevant information, facts, figures, ethical theories, moral principles in relation to subjects, objects, properties and events.	Organizational tacit knowledge and routines, skills, and procedure: corporate collective (e.g., board of directors) rationality of gathering, sorting, selecting, storing, archiving, retrieving, analyzing relevant information, facts, customs, traditions, ethical theories, corporate policies, and corporate moral principles regarding a given case or litigation.
	Moral and nonmoral criteria in reasoning.	
	Moral judgment calls.	
	Moral judgment justification.	
	Moral ignorance and weakness.	Moral reasoning can be refined and enhanced by

(Continued)

Table 3.1. (*Continued*)

Moral Responsibility Components	Corporate Individual	Corporate Collective
	Moral law compliance and abidance. Industry law compliance or defiance.	top management and board of directors, consulting, and research. Moral ignorance and compliance of regulations. Corporate moral congruence and convergence.
Moral coordination	Given moral perception and reasoning, moral coordination involves: Individual moral competence, moral intelligibility. Personal corporate goals and objectives. Individual motivation and autonomy. Individual efforts to corporate congruence and accord. Coordination in creativity, discovery, invention, and innovation. Coordination in explanation, prediction, monitoring, and control.	Given moral perception and reasoning, organizational moral coordination involves: Organizational moral competence. Shared plans and intentions. Shared vision/mission, goals, and objectives. Corporate motivation and autonomy. Corporate strategies for corporate congruence and accord. Corporate ambitions and aspirations. Shared corporate vision, mission, and identity. Corporate moral agreement/disagreement. Corporate moral journey, governance philosophy.
Moral projection	Moral projection from thought to action, individual to team and groups, microcosms to macrocosms. Moral conscience and moral intentions.	Organizational conscience. Corporate moral purpose and passion. Corporate conscience for local communities. Organizational moral climate.

Employee rights and entitlements.
Consumer rights and entitlements.
Local community rights and duties and entitlements.
National rights, duties, and entitlements.
Global community right, duties, privileges.
Global ecology and sustainability.
Cosmic ecology and sustainability.

Corporate social responsibility.
Corporate philanthropy and outreach.
Global community right, duties.
Global justice, harmony, and solidarity.
Global human equality and eradication of poverty.
Global ecology and sustainability.
Corporate contribution to employment and welfare.
Corporate influence on industry and community.

Moral implementation

Personal commitment/promise to worker/consumer safety and welfare.
Passionate commitment to corporate implementation of moral responsibility.
Individual commitment to creativity, discovery, invention, and innovation.
Commitment to enhancing corporate, brand, identity, and mission.
Commitment to global harmony, peace, and solidarity.

Institutionalizing worker/consumer safety.
Responding to employee and customer complaints.
Handling short-term versus long-term objectives.
Handling competitive pressures.
Handling litigation pressures and actions.
Sustainable competitive advantage (SCA).
Avoiding cost benefit analysis (CBA) by seeking newer alternatives.
Corporate tradeoffs for growth and survival.
Corporate returns to shareholders (return on equity [ROE], employee pension scheme [EPS], price-to-earnings [P/E] ratio, total shareholder return [TSR])

Source: Compiled by the authors. See also Goodpaster (1983).

Table 3.2. Constituents of Individual and Collective Moral Responsibility.

Responsibility Constituents	Individual Executive	Collective Corporate
Rationality (R)	Individual perception, reasoning, attitude. Individual market scanning, selection of markets, events.	Collective rationality represented by collective perceptions, collective reasoning, and explanation.
	Gathering information, description, analysis, explanation, rationalization, justification, prediction.	Collective attitudes, convictions, and beliefs. Shared market scanning and selection of market opportunities and territories.
	Individual problem identification, formulation, and resolving.	Collective information gathering for evaluation of problem solution alternatives.
	Seeking and evaluating problem solution alternatives and solution skills.	Collective agreement/disagreement patterns. Collective organizational learning and routines, tacit and overt knowledge, skills, IPR, and technologies.
	Individual learning, skills, expertise, intellectual properties, including patents (intellectual property rights [IPRs]).	
	Ability to make rational decisions and consider rational arguments (French, 1995).	
Intentionality (I)	The action in question was intended by the subject or that the individual intent and intentionality was marked by personal goals (French, 1979).	Collective shared intentions and intentionality characterized by group dynamics, corporate conduct, corporate vision, mission, identity, expectations, standards.
	Having "purposes, plans, goals, and interests" that control behavior (French, 1995).	Corporate codes, interpreting and complying with industrial codes, mores, conventions, injunctions.
	Marked by purpose, beliefs, values, family mores, and traditions, family dreams/ ambitions, personal expectations, standards.	Corporate involvement, commitment, dedication, contribution, promise.
	Individual commitment of expertise, skill,	Corporate challenges of being good (*dharma*).

	focus, dedication, and involvement. Individual challenge of being good (*dharma*). Individual autonomy, civility, integrity, and transparency.	Corporate civility, integrity, transparency, citizenship.
Freedom (F)	Individual autonomy and freedom to act or withdraw (avoidability) from acting. Utonomy is reinforced with discernment and deliberation to act or not to act.	Corporate autonomy and freedom to act or withdraw (avoidability) from acting. Corporate autonomy is reinforced with collective discernment, dialogue, and deliberation to act or not to act.
Causality (C)	Capable of acting so as to be the cause of an event (French, 1979), individual action composed of mind, heart and body (Velasquez, 1983). Individual choices, intentions, elections, votes. Individually foreseen and unforeseen consequences with social externalities. Individual insight, intuition, hindsight, abilities, skills, contributions, initiations, creativity, invention, discovery, innovation, ventures, and adventures. Understanding and taming risk, uncertainty, chaos.	Collective action marked by group decision-making via corporate choices, options, intentions, selection, elections, commissions, omissions, strategies, implementation, and control (French, 1979). Corporate rules, norms, standards, and expectations. Corporate mandates, policies and procedures, shared planning, goals, and objectives. Collective understanding/taming risk, uncertainty, chaos. Collective combatting of competitive pressures and environments.
Accountability (A)	Personal accountability and personal answerability. Personal attributions and appropriations of responsibility.	Collective accountability and answerability. Corporate attributions and appropriations of rationality. Corporate expectations, obligations, duties,

(Continued)

Table 3.2. (*Continued*)

Responsibility Constituents	Individual Executive	Collective Corporate
Causal agency = f (F, C)*	Individual expectations, obligations, duties, rights, community entitlements, social justice. Good (socially benefitting) outcomes – individual attribution/appropriation of praise/reward. Bad (socially harmful) outcomes – individual attribution/appropriation of guilt, blame/punishment. $\approx (F + C)$ Individual causal agency.	rights, entitlements, compensations, social justice, corporate justice. Good (socially benefitting) outcomes – corporate attribution/appropriation of praise/awards. Bad (socially harmful) outcomes – corporate attribution/appropriation of collective liability, guilt, blame/punishment. $\approx (F + C)$ corporate causal agency.
Moral agency = f(R, I, F, C)*	$\approx (I + F + C)$ individual moral agency.	$\approx (F + I + C)$ corporate moral agency.
Responsibility = f(I, F, C, A)*	$\approx (I + F + C + A)$ = Individual moral responsibility.	$\approx (I + F + C + A)$ = corporate moral responsibility.
Causal responsibility = f (R, C, A)*	$\approx (R + I + C + A)$ Individual causal responsibility as agents.	$\approx (R + I C + A)$ corporate causal responsibility as agents.
Moral persons and moral responsibility = f (I, R, F, C)*	$\approx (I + R + F + C + A)$ Individual causal, moral responsibility as moral persons. Admitting wrongdoing, and amending behavior if called for.	$\approx (I + R + F + C + A)$ = corporate causal, moral responsibility as corporate moral agents. Admitting corporate wrongdoing and amending behavior if called for by social accountability.

Source: Compiled by the authors.

Notes: (i) * Are more general functions that could be nonlinear and nonadditive. (ii) R, I, F, C, A are as defined in Column 1.

Exhibit 3.2. Assigning Legal and Moral Responsibilities to Various Actors by Their Antecedent Involvements.

Legend	NC = Necessary Condition; SC = Sufficient Condition; JC = Joint Condition; EC = Enabling Condition			
Possible Responsibility Antecedents	**Legal Liability to Concerned Stakeholders**	**Moral Responsibility to Concerned Stakeholders**		
		Individual	**Corporate**	**Joint**
Sole physical causality	NC	NC	NC	NC
Joint physical causality	JC	JC	JC	JC
Moral reasoning and rationality	EC	EC	EC	EC
Action: Physical avoidability of action	NC	NC	NC	NC
Action: Moral avoidability	EC	EC	EC	EC
Moral individual intentionality	EC	NC	NC	NC
Moral individual and joint intentionality	SC	SC	SC	SC
Collective dialogue, discernment, and deliberation	EC	JC	JC	JC
Moral discernment without lobbying deliberation	EC	EC	EC	EC
Moral accountability	EC	JC	JC	JC
Moral agency	EC	NC	NC	NC
Moral personhood	EC	SC	SC	SC
Moral considerability	EC	EC	EC	EC

Source: Compiled by the authors.

participants in "joint mechanisms" are individually responsible for their contributory actions. On the other hand, a joint mechanism is a set of interlocking and interdependent behaviors like a company's decision-making procedures used to coordinate actions and bring about certain types of outcomes. The "corporate actions" produced by mechanisms are irreducible to individuals' contributing actions because the joint mechanism allows for outcomes contrary to some of the participants' preferences (Miller, 2001, p. 174).

Critical Thinking Exercise 3.17

Apply critical thinking (see footnote 3 in Chapter 1) to Exhibit 3.2, which summarizes individual and corporate moral responsibility based on necessary condition (NC), sufficient condition (SC), joint condition (JC), and enabling condition (EC) at individual, corporate, and joint levels of an organization.

How can you improve on the categorization of Exhibit 3.2 to make it more realistic and objectively verifiable? Are these necessary and sufficient conditions cumulative and normative by columns, e.g., greater the number of NCs and SCs verified along any given column, stronger is the reason for assigning moral responsibility for that column subject?

Additionally, critically consider the following relevant observations:

- Corporations can act autonomously because the corporation's judgment cannot be reduced to the judgment of the individuals who comprise it. Thus, "autonomy is intuitively guaranteed by the fact that on one or more issues the judgment of the group will have to be functionally independent of the corresponding members' judgments, so that its intentional attitudes as a whole are most saliently unified by being, precisely, the attitudes of the group" (Pettit, 2007, p. 184).
- "If an agent knew, could have known, or should have known, that a certain action of hers could lead to a particular outcome, then we shall assess her responsibility for the outcome differently than if she could not possibly have known, or not known, or need not have known, that the outcome would have resulted. To avoid these circumstances, we could assume the agents had 'full information' and hence, ignorance cannot excuse" (Braham & Van Hees, 2012, p. 608).

Analysis of Four Mini Cases

For instance, consider the following four illustrative scenarios or cases of combinations of R, I, F, C, and A:

(1) *Case A:* As CEO and member of the governing board, John freely voted against certain actions of the corporation and board of directors and lobbied heavily against the action.

(2) *Case B:* As a member of the same governing board, John voted against this action but did not lobby against it as he should.

(3) *Case C:* As a CEO of the same company, at a pre-board of directors meeting, John voted for this action and lobbied heavily for it, and the board of directors also decided for the action.

(4) *Case D:* As a shareholder at the annual general body meeting (AGBM), John voted against it, but AGBM decided for it anyhow.

The same four cases with possible attribution of rationality (R), intentionality (I), freedom (F), causality (C), and accountability (A) states (see Table 3.2) would look like this:

(1) **A***: As CEO and member (I, F) of the governing board, John freely voted (F) against certain action of the corporation and the board of directors (−I, − C), and lobbied heavily against the action (R, −I, −F).
(2) **B***: As a member of the governing board, John voted against this action (R, F, −I, −C) but did not lobby against it as he should (−R, −F, −C), i.e., silence may be construed as consent (+R, +F) or complicity (C).
(3) **C***: As a CEO of the same company at a pre-board of directors meeting, John voted for this action (+I, +C, +F) and lobbied heavily for it (+I, +R, +F), and the board of directors also decided for the action.
(4) **D***: As a shareholder at the AGBM, John voted against the action (F, −I, −C), but AGBM decided for it anyhow (−A).

Let us assume the corporate decision resulted in significant social harm under all four cases (A to D). Further, there is moral culpability under all four cases, since John is a corporate member in all four, but the culpability varies by degrees depending on factors such as: (a) gravity and width/depth of harm resulting from the corporate decision, (b) length (duration), breadth, and depth of John's corporate involvement for or against this action, (c) what could have been done by John to avert the action (i.e., act of omission given "avoidability"), and (d) whether the corporate act that caused harm was endemic to the context, or chaotic, random, or influenced by other contextual circumstances corporates could not control.

In the first case, John did not intend the action (−I) by not voting for it (−C), and even lobbied heavily against it (R, −C) (i.e., John reasoned and argued against it indicating that he did not intend it [−I]), but the board of directors decided it anyhow. Thus, what is the degree of accountability (or its correlative, culpability) of John in the final outcome that *turned out to be socially harmful?* Minimal, but as CEO and a member of the board of directors, John must jointly, even if vicariously, accept blame and culpability for corporate actions beyond his control. Just based on the R, I, C, F, and A conditions attributable to John, one rank of perceived descending culpability among the four scenarios could be C, B, D, A. But if this allocation is weighed by the hierarchical importance or position of John as involved in the action, the rank of descending culpability would be A, C, B, D (i.e., John's accountability remains significant despite his voting and lobbying against it, as perhaps, John might have deservedly lost his power and credibility with the board of directors, or he could have deployed other promoter resources against the corporate action).

But what is the moral responsibility of each person in the final outcome that turned to be socially harmful? Again, just based on an objective predication of R, I, F, C, and A to A, B, C, and D, one rank of descending moral responsibility would be C, B, A, D. Now, assume that moral responsibility is proportional to the duration of involvement and level of control that John had before the action and the extent he used it both for stopping or redesigning the action. Further, if this allocation is weighed by the hierarchical importance of the person involved in the action, the rank order of descending moral responsibility would be C, A, B, D.

Thus far, in the allocation of accountability or moral responsibility as done above, the persons in cases A, B, C, and D and their actions and responsibilities are considered independently and not interactively, as the case most often is. But as Miller (2001) argues, being fully, individually responsible for their contributory actions such as votes, participants in joint mechanisms (e.g., discernment, deliberation, discussion, dialogue, voting, lobbying) are "jointly responsible" for the relevant corporate action, meaning that each member is morally responsible, but this responsibility is dependent on the other members' being equally responsible. Miller argues that even those whose preferences are not reflected in the joint mechanism's outcome, such as those on the losing side of a committee vote, are still morally and jointly responsible for the outcome. This follows because they committed themselves to abide by the corporation they chose to work for, and accepted the corporation's decision procedures and mechanisms with their outcomes and thereby, connected their own conscious agency with the power of the group. Here, even the opponent to a proposal is jointly responsible for the associated action when the majority of one's peers bring it about through a joint mechanism (Miller, 2001, p. 241). This could happen due to adverse selection or moral hazard, both results of noncritical thinking. Even Velasquez (2003, pp. 547–548) admits:

> When we attribute intentionality to a collection of people that cannot be attributed to the individual members of the collection, then, we generally do so because the actions of the collection meet certain conditions: they exhibit a pattern that we think is sufficiently analogous to the actions of intentional humans to merit describing them in that way…. The law, for example, attributes to sellers certain so-called "implied" promises of usability. Such laws are not saying that sellers have actually made such promises, nor that sellers behave as if they are making such promises. Instead, the law is simply declaring that sellers are to be treated as if they have made such promise.

Discussion

Parts II and III of this chapter reveal how complicated and involved the issues of individual, corporate, and joint responsibility, moral responsibility assignation, moral agency, moral personal responsibility, and the like are, especially when all these issues are scrutinized through the lens of critical thinking. Critical thinking also exposes us to the fallibility and liability of human judgment and that we can never afford to be dogmatic and absolute about our moral judgments, reflecting as they are turbulent markets wrought with randomness, Black Swans, uncertainty, unpredictability, and complexity that include chaos and ambiguity.

At the same time, responsibility bears many dimensions other than what we have considered. Table 3.3 explores an expanded domain, scope, and mandate of individual, joint, and corporate moral responsibility. It beckons all of us, consumers, workers, societies, executives, CXOs, and boards of directors/governors to go:

- beyond the realm of legal responsibility (that questions, *is this the **legal** thing to do?*);
- to ascend to the arena of ethical responsibility (that questions, *is this the **right** thing to do?*);
- to the complementary zone of moral responsibility (that questions, *how can we do the right thing **rightly**?*);
- to the lofty but necessary heights of spiritual responsibility (that questions, *how can we do the right thing **rightly for the right goals and intentions**?*);
- to the yet unexplored challenges of planetary ecology and cosmic sustainability (that questions, *are we doing the right thing rightly and for the right reasons **that include planetary ecology and cosmic sustainability**?*).

One moral lesson, however, we must learn from this chapter is that our executives, top management, and governing boards are heroes and heroines that battle for us in the arena of relentless competition, free entry–exit capitalist markets, increasing regulation amidst overwhelming globalization, ecologization, and international trade wars. Far from being judgmental and retributive on them with our arsenal of blaming, wrongdoing, guilt, and punishment, we might ourselves reflect what we would have done if we were in their shoes and predicament, day in and day out. Moralists and business ethicists cannot assume an adversarial role of "we saints" versus "they sinners" any more, but chose to be their grateful companions walking the same journey of global prosperity and destiny!

Ethics is fundamentally a science of individual, social, and collective (e.g., corporate) responsibility. Ethics concerns human behavior as responsible or accountable. Because of the nature of social interaction, certain members of the society will have greater involvement and higher authority, and hence, greater individual and social responsibility than others. In our world, personal responsibility and social responsibility are hardly separable. Personal responsibility becomes responsibility for the world because the person and the world are inseparable.

Although a corporation is a fluid institution with regularly changing office bearers, shifting approaches and principles, and a mutable identity, when is anything stable enough to accept and own moral responsibility? Irrespective of whether the necessary and sufficient conditions are verified, can we conclude that the corporation be legally held liable for its harmful effects, while its corporates be held additionally morally responsible for its harmful effects? Or, can we consider *joint attributions* to both corporations and corporates without necessarily reifying

Table 3.3. Domain, Scope, and Mandate of Individual, Joint, and Corporate Moral Responsibility.

Dimensions of Responsibility	Domain, Scope, and Mandate of Responsibility		
	Individual (Executive)	Corporate (Organizational)	Joint (Executive/Corporate)
Legal responsibility	Executive law awareness Executive law compliance Executive law abidance Executive unjust law defiance Executive nonmalfeasance Executive legal blameworthiness Executive legal liability	Corporate law awareness Corporate law compliance Corporate law abidance Corporate unjust law defiance Corporate nonmalfeasance Corporate legal blameworthiness Corporate legal liability	Shared law awareness Shared law compliance Shared law abidance Unjust law shared defiance Joint nonmalfeasance Joint legal blameworthiness Joint legal liability
Ethical responsibility	Did individual executives: *Do the right thing?* Avoid any wrong thing? Prevent people from all harm? Protect people from all harm? Execute teleological justice? Execute deontological justice? Foster distributive justice? Support corrective justice? Reduce buyer–seller information asymmetry (BSIA)?	Did corporations: Do the right thing? Avoid any wrong thing? Prevent all harm to society? Protect people from all harm? Fulfill teleological justice? Execute deontological justice? Work toward distributive justice? Support corrective justice? Collectively reduce BSIA?	Did corporations and its executives: Do the right thing? Jointly avoid any wrong thing? Jointly prevent all harm? Protect people from all harm? Fulfill teleological justice? Bring about deontological justice? Promote distributive justice? Support corrective justice? Be transparent and reduce BSIA?

Moral responsibility	Executives are full moral persons, hence, do they: Do the right thing rightly? Deserve moral praiseworthiness? Respect human dignity of all? Live the cardinal virtues of prudence, justice, temperance, and fortitude? Have moral intent and intentions? Have moral vision and mission? Internalize categorical imperatives?	Do corporations: Do the right thing rightly? Deserve moral praiseworthiness? Respect human dignity? Foster cardinal virtues? Restore human equality? Uphold moral plans and intentions? Promote moral vision and mission? Nurture moral brand identity? Institutionalize categorical corporate imperatives?	Do corporations and their executives as moral institutions: Do the right thing rightly? Jointly deserve moral praiseworthiness? Promote equal human dignity of all? Jointly nurture cardinal virtues? Jointly restore human equality? Share corporate moral plans and goals? Foster moral vision and mission? Nurture moral brand identity? Share categorical imperatives?
Spiritual responsibility	As moral persons, did individuals do the right thing rightly and for the right reasons? Thus, did they: Cultivate interpersonal trust? Live immanence and transcendence? Live personal honesty and integrity? Live national and global citizenship? Restore human equality of all?	As quasi-moral persons or as moral agents, did the corporations do the right thing rightly and for the right reasons? Thus, did they: Cultivate interpersonal trust? Live corporate transcendence? Value integrity and honesty? Uphold corporate citizenship? Combat all forms of human inequalities and inequities?	As moral institutions, do corporations and their executives do the right thing rightly and for the right reasons? Thus, did they: Nurture corporate interpersonal trust? Share corporate transcendence? Witness integrity and honesty? Value corporate citizenship? Uphold human equality?

(Continued)

Table 3.3. (*Continued*)

Dimensions of Responsibility	Domain, Scope, and Mandate of Responsibility		
	Individual (Executive)	Corporate (Organizational)	Joint (Executive/Corporate)
Responsibility for planetary ecology	As individual corporate executives, were they doing the right thing rightly and for the right reasons that include planetary ecology? Thus: Were they aware of ecological concerns? Did they fulfill ecological obligations? Did they seek partnership with nature? Did they restore and recreate nature? Did they develop and transform nature? Did they eradicate or alleviate poverty? Did they combat pandemic disease? Did they assure housing, nutrition, and healthcare skills for all workers?	As a global citizen, did the corporation: Respond to ecological concerns? Fulfill all ecological obligations? Nurture partnership with nature? Restore and recreate nature? Develop and transform nature? Eradicate poverty under all forms? Combat pandemic disease? Assure housing, nutrition, and healthcare skills for all workers? Ensure legacy of restored nature to posterity?	Did corporations and their executives, as moral institutions: Address most ecological concerns? Fulfill most ecological obligations? Strive for partnership with nature? Restore and recreate nature? Develop and transform nature? Eradicate poverty as social violence? Combat pandemic disease? Ensure legacy of restored nature to posterity?

Responsibility for cosmic sustainability	As cosmic citizens, are individual corporate executives doing the right thing rightly and for the right reasons that include planetary ecology and cosmic sustainability? Thus, do they: Seek cosmic conservation? Fight cosmic anthropocentrism (man is superior and heir to central to nature and animals) and cosmic anthropomorphism (the universe is for man)?[3] Foster cosmic spirituality? Nurture cosmic partnership?	As a cosmic citizen, did the corporation: Engage in cosmic conservation? Decrease planetary extraction? Fight cosmic anthropocentrism? Fight cosmic anthropomorphism? Foster cosmic spirituality? Seek cosmic partnership? Promote cosmic harmony and peace? Respect cosmic fulfillment and happiness?	Did corporations and their executives, as moral institutions: Engage in cosmic conservation? Progressively decrease extraction? Fight cosmic anthropocentrism? Fight cosmic anthropomorphism? Foster cosmic spirituality? Ensure cosmic partnership? Promote cosmic harmony and peace? Respect cosmic fulfillment and happiness?
Did they assure legacy of renewed nature to posterity?			

Source: Compiled by the authors.

[3] Anthropocentrism, in its original connotation in environmental ethics, is the belief that all value is human-centered and that all other beings are means to human ends. Environmentally concerned authors have argued that anthropocentrism is ethically wrong and at the root of ecological crises. A philosophical version of anthropocentrism believes that human beings are the only species that are and can be moral by nature, and hence only humans have rights and duties, privileges, and entitlements, which is equally controversial. That is, moral considerations cannot be realistically attributed only to humans. Animal ethics rejects this extreme position as presumptive and unnecessary. Anthropomorphism, on the other hand, is a philosophy that sees human form in nonhumans (especially pet animals), which often turns out to be projective. We believe that it is too early for critical thinking to take a definitive stance on these highly debated issues. However, we believe that morality and its rights and duties need not be the exclusive domain of humans. We do not have reasons or evidence to affirm this. We return to anthropocentrism and its opposite, nonanthropocentrism, in Volume 3 of this series on critical thinking.

the necessary condition and sufficient condition or overdetermining them or underdetermining or vilifying them?

Some of these have good processes (e.g., research, rationality, intentions, discernment, deliberation, appropriation, attribution, discussion, dialogue) and good outcomes (revenues, profits, dividends, growth), while other choices are riddled with bad processes (e.g., fraud, corruption, avarice, envy, bribery, misleading, deception, opacity, cheating, obfuscation) and bad outcomes (e.g., money laundering, embezzlement, losses in reputation, equity and market capitalization, that lead to insolvency and/or bankruptcy). Corporations as individual executives or collective groups can assess bad processes (such as confusing policies, frozen unexamined procedures, routines, and rituals) and avoid them and thus minimize bad outcomes. This is their individual and collective – causal and moral – agency and responsibility. Even if it is "as-if" or metaphorical rationality and intentionality, corporations cannot be totally exonerated from moral and agent accountability and responsibility (see Mascarenhas, 1995). Neither should responsibility of corporate executives be exaggerated since they clearly exhibit intrinsic rationality, intentionality, freedom, autonomy, causality, and accountability.

Individuals and corporate collectives can both exhibit enough of rationality, intentionality, causality, and accountability to be assigned causal and moral responsibility for certain outcomes they initiate, process, and cause. In most of these collective deliberations, individual executives are best positioned to objectively assess their own role and contributions and accordingly, accept appropriational (over and above attributional) responsibility that freely extends moral ownership of corporate actions and outcomes. This is objective critical thinking. This is moral integrity and democratic citizenship and responsibility.

Prescriptive attributions are also the prelegal basis of a certain legal device that we noted earlier: the device of declaring that some entity is to be treated as if it had characteristics that it does not in reality have. According to Velasquez (2003, p. 559, footnote 45):

> Intentional characteristics are not the only kinds of features that can be prescriptively attributed to persons, groups, or objects. We can prescriptively attribute to persons, groups, or objects virtually anything at all, including actions, functions, emotions, rights, obligations, liabilities, relationships, and so on. In adoptions, for example, the law prescriptively attributes to certain individuals the relationships (along with its attendant rights, obligations, and liabilities) of father, mother, son, or daughter. In certain cases, the law of torts prescriptively attributes to a parent the actions of his or her child, along with their attendant legal consequences. The law can attribute to corporate groups the status of personhood (along with its attendant legal rights and obligations), and it attributes to that fictitious legal entity we call a "corporation," the actions of its officers.

Responsibility, whether legal, ethical, moral, spiritual, ecological, or cosmic sustainability, is market contextual. We need to restudy the scandals or tragic events in terms of their randomness or Black Swan content so that we might be better equipped to explain, predict, detect, prevent, monitor, and control such events far before they get slammed upon their victims. In this connection, the theoretical discussions by Nassim Nicholas Taleb in *Fooled by Randomness* (2004) and *The Black Swan: The Impact of the Highly Improbable* (2010) are very valuable and offer directions for future research.

Concluding Remarks

While most necessary and sufficient conditions argued by earlier studies of moralists such as Goodpaster (1983), Velasquez (1983), Donaldson (1982), Werhane (1985), and Pettit (1995), such as rationality, intentionality, autonomy, subjective causality, and accountability are more subjective and reflect internal/mental conditions of actors, agents, and corporations that we have no direct access to for verification, later moralists such as French (1995), Braham and Van Hees (2012), Pettit (2007), Hasnas (2012), and Sepinwall and Orts (2017) have based necessary and sufficient conditions on objective market conditions accessible to all for objective assessment and analysis, such as corporate internal decision structures (French, 1995), causal relevancy condition and avoidability (Braham & Van Hees, 2012), value relevance, value judgment, and value sensitivity (Pettit, 2007, p. 175), and objective evidence (Hasnas, 2012; Sepinwall & Orts, 2017). Accordingly, the former group has tended to be retributive, judgmental, and punitive (Hasnas, 2012), while the latter has been more sympathetic, intuitive, and understanding.

Hence, in this chapter we have, despite critical thinking, have argued that corporations and their executives are often so overwhelmed and fooled by randomness (Taleb, 2004) or affected by Black Swan–infested markets (Taleb, 2010), that they should not only be partly exonerated from full corporate moral blame and guilt (Mascarenhas, 1995) but that we should even commend them for their fortitude and moral audacity in confronting and braving these turbulent markets with the best of their taming abilities and skills and still continue to creatively innovate new products and service offerings beneficial to society. In this connection, most corporate executives have been our frontline ambassadors defending capitalism despite its problems and challenges. They have been our advocates of capitalist peace and prosperity for over 200 years. Of course, there have been companies infected with greed, fraud, envy, and bribery, but the law (in the United States and Europe) has adequately dealt with them both with mere compensatory (or hefty) punitive liabilities. But the best of capitalism – which currently is conscious, Mackey and Sisodia (2014) and inclusive (Hammond & Prahalad, 2004; Prahalad & Hammond, 2002)) – has triumphed and has proved both corporates and corporations to be nonmalicious and nonmalevolent.

We analyze too much, and in the process, we over dissect the single act of corporate decision-making into discrete acts such as rationality, intentions, intentionality, autonomy, freedom, causality, responsibility, and accountability, and then we also differentiate people into moral actors, moral agents, moral persons, moral responsible agents, primary actors and secondary actors, with individual intentions versus corporate intentions versus joint (individual/executive/corporate) intentions, individual executive decision-makers versus corporate or governing body decision-makers. Though the essence of philosophy is to make distinctions, yet too many distinctions can evade, confuse, and obfuscate assigning moral responsibility for harmful consequences of corporate actions. Hence, despite raging debates for more than half a century, the concept and cognates of moral responsibility are still ambiguous and there exists no standard terminology (Braham & Van Hees, 2012, p. 604).

In saying that an individual is morally responsible, are we primarily describing certain of their cognitive, emotional, or decision-making characteristics or are we instead (or also) commending and recommending them? To put it differently, is the concept of moral responsibility, as we are pursuing it, a normative concept or a descriptive concept or some mixture of the two? The last seems more encouraging.

Moral responsibility understood among ethics scholars is primarily for harmful social outcomes that have already happened, normally designated as *retrospective responsibility*. While taking blame or responsibility for prevention of harm or violation of one's duties toward others is *prospective responsibility*, also called "substantive responsibility" or "attributive responsibility" or "accountability" (Watson, 2004), this type of responsibility does not get the attention it deserves (Scanlon, 1998). Further, by asking for states of full willing, causation, and avoidance as necessary or sufficient conditions of moral responsibility, we are "overdetermining" moral responsibility, thus, unwittingly seeking to exonerate executive responsibility (Braham & Van Hees, 2012, p. 607) and let many guilty "off the hook" (Velasquez, 1983).

Much of the literature speaks about moral responsibility as blameworthiness for bad outcomes; it is retrospective and predominantly retributive. Its target is to load the victim with guilt and punishment. Moral responsibility is hardly treated in a prospective context that deals with other notions such as promise, commitment, dedicated planning for the future and the like.

Often, the conditions for corporate moral and turbulent responsibility postulated have been so overdetermining that unwittingly tended to exonerate corporates from moral responsibility, or, on the other hand, they have been so underdetermining that moral blame, guilt, and costly forms of responsibility were freely imposed on guilty or innocent executives alike.

Could prescribing weak necessary and sufficient conditions so underdetermine moral responsibility that individuals and corporates could be too quickly blamed or held morally responsible? Further, can the corporation be held morally (and not only legally) responsible, even though legally it may not be a moral agent or a moral person? For instance, if a majority vote decided the choice that resulted in the execution of an action that produced harmful consequences, and any individual abstaining from vote would not have changed this choice, then is seeking to verify all three conditions from each corporate agent for unilaterally controlled outcomes not too strong a condition of overdetermination?

Moreover, moral responsibility is mostly defined in terms of past actions as commissions. There is hardly any moral responsibility taken for omissions. In which case, we are far better off by attributing "joint moral responsibility" to all the "co-authors" of "crime," rather than victimize and chastise each to full causality. This was a suggestion independently arrived by McKenna (2006), Wyma (1997), and Otsuka (1998). Even if a given executive acted autonomously under nonautonomous conditions, we can still assign some "joint responsibility" to that individual. Alternatively, even if an autonomous agent acted non-autonomously under certain circumstances, we can still ascribe "joint responsibility" to that person on the grounds he did not vote or act, but was still part of the team and bylaws that sanctioned the action.

No matter how elaborate or simplified the processes of identifying the domain, scope, and allocation of moral responsibility, the final critical point is how willing we are to appropriate legal, ethical, moral, spiritual, planetary, ecological, and cosmic sustainability as individuals, corporations, or joint corporate organizations and members. When everything is said and done, as corporates, individually or collectively, we know best our own states of rationality, intentionality, freedom, causality, accountability, and responsibility when we acted, and accordingly accept, appropriate, and own responsibility much before it is attributed to us. In this sense, appropriational (i.e., willing and personal ownership of moral responsibility and implementation of causal responsibility) is the most human and humanizing form of responsibility compared to attributional (assigned) responsibility. What is taken back from the society in the form of greed, fraud, corruption, money laundering, safety violations, system breakdown, wanton outsourcing, relocation, plant closure, insolvency, and bankruptcy *must be restored to society as its due entitlement and not as charity.* The world and its corporations will have a better future, and mankind better peace and posterity, if all the agents involved in a given scandal or tragic or Black Swan events take full responsibility for their role, actions, and consequences.

Chapter 4

Critical Thinking for Redesigning the MBA Program: A Paradigm Shift to Respond to Its Major Criticisms

Executive Summary

The 170-year-old Master in Business Administration (MBA) program is becoming obsolete and inefficient to address today's real-world problems, and is facing mounting criticism from business scholars, management deans, and academic scholars alike. Reviewing major criticisms, this chapter suggests a new design for the MBA program that will not only address the criticisms but also accept a paradigm shift that will spearhead it in coming decades. The redesigned MBA "structure" proposes a four-semester full-time program, during which each semester delves into deeper marketplace problems of increasing complexity (i.e., from simple to complex to unstructured to wicked problems) and deals with these problems with new levels of critical thinking skills and ethical reasoning processes tempered by corresponding entrepreneurial knowledge, skills, and values. The "content" of the redesigned program is anchored around five major themes of business learning: namely, intrinsic motivation management, creativity and innovation management, productivity management, revenue management, and eco-sustainability management, each geared to generate professional entrepreneurial knowledge, and skills and values urgently needed today. Numerous beneficial features of this newly redesigned integrated business management program (MBA) are also discussed.

Introduction

The Master in Business Administration (MBA) program was arguably designed and promoted some 170 years ago by Harvard University against the backdrop of a strong agricultural economy, supported by a rudimentary manufacturing economy in the United States and the United Kingdom. Since then, the *agricultural economy* transformed into an *industrial manufacturing economy* (1950s), to a

A Primer on Critical Thinking and Business Ethics, 111–145
Copyright © 2024 Oswald A. J. Mascarenhas, Munish Thakur and Payal Kumar
Published under exclusive licence by Emerald Publishing Limited
doi:10.1108/978-1-83753-312-120231004

services economy (1980s), to a *globalized information-communication economy* – internet, e-commerce, e-marketing, and e-business (1990s), and a *social e-entertainment networking experience economy* – iPod, iPhone, iPad, Blackberry, PlayStation, Nintendo, Facebook, Instagram, and Twitter (2000s). Currently, we are unwittingly propelled into a *carbon emissions reduction and carbon trading economy* that seeks long-term strategic eco-sustainability management (Sandour, 2008). The MBA program, for the most part, has not significantly changed to reflect and proactively incorporate the changing economies since its origins in the 1880s. In the wake of several scholarly criticisms that seriously question the existing MBA model (e.g., Bennis & O'Toole, 2005; Hamel, 2006; Khurana, 2007; Marti & Scherer, 2016; Neumeier, 2009; Podolny, 2009), the MBA program should seek to update, upgrade, and transform itself to reflect critical thinking and address these market and economic generational challenges of the last 200 years and more. This chapter is an initial attempt in this direction. Chapter 5, which follows, will revisit the project of redesigning the MBA curriculum and pedagogy, especially incorporating the theory and challenges of addressing the "wicked problems" that uncontrolled corporate capitalism has created since the dawn of the manufacturing industry.

Major Problems With Higher Education in General

Our higher education needs to undergo radical change. The core university has seen only minor changes over the last millennium, said Henry Cardinal Newman in his 19th century discourses on *The Idea of the University* (1982). The core university made even fewer minor adjustments in the 20th century. The change is much more urgent now. A radical change is long due. The role of a university will always be *knowledge creation.* We now live in a world that is increasingly dependent upon knowledge-based industries and markets. What must change is not the role of the university (i.e., knowledge creation) but *the way it fulfills its role* (Penley, 2009, p. 32). Universities must offer a wider assortment of basic and applied knowledge–based degree programs. Business schools in particular must challenge students to critical thinking and ethical thinking, which address the wicked problems created by corporate capitalist economies with social account-ability and moral leadership. Economic prosperity will follow, and so will global economic equality of opportunity.

In their book, *Turning Learning Right Side Up: Putting Education Back on Track*, Russell Ackoff and Daniel Greenberg (2008) warn us that real education is not teaching but learning. Traditional education focuses on teaching, not learning. It incorrectly assumes that for every ounce of teaching, there is an ounce of learning by those who are taught. On the contrary, most of what we learn before, during, and after attending schools is learned without it being taught to us. A child learns such fundamental things as how to crawl, walk, talk, eat, drink, and so on, without being taught these things. Adults learn most of what they use

---

Critical Thinking Exercise 4.1

Apply critical thinking (see footnote 3 in Chapter 1) to our current institutions of teaching and presumed learning, as judged by Russell Ackoff and Daniel Greenberg (2008):

- In most schools, including business schools, memorization is mistaken for learning. Most of what is remembered is remembered only for a short time but then is quickly forgotten.
- Computers, computer software, recording machines, cameras, blogposts, and the like can do better in teaching the stuff that we normally teach in our classrooms.
- Most often, teachers are poor surrogates for such machines, equipment, and instruments. Why should students – children or adults – do something in classrooms that computers and related equipment can do much better than teachers can either in or out of classrooms?
- What education should focus on, therefore, is what humans can do better than the machines and instruments they create. When we ask those, whom we taught, about who in the class learned most, virtually all of them say, "The teacher."
- It is apparent to those who have taught that teaching is a better way to learn than being taught. Teaching enables the teacher to discover what one thinks about the subject being taught.
- Schools are upside down: students should be teaching and faculty learning.

---

at work or at leisure, while at work or leisure. Most of what is taught in classroom settings is almost forgotten, and much of what is remembered may be irrelevant.

While these provocative remarks are highly pertinent to high school and college curricula and pedagogies in general, there are some specific indictments against the MBA programs that we must review.

Problems With Management Education Today

Corporate accounting irregularities peaked in the United States during 2000–2008. Early 2000 marked the beginning of some of the worst corporate security irregularities in history. Most of the largest frauds uncovered were in the utility business (for details on pioneering fraudulent companies, see Forbes, 2002; Fortune, 2002). Enron, Tyco, and World.com spearheaded the scandals. Such irregularities included overselling shares to depress stock prices, overstating financial worth to boost stock prices, and overstating revenues by "round-trip" sales, understating debt, and overstating equity, or, in general, "cooking" the books to influence better Securities and Exchange Commission (SEC) ratings.[1]

The year 2008 will go down in American and global economic history as the worst since 1931. The year began with a shock – Société Générale of Paris lost 4.9 billion Euros (then about US$ 6.8 billion) on the unauthorized speculative positions held by a low-level trader. This presumably gigantic loss was quickly dwarfed by a series of disasters that followed. Financial investment corporations which together had a market-capitalization total of over US$ 1.6 trillion on October 9, 2007, found that their value evaporated *within a year* to a total of US$ 865.6 billion by September 12, 2008, a total loss of US$ 791.72 billion (47.8%), or an average of US$ 46.6 billion loss per mega financial company. Global financial crisis entered a potentially new phase when many credit markets stopped working normally, as investors around the world moved their money into ultrasafe investments such as Treasury bills (Bajaj, 2008). This, in turn, sent the yield on one-month Treasury bills from 1.507% a week earlier to 0.259%, down by almost 53% within the space of three business days. Consequently, the cost of borrowing soared for many companies, and global financial investment companies, such as Goldman Sachs and Morgan Stanley, which had declared themselves relatively strong a week before, came under assault from waves of selling.

Critical Thinking Exercise 4.2

- Apply critical thinking (see footnote 3 in Chapter 1) to our current institutions of business education and presumed learning (e.g., celebrated business schools), as judged by the following remarks from experts:
- A myth of higher education, points David Orr (1991), was that we can adequately restore that which we dismantle. For instance, in the business management curriculum, we have fragmented business knowledge into disciplines and subdisciplines of economics: strategy, business law, human resources management (HRM), accounting, finance, production, marketing, sustainability, and the like. Consequently, most business students graduate without any broader integrated sense of the unity of things or the multidimensional nature of business markets and problems.

---

[1]The United States Federal Energy Regulatory Commission (FERC) defines *wash trading*, also known as "round trip" or "sell/buyback" trading, as the sale of a product (e.g., electricity) to another company with a simultaneous purchase of the same product at the same price. Essentially, wash trading is false trading because it boosts the companies' trading volume, or even sets benchmark prices, but shows no gains or losses on the balance sheets. While this kind of trading may not be explicitly illegal or illicit as per generally accepted accounting principles (GAAP), it can manipulate the power market, which is illegal. But markets are amoral, and the line between shading earnings and committing outright fraud is not always clear (Gardner, 2007, p. 53).

(Continued)

- For example, we routinely produce economists who lack the most rudimentary knowledge of ecology or eco-sustainability. Our national accounting systems do not subtract the costs of biotic impoverishment, soil erosion, poisons in the air or water, and resource depletion from gross national product (GNP). We add the price of a sale of a bushel of wheat to GNP while forgetting to subtract the three bushels of topsoil lost in its production. As a result of this incomplete education, we have fooled ourselves into thinking that we are much richer than we are.
- The financial recession and depression that followed has affected not only the United States (with millions of job and income losses) but also the rest of the world – about 40% of the global gross domestic product (GDP) and currencies were negatively impacted. Stocks throughout the world lost 42% of their value in 2008 as calculated by the Morgan Stanley Capital International World Index, erasing more than US$ 29 trillion in value and all of the gains made since 2003.
  - The Shanghai Composite Index fell by 65.4%.
  - The Russian RTS Index fell by 72%.
  - The Sensex 30 in Mumbai fell by 52.4%.
  - The Dow Jones Euro Stoxx 600 Index, a measure of the broad European market, closed 2008 with a loss of 46%.
  - The US Dow Jones industrial average lost 33.8%, its worst year since 1931.
  - The broader Standard & Poor's 500-stock Index plummeted by 38.5%. (*The New York Times*, September 18, 2008).
- What went wrong and why? One would not be totally wrong in assuming that much of the financial disaster could be traced to greed and mismanagement by hundreds of executives holding MBAs from prestigious business schools, who ran these gigantic commercial and investment banks. Most top executives of these fraudulent firms and investment banks were trained in the top business schools in the United States.
- To what extent can business schools claim exoneration from and be indifferent to the role that hundreds of MBAs played in these corporate scandals?
- Many people believe that management education has contributed to the systemic failure of leadership that led to the financial crisis or the Wall Street meltdown. The crisis is clear proof that business schools have not done enough to equip students with the required modicum of integrity, honesty, moral courage, and moral reasoning. The degree of contrition at business schools seems small compared with the magnitude of the offense (Podolny, 2009, pp. 63–65).

Edward Deming, a celebrated production management and total quality management (TQM) guru, in writing an introduction to Peter Senge's bestseller book (1990), *The Fifth Discipline*, said:

> Our prevailing system of management has destroyed our people. People are born with intrinsic motivation, self-respect, dignity, curiosity to learn, joy in learning. The forces of destruction begin with toddlers – a prize for the best Halloween costume, grades in school, gold stars – and on up through the university. On the job, people, teams, and divisions are ranked, with reward for the top, punishment for the bottom. Management by objectives, quotas, incentive pay, business plans, put together separately, division by division, cause further loss, unknown and unknowable.
>
> (Cited in Senge, 2006, p. xii)

Change in Management Education Is Long due

Edward Deming (1994, p. 143) wrote:

> Schools of business teach how business is conducted at present. In other words, they teach perpetuation of present style of management. They teach perpetuation of our decline. A school of business has an obligation to prepare students to lead the transformation, to halt our decline and turn it upward. They ought to teach the theory of a system and the theory of profound knowledge for transformation.

Critical Thinking Exercise 4.3

Apply critical thinking (see footnote 3 in Chapter 1) to the current business school curriculum, which claim to impart – but may not – business education and student learning, as judged by the following remarks of management gurus.

Management in the manufacturing world was originally invented to solve two basic problems – production and distribution. The former was solved using material and process technologies, repetitive skills management, economies of scale, and inventory management. The latter was solved by warehousing, transportation logistics, and retailing. Management in the information explosion world of today faces a new set of problems (see Hamel, 2006; Khurana, 2007; Marti & Scherer, 2016; Podolny, 2009):

- In an age of rapid change, how can we create organizations that are both adaptable and resilient as they are focused and effective?
- In an age of rapid innovation or "creative destruction" and even more rapid technological obsolescence, how can companies innovate quickly and boldly enough to stay relevant and profitable?

(Continued)

- At a time when the hidden social costs of rapid industrialization have become distressingly apparent, especially via the internet and social networks, how do we encourage executives to fulfill their corporate social responsibilities toward all stakeholders?
- The industrial age, that was built on the principles of standardization, specialization, hierarchies and bureaucracies, anti-competition and barriers to new market entrants, corporate power and control, sovereignty and primacy of shareholder interests, is becoming ineffective and irrelevant to respond to these questions. *Tomorrow's business imperatives lie outside the performance envelope of today's best management practices* (Podolny, 2009).
- Managers and students of management cannot be paralyzed by the hidden mind traps of anchoring, status quo, sunk costs, evidence management and framing, and preoccupation with the bottom line (Hammond et al., 1998) that have characterized the old management school.
- Pressures of globalization, changes in workforce demographics, and knowledge-based economy have made talent development and talent search not only extremely difficult and but also a competitive asset.
- According to an Accenture study, most top executives affirm that talent-related capabilities are important to achieving high performance in companies, but there is poor execution in developing that talent (Cappelli, 2008).
- Having the right talent, both aligned and engaged, is crucial to achieving strategic corporate objectives, but fragmented talent management systems, processes, and practices are still the norm in many organizations. Companies have not adequately focused on building talent management capabilities across the organization.
- As competition for high-potential talent increases, there is an increase in talent gap in critical workforce segments. What type of talent do we produce through MBA programs? To begin with, how do we attract, develop, and retain high-potential talent capability through MBA admission processes?

Major Indictments of the Traditional MBA Program

Business schools are facing intense criticism for failing to impact society positively and failing to impart useful skills to students, failing to prepare leaders for tomorrow, failing to instill norms of ethical behavior, and even failing to place graduates in good and meaningful corporate jobs. Such criticisms come from a variety of stakeholders – students, employers, media, and even the deans of some of the best business schools in the world. Several academic business scholars have addressed this criticism and have identified different root causes to the crisis in management education. We review some of these criticisms.

MBA Imperatives Based on Major Expert Criticisms: Professionalizing the MBA Program and Curriculum

---

Critical Thinking Exercise 4.4

Apply critical thinking (see footnote 3 in Chapter 1) to the current business school curriculum that claims to, but may not, impart business education and real student learning, as judged further by the faculty of business schools.

- According to Bennis and O'Toole (2005), business schools have adopted a wrong – and self-defeating – model of academic excellence based solely on the scientific rigor and number of publications of its faculty.
- This model is based, in turn, on the unquestioned assumption of business schools and faculty that business is an academic discipline (like any other science, such as biochemistry or physics), which implicitly denies that business is a profession, and that business schools should be professional schools (similar to medicine, law, or architecture).
- Instead of benchmarking business schools in terms of the competences of their graduates, and how well the faculty understands important drivers of business performance, business schools and faculty indulge in the academic veneer without checking against the demands of market reality.
- Bennis and O'Toole (2005), accordingly, suggest that without regressing to convert business schools into glorified trade schools, they should regain relevancy by rediscovering the practice of business management while pursuing the dual roles of educating practitioners and creating new business knowledge through research.
- According to Khurana (2007), all university-based business schools were founded to train a professional class of managers in the mold of doctors and lawyers. They have effectively retreated, however, from that goal, leaving a gaping moral hole at the center of business education and perhaps in management itself.
- Khurana argues that business schools have largely capitulated in the battle for professionalism and have become mere purveyors of a product, the MBA, with students treated as consumers.
- Professional and moral ideals that once animated and inspired business schools have now been just about obliterated (Khurana, 2007), by a doctrine that managers are merely agents of shareholders, beholden to the cause of the bottom line and profit sharing (Khurana & Nohria, 2008).
- This trend has spurred corporate fraud or malfeasance (Khurana & Nohria, 2008). The time has come to rejuvenate intellectually and morally the training of our future business leaders (Khurana, 2007).

Breakthrough Innovative Talent Management and Development

- Every talent management process in use today was developed half a century ago, and it is time for a new model, says Peter Cappelli.[2] Large Fortune 500 companies still rely on complex and bureaucratic models from the 1950s for forecasting and succession planning – legacy systems that grew up in an era when business was highly predictable and controllable. These models fail now because they are inaccurate and costly in a very volatile market environment. Hence, Cappelli concludes, it is time now for a fundamentally new approach to talent management that takes into account the uncertainties and ambiguities that businesses face today (Cappelli, 2008, pp. 74–75).
- Most fundamental breakthroughs in management occurred decades ago, writes Gary Hamel.[3] For instance, workflow design, annual budgeting, return on investment analysis, project management, centralization and decentralization, backward, forward, and horizontal integration, brand management, and a host of other indispensable tools of management have been around since the early 1990s. The evolution of management has traced a classic S-curve. After a fast start in the early twentieth century, the pace of innovation gradually decelerated and in recent years has slowed to a crawl (Hamel, 2009, p. 91).

Humanizing Management With Charismatic Leadership

- The model for 20th century management was not the warm humanism of the Renaissance but the cold mechanics of the assembly line, the laser-like focus of Newtonian science applied to the manufacture of wealth. The assembly line was intentionally blind to morality, emotions, and human aspiration – all the better to make your competitors and customers to lose so you can win (Khurana & Nohria, 2008).
- Yet business is not mechanical but human. Innovation without emotion is uninteresting. Products without aesthetics are not compelling. Moreover, a business without ethics is unsustainable.
- The management model that got us here is underpowered to move us forward. To succeed, the new model must replace the win–lose nature of the assembly line with the win–win nature of the network (Neumeier, 2009, pp. 4–5). This is precisely the challenge of executive critical thinking and executive spiritual development.

---

[2]Professor of Management and the Director of the Center for Human Resources, Wharton School, University of Pennsylvania in Philadelphia, PA.

[3]Ex-Professor (and now visiting professor) of Strategic and International Management, London Business School, and Director of The Management Lab, a Silicon Valley–based nonprofit research organization that focuses on management innovation.

Critical Thinking Exercise 4.5

Apply critical thinking (see footnote 3 in Chapter 1) to current business school curriculum that claims – but fails – to impart business ethics education and genuine learning, as further judged by the remarks of deans of business schools, such as Martin and Podolny.

Learning From Outlier Student Performance: Mysteries Beyond the Normal Curve

- The orthodoxy in business is to use what we already know, hone, and refine it. We attack the "mystery" of the business world by what was true (in the past) rather by what could be true (in the future). Business scholars and practitioners look for templates, PowerPoint summaries, typical cases, known algorithms, fixed formulae, and canned or written scripts to follow, as there are enormous time savings.
- The danger of this orthodox traditional approach, argues Roger Martin, is that conditioned by bell curve and normal data, people stop looking for oddball or outlier data and mysteries entirely.[4] Real discovery and exploration narrow the field of complex inquiry to the oddball data of anomalies and mysteries, and then derive evidence-based heuristics that could unravel the mystery down to a manageable size.
- Instead, most business school researchers ignore business and marketplace outliers or oddball data, and focus on the obvious, expected, and the replicable, thus truncating advances in real learning (Marti & Scherer, 2016).
- Most research is focused on creating reliable outcomes that can be consistently replicated. That is the big part of the so-called "scientific method." But major leaps forward in knowledge come from focusing on achieving a valid outcome, the one that actually answers the question and provides the information we really need. Quantitative methods that produce reliable outcomes often strip away nuance and context, and thus prevent the discovery of a valid outcome. By emphasizing validity, even at the expense of reliability, one can develop a heuristic that moves the work forward.

Radical Integration Management Sans Compartmentalization

- Hence, Joel Podolny argues, "Unless American business schools make radical changes, society will become convinced that MBAs work to serve only their own selfish interests" (2009, p. 62).[5]

---

[4]Formerly Dean of the Rotman School of Management, University of Toronto.
[5]Joel M. Podolny is the current dean and vice president of Apple University in Cupertino, CA, and former dean of the Yale School of Management (2005–2008) and quondam professor at Harvard Business School and the Stanford Graduate School of Business.

- Podolny is disturbed about the inattention to ethics and values–based leadership in business schools. He is exasperated about the disciplinary silos in which business schools teach management.
- Additionally, too much compartmentalization of management education has left academics without a holistic appreciation of the challenges MBAs face. Academicians are not curious about what really goes on inside companies. They indulge in conceptual and theoretical models that obscure rather than clarify the way organizations work.
- Podolny feels that business schools, as they stand today, are harmful to society, fostering self-interested, unethical, and even illegal behavior by their graduates.
- The MBAs are part of the problem rather than the solution (Podolny, 2009, p. 63). The world of consumers and markets, producers and suppliers, traders and distributors, banks and creditors, domestic and international governments is constantly changing. Are business schools keeping up with change? How do we rethink the MBA program, content, curriculum, and delivery to align with these changes?[6]

Toward Redesigning the MBA Program

Table 4.1 summarizes major criticisms of the MBA program that we have covered thus far.

Critical Thinking Exercise 4.6

Apply critical thinking (see footnote 3 in Chapter 1) to the following corporate challenges and social responsibilities.

With the changing world, there naturally arise new corporate social responsibilities. Thus, for instance:

- Can one make money and save the planet at the same time?
- Can one do well in business by doing good?

---

[6]Specifically, how do we rethink business education in the over 100 Graduate Jesuit Business Schools and Universities of the world? In his vision-business plan for a brand-new MBA program for Jesuit schools of business, Mascarenhas (2009a) explores some new paradigms and ethical imperatives based on Jesuit mandates that emerged in the Thirty-Second "General Congregation." (The GC is the supreme legislative body of the Society of Jesus and reiterated in the subsequent General Congregations 33, 34, and 35 – justice in the service of faith.) Specifically, Mascarenhas (2009a) examines two paradigms for rethinking MBA in Jesuit business schools – achieving business justice and fostering business faith. Both paradigms invite immersive and engaging experiences in the economic realities of where our faculty and students live, thus making coursework come alive. Business issues interconnect globally and so do global business strategies and responsibilities.

Table 4.1. A Synthetic Summary of Major Criticisms Against Traditional Master in Business Administration (MBA) Programs.

Author(s) (Year of Publication)	Major Criticism of MBA	False Assumptions About MBA	Suggested Reforms for MBA
Bennis and Toole (2005)	Academic excellence is based solely on scientific rigor and the number of journal publications of its faculty.	Business is an academic discipline (like any other science) and not a profession (like law or medicine).	Make business schools *professional* schools. Benchmark business schools by competencies of their graduates and their contributions to social progress, and how well the faculty understands important drivers of business performance in the marketplace.
Khurana (2007); Khurana and Nohria (2008)	University-based business schools were meant to train a professional class of managers *a la* doctors and lawyers. They have effectively retreated from that goal, leaving a gaping moral hole at the center of business education and perhaps in management itself.	Managers are merely agents of shareholders, beholden to the cause of the bottom line and profit maximization. Professional and moral ideals that once animated and inspired business schools have been abandoned or obliterated. This trend has spurred corporate fraud and malfeasance.	Rejuvenate, intellectually and morally, the training of future business leaders as a profession. Business schools have capitulated in the battle for professionalism and have become mere purveyors of a product, the MBA, with students treated as consumers.

Table 4.1. *(Continued)*

Author(s) (Year of Publication)	Major Criticism of MBA	False Assumptions About MBA	Suggested Reforms for MBA
Cappelli (2008)	Every talent management process in use today was developed more than half a century ago. Large Fortune 500 companies still rely on complex and bureaucratic models from the 1950s for forecasting and succession planning. A new model is long due.	Business is highly predictable and controllable, and the legacy models will continue to work, even when business is unpredictable and uncontrollable, inaccurate and costly, and in a very volatile market environment.	Have a fundamentally new approach to talent management that considers the uncertainties and ambiguities that businesses face today.
Hamel and Breen (2007)	Most fundamental breakthroughs in management occurred decades ago. The evolution of management has traced a classic S-curve: after a fast start in the early 20th century, the pace of innovation has gradually decelerated to a crawl.	Workflow design, annual budgeting, return on investment (ROI) analysis, project management, centralization and decentralization, backward, forward and horizontal integration, brand management, and other tools, dated from the early 1990s, are still relevant.	Redesign the MBA program in order to make it relevant to the current and future dynamically changing times.

(Continued)

Table 4.1. *(Continued)*

Author(s) (Year of Publication)	Major Criticism of MBA	False Assumptions About MBA	Suggested Reforms for MBA
Neumeier (2009)	Management models are mechanical, not human, built on deterministic assembly lines since Henry Ford's assembly lines.	Business management is deterministic; it is a "win–lose" game.	Humanize management styles and models, as also management education and content. Transform all into win–win human systems.
Marti and Scherer (2016)	Most business school research is focused on creating reliable outcomes that can be consistently replicated. That is the big part of the so-called "scientific method."	That major leaps forward in knowledge do not come from focusing on achieving a valid outcome, the one that actually answers the question and provides the information we really need to uphold basic human equality.	Emphasize validity, even if it is at the expense of reliability, so as to develop a heuristic that moves the work forward, because quantitative methods that focus on reliable outcomes discount nuance and context and prevent the discovery of a valid outcome.
Podolny (2009)	Unless business schools make radical changes, society will become convinced that MBAs work to serve only their own selfish interests.	Compartmentalization of management education without a holistic appreciation of the challenges MBAs face is necessary for management education. The MBAs are part of the solution	Foster an integrated business management (IBM) education with a heavy emphasis on ethics. Academicians must be curious

Table 4.1. *(Continued)*

Author(s) (Year of Publication)	Major Criticism of MBA	False Assumptions About MBA	Suggested Reforms for MBA
	Business schools, as they stand today, are harmful to society, fostering self-interested, unethical, and even illegal behavior by their graduates.	and not part of the problem.	about what really goes on inside companies. Rather than indulge in conceptual and theoretical models that obscure, they should question the way organizations work.
Mascarenhas (2009a, 2009b)	The world of all stakeholders, domestic and global, is constantly changing before our eyes. Are business schools keeping up with change?	Rethinking the MBA content, program, curriculum, and delivery to align with these changes, especially those that increase inequality and injustice of the marginalized, is not possible.	Redesign the entire MBA program around two critical paradigms: *business faith* (mutual trust) among all stakeholders to foster *business justice.*

Source: Compiled by the authors.

- Can one do fair trade and carbon neutralizing at the same time?
- Can sustainable competitive advantage (SCA) coexist and stimulate sustainability of the national and global economies?
- Can one do well in business by reducing gaping income inequalities between the rich and the poor, or while striving for social progress and economic development of all?
- Can one realize happiness of all people alike with carbon neutrality and eco-sustainability?

These are current concerns of corporate social responsibility. These are clarion calls of corporate citizenship. Publicly held corporations are creations of the state. In return for the privilege of limited liability, the society has always demanded at least vaguely good corporate behavior. The cost of this implicit social franchise is corporate social responsibility rooted in business faith that leads to business justice.

Critical Thinking Exercise 4.7

Apply critical thinking (see footnote 3 in Chapter 1) to analyze how redesigning the MBA curriculum would respond and safeguard to the following imperatives of deeply concerned management critics.

Lack of Intrinsic Motivation That Encourages Fraud and Money Laundering

- According to Deming (2006), the prevailing system of management has destroyed people by reward–punishment systems. People are born with intrinsic motivation, self-respect, dignity, curiosity to learn, and joy in learning. The MBA program should generate and sustain intrinsic than external (rewards/ punishment) motivation among all stakeholders.
- The MBA program cannot be confined to teach today's management styles, even its best management practices, since – as Deming (1994) rightly observed – today's management is on the decline (increasing corporate fraud, fragmented talent management systems, institutionalized bribery systems, deceptively defective products), and tomorrow's business imperatives lie outside the performance envelope of today's best management practices.
- When it originated, the traditional MBA program trained its charges to confront only two problems: production and distribution. Today, the MBA program and paradigm must, at the minimum, confront many and different problems such as consumption welfare management, IT management, uncertainty management, motivation management, new skilling and upskilling management, social progress and development management, work from home management, and work–life balance management.
- In an age of rapid change and technological obsolescence, the redesigned MBA program should train students to create resilient organizations that are focused and effective to innovate quickly, boldly, and be profitable and socially responsible at the same time (Hamel, 2006, 2009; Hamel & Valikangas, 2003).
- According to an Accenture study, most top executives affirm that talent-related capabilities are important to achieving high performance in companies, but there is poor execution in developing that talent. The MBA program should focus on integrated talent management (see Cappelli, 2008).
- Universities must offer a wider assortment of basic and applied knowledge–based degree programs, and business schools in particular must challenge students to critical thinking, social accountability, moral leadership, and national development.

De-mechanize Education to Make it Resilient and Creative

- According to Ackoff and Greenberg (2008), the industrial age has imposed upon us a mechanized form of education that requires all human skills to be honed and readied for the machine age. Incoming students are very much treated as raw materials to be converted into products that would be readily absorbed into the workforce.

- Hence, fixed textbooks, frozen teaching materials, closed book exams, tests based on memory-retrieval, and accurate reproduction have become the tools, techniques, and highlights of educational success. This pedagogy has also infected the MBA program from which it must be liberated (Ackoff & Greenberg, 2008).
- Moreover, in the industrial education system, argue Ackoff and Greenberg (2008), the right subject skills must be mastered in the right way and at the right time, with codes of well-defined, acceptable modes of public behavior. The impact of this mechanized system is that students and professors challenging the business school "official curriculum" are labeled as unorthodox and mavericks.
- The dominant form of learning in business schools, purged from rewards and punishments (e.g., grades and ranks), must go beyond the instruction in yesterday's skills to learning through self-exploration and other intrinsic motivation activities. Creative and innovative forays into physical, intellectual, and spiritual territories, not encouraged by the current official curriculum, should be encouraged and recognized.

Critical Thinking Exercise 4.8

In actually redesigning the MBA curriculum, how would you apply critical thinking (see footnote 3 in Chapter 1) in responding to the following concerns expressed by serious business school scholars?

- Academic excellence is solely based on the scientific rigor and the number of publications of its faculty (Bennis & O'Toole, 2005).
- MBA programs do not train students to be professionals, just management-discipline savvy (Khurana, 2007).
- Several talent management tools of current MBA programs are almost 50 years old (Cappelli, 2008).
- Most fundamental breakthroughs in management occurred decades ago (Hamel, 2009).
- The management model is mechanical not human, built on the deterministic auto assembly line of Ford's T-model of 1908 (Ackoff & Greenberg, 2008; Neumeier, 2009).
- Its scientific method and research methodologies focus on generating reliable and duplicable outcomes without concentrating on market validity and relevance (Marti & Scherer, 2016).
- Business schools, as they stand today, are harmful to society, fostering self-interested, unethical, and even illegal behavior by their graduates (Podolny, 2009).
- While the world of all stakeholders, domestic and global, is constantly changing, business schools have not adapted to change nor are they promoting business trust and business justice.

Given these criticisms of business schools in general, and the MBA program in particular, it is imperative for us to deploy critical thinking in redesigning the MBA program that adequately addresses most major criticisms leveled against it. According to Neumeier (2009, pp. 4–5), the management model that got us up to this point is underpowered to move us forward. Hence, any new model must replace the win–lose nature of the assembly line with the win–win nature of newly created "blue oceans" (Kim & Mauborgne, 2004) that will empower administrators, teachers, and students to include social progress and national development as part of the MBA curriculum via social networking and integrated management systems. In this connection, Table 4.2 unfolds biases, assumptions, presumptions, and presuppositions of the current MBA program that is implicitly committed to profit-maximization.

Critical Thinking Exercise 4.9

In actually redesigning the MBA curriculum, how would you identify, analyze, and counteract its current implicit biases, assumptions, presumptions, and presuppositions, some of which are listed in Table 4.2? Are there other subtle biases, assumptions, presumptions, suppositions, and presuppositions that we have missed? If so, can you identify them and assess their impact on the current MBA curriculum?

Why do We Need a Paradigm Shift?

With so many major criticisms of the existing MBA programs, we cannot respond to them by patchwork, band-aided, or disconnected symptomatic solutions; we need a paradigm shift. While most of the world believes in customization, personalization, and individualization, we have on the pretext of making it professional, standardized business education, at the undergraduate, graduate, and doctoral levels. The costs are many: a standardized program, howsoever innovative, can standardize the minds and mindsets, and freeze mental models or mental prototypes of our brilliant students, thus destroying their capacity for creativity, discovery, invention and innovation, entrepreneurship, and experimentation. We cannot look for standardized solutions to unstandardized problems; the real problems of the business world are most often "wicked" problems that are mostly unstructured and complex (Rittel & Webber, 1973). A good shot of liberal arts education in the MBA program (e.g., in business logic, history, classical poetry, drama and theater, managerial philosophy, educational psychology, business anthropology, and the like) can restore or trigger creativity, imagination, exploration, discovery, experimentation and innovation, freedom, play and fun in MBA learning.

Table 4.2. Typical Sets of Biases, Prejudices, Presumptions, and Presuppositions in Current Business Education and Learning.

Component of Uncritical Thinking	Management	Marketing	Labor Economics, Accounting, and Finance	Technology and Information Systems
Structural Biases	Humans are not equal. Men are superior to women. Caucasians are superior to others. Western models of freedom, democracy, and civilization are benchmarks for other countries to follow. Work is duty; wage is privilege. Education/employment are more rights than privileges. Access to health care is a right.	Consumers are only means and not ends-in-themselves. Consumption is ultimate progress and happiness. Higher consumption implies growth. Immediate gratification checks better than its delay. *Consumers: be aware.* Planned product obsolescence is growth. Outdated products are best exported to developing nations.	Human labor is a mere factor of production; hence, exploitable. Plant closings, mergers, acquisitions, outsourcing, etc. are necessary and natural means of growth. Granting credit spurs consumption. Debt-leverage is better than equity-leverage. Seeking bankruptcy protection is normal. Federal and trade deficits are normal.	Innovation is power. Innovation is ethics neutral. Automation and robotics spell growth and human dignity. Innovation is conquest and control of nature. Planned technology and skills obsolescence are growth and progress. Outdated technologies should be exported to developing countries than retired. Heightened energy consumption is progress, not a hazard.

(Continued)

Table 4.2. (*Continued*)

Component of Uncritical Thinking	Management	Marketing	Labor Economics, Accounting, and Finance	Technology and Information Systems
Social Prejudices	American capitalism is the best free market system in the world. Big is better and beautiful. More is satisfying. Higher market demand is growth and prosperity. The Western paradigm of capitalism and its business school curriculum is the best in and for the world.	Consumer delight and satisfaction is the goal of marketing. American fads and fashions are the norm for the world. Predatory and exorbitant pricing are normal and driven by markets. Not all product defects and risks can be eliminated.	Labor is just a cost and not talent development. Dignity of labor is its productivity. Unproductive labor is best fired or retired. Labor should be paid by efforts and outputs, not by family needs and conditions.	All technology implies an ecological cost. Harmony with nature is weakness. Innovation is useless without commercialization. Human/market success demands innovation new patents and new technologies.
Imperial Presumptions	The United States is *the* superpower. World's energy resources should be governed by a superpower. The United States as superpower should	Consumer risk is acceptable. Credit based consumption is growth. Only allopathic medicine is the best and should be	All work is a duty. No work is risk-free. No working conditions are totally safe. Total worker safety is a utopian luxury that stalls	The larger the number of new products and services the market offers each year, the better the world is. Globalization is progress.

Self-serving Presuppositions	control nuclear weaponry and proliferation. Humans can be used for experimentation. Stem-cell research is a necessity. This planet is for humans; posterity will take care of itself. Anthropocentricism is nature's law for us.	nationally insured and institutionalized. Fast foods do not lead to obesity or laziness. Tobacco products do not necessarily lead to cancer. Some drugs need to be legalized. Product safety is a consumer duty.	productivity. *Workers: be aware!* Shareholder profitability is the only end of capitalism. Corporations exist for shareholders. All corporate responsibility is for shareholders.	Globalization eliminates global inequalities. Consumer privacy is a consumer problem. Privacy invasion is a necessity to combat terrorism. Environment-friendliness is a weakness ultimately.

Source: Compiled by the authors.

At the minimum, we need a paradigm shift for overcoming the multitude of criticisms and shortcomings of the existing MBA programs, pointed by experts and listed above, so as to foster positive directions, as provided in Exhibit 4.1.

Critical Thinking Exercise 4.10

In actually redesigning the MBA curriculum, how would you incorporate the positive directions suggested by the following expert sources in Exhibit 4.1? Are there other positive suggestions that we have missed? If so, can you identify them and assess their positive impact on the current MBA curriculum?

Exhibit 4.1. Scholarly Positive Directions for Redesigning the Master in Business Administration (MBA) Program.

(1) In an age of rapid change, students must be trained to create and energize organizations that are both adaptable and resilient as they are focused and effective (Hamel, 2006, 2009; Hamel & Prahalad, 1994; Hamel & Valikangas, 2003).

(2) In an age of rapid innovation or "creative destruction" (Schumpeter, 1934) and even more rapid technological obsolescence, the newly designed MBA programs should empower students to create organizations that can innovate quickly and boldly enough to stay relevant and profitable (Neumeier, 2009).

(3) The notion of educating the "whole person" to "educating the whole person in solidarity for the real world" (Newman, 1982) should be expanded.

(4) This solidarity must be learnt through "contact" rather than through "concepts." The challenging role for the faculty today whose mission is to pursue the truth and to form each student into an integrated whole person of solidarity who will take responsibility for the real world.

(5) That is, students/teachers/researchers "must immerse themselves in the gritty reality of this world which they must experience into their lives so that they can learn to feel it, think about it critically, respond to its suffering, and engage it constructively," (https://www.xavier.edu/jesuitresource/jesuit-a-z/terms-s/solidarity).

(6) In a socially conscious university, faculty research must not only obey the canons of each discipline but ultimately embrace human reality in order to help make the world a more fitting place for six billion of the poor to habit (Hammond & Prahalad, 2004).

Exhibit 4.1. *(Continued)*

(7) In an era of sustainability consciousness and transparency imperatives, especially demanded by open system internet and social media networks, future executives must be trained to fulfill their corporate social responsibilities to all stakeholders, besides shareholders (Podolny, 2009).

(8) In an age of fragmented talent management, systems, processes, and practices reinforced by compartmentalized disciplines of business management (such as production, accounting, finance, human resources, business law, and marketing), students must be trained with the right talent of designing IBM solutions and operations that require interactive synergies of all business disciplines fused together (Cappelli, 2008; Neumeier, 2009).

(9) Universities must offer a wider assortment of basic and applied knowledge–based degree programs, and business schools in particular must challenge students to critical thinking, social accountability, and moral leadership (Khurana, 2007).

(10) The concept of a frozen "official curriculum" for business schools must be abandoned, and instead, individualized and mentor-based learning through self-exploration and other self-motivated activities must be fostered, which foray into personal, family-supportive, self-actualizing, intellectual, creative, innovative, and spiritual territories of business markets and management (Ackoff & Greenberg, 2008; Mascarenhas, 2010).

(11) A "creative destruction" of the old with creative designing of the new MBA program and curriculum is needed (see Christensen et al., 2006).

Source: Compiled by the authors.

Applying critical thinking, Table 4.3 tentatively contrasts the mindset, mental models, self-mastery, team learning, and team visions of the traditional MBA program with those of the proposed redesigned MBA program, such that most of the criticisms and positive suggestions for a newly designed MBA program are duly addressed.

Critical Thinking Exercise 4.11

Critically analyze the veracity, validity, and credibility of the contents of Table 4.3. Are there other aspects we have missed? Please identify them and assess their positive or negative impact on the current MBA curriculum?

Table 4.3. Critical Differences Between the Traditional and the Proposed Redesigned Master in Business Administration (MBA): A Paradigm Shift.

Domain	Traditional MBA	Redesigned MBA	Implications of Redesigned MBA
Mindset	Old constraining, inherited orthodoxies of status quo, resistance to change, sunk costs, anchoring, framing, evidence management, and risk reduction. The business bottom line is profits via market entry barriers and SCA.	New liberating self-regulating imperatives of resilience and adaptation, seeking change, new anchors, new investments, new frames, new intuition and imagination, exploiting risk, uncertainty, and ambiguity. Bottom line is lasting values to all stakeholders.	A newly designed MBA paradigm should thrive on a totally liberating and humanizing mindset of imagination, exploration, invention, discovery, experimentation, trial and error, learning from mistakes, thinking out of the box, and creativity as well as innovation. The bottom line is eco-sustainability and corporate social responsibility, both of which can be profitable, with corrective and protective justice for all.
Mental Models	Old mechanistic assumptions and presuppositions that represent win–lose and market barrier systems, ethnic biases, racial stereotypes, zonal rules and regulations, market protection, farm subsidies,	New nondeterministic assumptions that are very necessary, axiomatic, intuitively valid, liberating, and humanizing, that affirm unity amid diversity, growth via sustainability, and profitability via performance.	All humans are equal (biologically, genetically, racially, and geographically). Equality of opportunity for all. Nobody should be left behind. Everybody matters, including the bottom of the pyramid, and the poor can be profitable to the

	unfair trade terms, and questionable negotiations.		corporations and to themselves (Prahalad, 2004). Diversity is strength. Small is better. Slower but steady is the speed of efficiency. Distributive and preventive justice for all.
Learning Models	Teaching is learning. Learning by memory, retrieval and reproduction. Learning by domains and disciplines, fragmented and compartmentalized knowledge silos. Obsession for scientific proof and vigor. Assessment by quantitative measures.	Learning is teaching yourself. Learning is imagination, design, fantasy, fun and play, freedom with creativity, innovation, discovery, exploration, and experimentation, questioning and challenging old orthodoxies, and exploring new shared meanings and visions.	Students teach themselves and faculty learn by observation and student empowerment. Learning is "edu-cation" – extracting and mining truth and love from the original well-endowed creative mind of all individuals. Hence, learning is the realization of one's potential for others. Learning is giving more than receiving, more equalizing than nonequalizing, progressive than retrogressive, and uniting than disuniting. Enhancing and empowering justice for all.

(Continued)

Table 4.3. (*Continued*)

Domain	Traditional MBA	Redesigned MBA	Implications of Redesigned MBA
MBA Curriculum and Syllabus Models	Based on fixed, boundaries, domains and disciplines of data, information, metrics, knowledge, concepts, hypotheses, theories, models, strategies, and cases delivered and tested in classrooms, number crunching for verification and falsification, and building knowledge silos.	New MBA is based on fluid, changing, expanding paradigms of self-identity, self-esteem, skills and competencies, talent management and creativity, new market spaces, market drivers, market intelligence, new knowledge, new humanizing values, virtues and wisdom, interactively shared in and outside, in-person and online classrooms.	Teaching from textbooks only is confining, constraining, obsolescing, and indulgent. Learning from recent top tier journals is a mandate. Learning by intuition and imagination, fancy and fantasy, fun and freedom, creativity and innovation, exploration and experimentation, animation, verbalization and visualization, imaging and graphics, humor and drama . . . is humanizing and self-actualizing. Humanizing justice for all.
Performance Assessment Models	IQ tests and batteries, closed-book classroom exams. Entry and exit criteria of quantitative test scores, ranks, and salaries.	PQ and EQ tests of holistic development of personality and character, market-relevant skills and competencies, talents and virtues, values and wisdom.	Health over wealth, value over money, virtue over greed, giving over receiving, win–win over win–lose, cooperation over competition, prudence over valor, simplicity over ostentation, frugality over indulgence, and

Self-Mastery and Executive Spirituality Models	Success measured by money and wealth, power and dominance, commanding leadership and followers, powered by influence and individualism, colonization and balkanization, with consequent marginalization totally ignored.	SQ tests of humanity and integrity, racial harmony and solidarity, shared vision and team building, learning and unlearning, steward and servant leadership, collective generosity and self-sacrifice.	wisdom over knowledge. Equalizing justice for all. Planet Earth is for all to share and live in. All human beings are ends in themselves with no built-in servile instrumentalities. One person is better than the world. Hence, nobody should be excluded or exploited; Everybody counts, matters, and is special. Total humanity and opportunity for all. Humanity is a sacred, blessed, and anointed gift for all. The world is a family with destiny for all. Beneficent justice for all.

Source: Compiled by the authors.

Notes: IQ = intellectual quotient; PQ = physical quotient; EQ = emotional quotient; SQ = spiritual quotient; see Stephen Covey (2004).

A Strategic Change in the MBA Program to Match Our Era

Every strategic change belongs to a certain economic era or stage of industry evolution. Richard Sandour (2008) distinguishes various eras of wealth and value creation since 1945.[7] For instance, during the post–World War II era of 1945–1970, manufacturing dominated the US economic scene, with nearly 70% of employment and wealth generated by this sector. The primary strategy was to create new structures for maximizing manufacturing productivity such as refineries, factories, coal-fired energy, assembly lines, labor unions, transportation logistics, railroads, and highway network. The United States commanded close to two-thirds of world's GDP. This manufacturing dominance of the economy is no more. In contrast, in the United States today, the manufacturing sector generates less than 20% of national employment; in the world, it is around 35%; the rest comes from the service sector that includes governments. The traditional MBA program reflects this manufacturing bias; accordingly, the new MBA program should be attuned to subsequent transitions of the manufacturing economy to: the service sector economy (1960–), to the information economy (1980–), to the knowledge-based industry economy (1990–), to an ecofeminist-conscious sustainability economy (2000–2020), and to the entertainment and happiness economy (2000–).

Given the rapid transition sequences of various economies in the world, there have synchronously generated new complex, unstructured, and "wicked" problems that the redesigned MBA program must learn to recognize, resolve, or tame. Increasingly, today's CEOs as strategists face wicked problems for which they are ill-equipped (Camillus, 2008). Too often, even economic or financial scholars succumb to problem complexity by offering simplistic, reductionistic solutions to incorrectly defined problems (Christensen et al., 2009, p. iv).

Design Structure of the Proposed New MBA Program

Given the above discussion of the major problems associated with the current MBA program, we now can outline a redesigned "integrated business management" MBA program as follows. The crux of this is to professionalize the business school curriculum and pedagogy.

Professionalizing MBA Program and Curriculum

Profession comes from two Latin words, *profiteri* (as past participle of profitēri, it means to profess, confess) and *profateri* (from pro-before + fatēri to acknowledge) – which when combined bear at least three meanings: (a) to research,

---

[7]Richard L. Sandour is the founder of the world's first and North America's only voluntary, legally binding, integrated greenhouse gas emissions reduction, registry, and trading system. He is the father of carbon trading, and currently, Chairman and CEO of the Chicago Climate Exchange, a financial institution that administers the carbon emission-reduction "cap and trade" program.

develop, and create new knowledge in depth which you profess it as your final word in the field; (b) you should be able to prophecy or predict the path of future knowledge and its challenges; and (c) a more serious moral requirement of professionalism is that it acknowledges and prepares students to practice the management profession, enriched and ennobled by its specific professional ethical and moral code of conduct with high and demanding standards. Thus, knowledge itself is professional, which needs to be professed and confessed; that real knowledge is prophetic – it peers into, predicts (projects) into real futures; hence, profession is moral and lives the demands of ethicality and morality. A newly designed MBA program and curriculum should prepare students for a life-time professional development in all three directions, as outlined in Exhibit 4.2.

Initial Assessment of Redesigned MBA

Exhibit 4.2 plans to train students to profess and practice management discipline given its built-in values and professional imperatives (see Column 4, Professional Imperatives). Following the Western MBA structure, we propose an MBA program to run in four semesters each about five months long, with at least five thematic courses (with three credits per course). Five themes, namely, intrinsic motivation management, CIM, productivity, revenue management, and sustainability management, in which students critically need training, are proposed. Exhibit 4.2 illustrates only the motivation and the CIM modules. (*Course development along three other areas suggested is left as a critical thinking exercise to faculty, students, and stakeholders.*)

Exhibit 4.2 makes the following assumptions.

- Professional management knowledge is both academic (descriptive and analytic knowledge emphasized in Semesters 1 and 2, respectively) and professional/practitioner wisdom (inculcated via experiential and sapiential knowledge in Semesters 3 and 4). Thus, we address the criticisms that bemoan lack of professionalism in the current MBA program.
- We assume professional executive business knowledge and practice are sufficiently enshrined in the five major themes selected; each major theme is delivered in four levels of increasing challenge and interconnected relevance (i.e., as descriptive knowledge, analytical knowledge, experiential knowledge, and sapiential knowledge or wisdom) – this process enables IBM. Other themes, contextually more urgent and relevant, could be adopted for future MBA programs; thus, this process does not freeze the MBA program but keeps it open, dynamic, and flexible (see positive suggestions 2, 4, 8, and 10 in Exhibit 4.1). Other competing themes are life quality management, risk management, national growth and prosperity management, nation-building management, global equality management, happiness/mindfulness management, etc.
- The MBA program emphasizes IBM that requires interactive synergies of all business disciplines fused together (see positive suggestion 10); that is, the five chosen themes could incorporate appropriate concepts, theories, cases, skills,

Exhibit 4.2. Template for Professional Development of Master in Business Administration (MBA) Students: Motivation and Creativity–Innovation Management (CIM) Modules.

Knowledge Level Pedagogy Level	Program Content and Challenge — Knowledge as Concepts, Interpretation, Constructs, Axioms, Theories, Paradigms, Paradigm Shifts, Experiences, Realizations, Comprehensions, New Skills and Upskilling, and Talent Development; Assurance of Learning via *Intrinsic Motivation*	Professional Imperatives — **Knowledge as Ethical, Moral, and Spiritual Values and Attitudes, Skills and Drives**
Semester 1: *Descriptive* Knowledge Core courses	*Motivation I:* *Focus: Personal motivation (PM) and personal psychology* Develop the art of PM via excursions in classical prose, poetry, drama, theater with PM legends and legacies across disciplines, enlivened by classical and modern business cases, essays, narratives, and exemplary stories in PM. *Creativity–Innovation Management (CIM I):* Focus on personal CIM; CIM psychology; develop the art of CIM via excursions into lives of recent Nobel prize winners and their legacies, recent manager-of-the-year awardees and their legacies, recent pro sports hall of famers and their achievements, recent brilliant new product development successes and success stories, recent highest growth cities and their sagas, recent brilliant entrepreneurs and their adventures, recent nongovernmental organisations (NGOs) and their narratives, and the like.	Executive self-development in excellence of thought, expression, achievement, communication, argumentation and persuasion, listening and learning, professional courtesy, etiquette and hospitality management; self-development in excellence of creativity and innovation management. The semester should enable self-discovery, self-invention, self-enlightenment, and self-mastery.

Semester 2: *Analytical* Knowledge Core courses and electives, add-ons	*Motivation II:* *Focus: Employee/employer* *motivation* via theories and schools of thought and traditions (Maslow, Herzberg, Argyris), analysis of top HR authors, top journal articles, deriving/ extracting new HR constructs, paradigms and paradigm shifts.	*CIM II:* Focus on people behind success stories; why were these success stories selected; selection bias; success and justification criteria; their social progress impact besides GDP/GNP; their nation-building impact beside wealth creation; their employment generation impact; their national peace and prosperity impact; their impact on young entrepreneurs; their impact on education of youth.	Executive understanding, critical thinking, explanation, prediction, monitoring, metering, supervision, and benign leadership of nonshirking labor; professionalization of gifted employees; humanization of work and labor; work–home spirituality.
Semester 3: *Experiential* Knowledge derived from behavior skills labs, search engines; seminars, webinars, think tanks, workshops; incubation centers; summer internship evaluation	*Motivation III:* *Focus: Customer Motivation* via total customer experience (TCE) management; know your customer (KYC) and TCE experiments and success stories, entrepreneurship, incubation centers, experiments, knowledge reliability and validity tests;	*CIM III:* Focus on actors (in CIM I–II) via experiential knowledge; internalizing their hard and confining work in creation-innovation labs; their long practices and drills and sacrifice stories; their incubation venture stories; their funding and financing	Executive creativity and imagination, discovery, invention, and innovation for KYC/TCE via new and safe product development; innovative leadership and corporate adventure; with moral fortitude deal with risk, uncertainty, and ambiguity management; going beyond

(Continued)

Exhibit 4.2. (*Continued*)

Knowledge Level Pedagogy Level	Program Content and Challenge **Knowledge as Concepts, Interpretation, Constructs, Axioms, Theories, Paradigms, Paradigm Shifts, Experiences, Realizations, Comprehensions, New Skills and Upskilling, and Talent Development; Assurance of Learning via *Intrinsic Motivation***	Professional Imperatives **Knowledge as Ethical, Moral, and Spiritual Values and Attitudes, Skills and Drives**
	business corporate legitimacy tests	customer and product to nobler and artistic aspects of consumption.
	experiences; their breakthrough innovation impact on markets and the country; their impact on sustainability and carbon neutrality.	
Semester 4: *Sapiential* Knowledge via inspirational and motivational talks, dialogue and discussion; sharing with experts and industry icons; executive shadow learning with industry champions and legends of intrinsic motivation.	*Motivation IV:* *Focus: Corporate/ organizational/local community motivation* Cultivation of wisdom, prudence, moral/enlightened decision-making for growth and prosperity strategies; intrinsic motivation, deriving just ethical and moral judgments and performance appraisals; executive virtues	*CIM IV:* Focus on their humanization impact; their leadership impact of virtue, courage, fortitude, and perseverance; their impact on customer/ employer happiness and mindfulness; their contribution to national happiness and harmony; their humanizing impact on the poor and the marginalized;	Executive organizational compassion expressed in virtue, respect, trust, love, loyalty, responsibility, honesty, transparency, authenticity, sincerity and integrity, commitment and dedication; anti-fraud and anti–money laundering codes of executive ethics; organizational commitment to sustainability, greening,

and other executive imperatives. The mystery and paradox of human motivation.	their impact on global poverty reduction; their impact on human equality and egalitarianism and libertarianism; their impact on human dignity, freedom, and rights, wisdom, and prudence; their impact on democracy of being and becoming.	quality of community life and integrity, good neighborhood, peace and tranquility.

and knowledge from almost all currently compartmentalized disciplines such as accounting, finance, marketing, organizational behavior, human resources, production, and the like (see Cappelli, 2008; Neumeier, 2009).

- The redesigned MBA program demands high involvement in the program by developing, testing, and validating new courses (e.g., Motivation I–IV, and CIM I–IV, Productivity Management I–IV, Revenue Management I–IV, and Eco-Sustainability Management I–IV, each anchored on personal, employee, customer, and organization/executive/community/environment management, suggested in Exhibit 4.1). This requirement will, presumably, generate much creative and innovative programs fulfilling the knowledge creation goal of the university. One hopes that this research will generate knowledge that fulfills the vision and mission of the business school, rather than just feed academic journals.

- The redesigned program is founded on intrinsic motivation (i.e., discouraging extrinsic motivation) all through the four semesters. Hence, implicitly, the program discourages exams and evaluations via closed-∂book, memory-based, in-class exams, discourages ranks and gold medals and trophies based on them, discourages curbing of grades to fit normal curves, and includes outlier students. We encourage open-book, take-home research-based exams performed by student-selected teams or random groups on the five domain topics.

- Each of the four semester levels prepares students through several substantive value imperatives: being *ethical* (i.e., learning right skills), *moral* (i.e., deploying these skills rightly), and *spiritual* (i.e., executing these right skills rightly and for the right reasons and intentions) (see Column 4 of Exhibit 4.2). This addresses concerns raised by MBA program critics regarding lack of moral and ethical training in the current MBA program and curriculum (see positive suggestions 4 and 9). The program advocates anti-fraud and anti–money laundering behaviors.

Concluding Remarks

If Exhibits 4.1 and 4.2 are seriously followed, the redesigned MBA program will progressively cease to be a mere academic product crafted in a mere academic discipline geared to MBA students as customized, individualized, and personalized consumers, and will restore its professional status, which it had retreated from decades ago. In the long run, if Exhibit 4.1 is strenuously implemented by business school administrators, faculty, and students, it will disprove the doctrine that managers are merely agents of shareholders, beholden to the cause of the bottom line of profits to them, but also rejuvenate intellectually and morally the training of our future business leaders (Khurana, 2007; Khurana & Nohria, 2008).

Professionalization needs depth, width, experience-innovation, and quality. Ideally, the same template of intrinsic motivation and CIM modules illustrated in

Exhibit 4.1 could be developed and consistently pursued along other proposed themes such as productivity management, revenue management, and eco-sustainability management, pursued along all four ascending levels of knowledge commitment, as indicated along the four semesters in Exhibit 4.1. We hope that training imparted along all five major themes and along all four semester levels will adequately respond to concerns on lack of professionalism in the current MBA program.

Chapter 5

Critical Thinking to Harness Global Social "Wicked" Problems: New Curriculum, Content, and Challenges in the Redesigned MBA Program

Executive Summary

We revisit the problem of redesigning the Master in Business Administration (MBA) program, curriculum, and pedagogy, focusing on understanding and seeking to tame its "wicked problems," as an intrinsic part and challenge of the MBA program venture, and to render it more realistic and relevant to address major problems and their consequences. We briefly review the theory of wicked problems and methods of dealing with their consequences from multiple perspectives. Most characterization of problems classifies them as simple (problems that have known formulations and solutions), complex (where formulations are known but not their resolutions), unstructured problems (where formulations are unknown, but solutions are estimated), and "wicked" (where both problem formulations and their resolutions are unknown but eventually partially tamable). Uncertainty, unpredictability, randomness, and ambiguity increase from simple to complex to unstructured to wicked problems. A redesigned MBA program should therefore address them effectively through the four semesters in two years. Most of these problems are real and affect life and economies, and hence, business schools cannot but incorporate them into their critical, ethical, and moral thinking.

Introduction: The Theory of Wicked Problems

Russell Ackoff (1974), one of the early founders of systems thinking, defined a problem in general as a "system at unrest." A system, according to him, was any set of two or more interacting parts, where the efficiency of a system is more than a mere sum of the efficiency of its parts owing to interacting effects. A system at unrest is when its equilibrium is disrupted by other systems such as competition,

A Primer on Critical Thinking and Business Ethics, 147–188

Copyright © 2024 Oswald A. J. Mascarenhas, Munish Thakur and Payal Kumar

Published under exclusive licence by Emerald Publishing Limited

doi:10.1108/978-1-83753-312-120231005

inflation, industrial concentration, or labor problems; all systems try to restore balance through feedback systems. The free enterprise competitive market system is an excellent example of a system that is frequently in a state of unrest.

In a landmark article in 1973, Horst Rittel and Melvin Webber, both urban planners at the University of Berkley in California, defined the notion and domain of what they called "wicked" problems as opposed to ordinary simple problems. They observed that there are a set of problems that cannot be resolved with traditional analytical approaches. For the first time, problems that are neither formulatable nor resolvable by known analytical methods were characterized as "wicked problems." Rittel and Webber (1973) were the first to introduce the notion of "wicked" in relation to social problems as opposed to "ordinary" problems. A year later, Ackoff (1974) called such problems a "mess," and many years later, Horn (2001) called them a "social mess."

Ackoff (1974) distinguished between puzzles, problems, and messes as follows:

- *Puzzles* are well-defined and well-structured problems with a specific solution that can be worked out.
- *Problems* are well-formulated or defined issues but with no single solution – different solutions are possible.
- *Messes* are complex issues that are not well formulated or defined.

Complexity comes from the multiplicity of variables involved in a problem (*detail complexity*) and from the multiplicity of interactions that occur between the variables over time (*dynamic complexity*).

From a systems-thinking perspective, dynamic complexity arises from many factors (Senge, 1990, 2006):

- Causes and effects are subtle, separated in time and space, and the effects of interventions are not obvious.
- The same cause or action has dramatically different effects in the short run and in the long run.
- An action or strategy has one set of consequences locally and a very different set of consequences in another part of the system or the world (this was obvious with COVID-19).
- Obvious interventions or resolution strategies produce nonobvious consequences (this was also apparent with COVID-19).

For instance, wicked problems arise amid market uncertainty and turbulence, excessive shareholder pressure, undue Securities and Exchange Commission (SEC) vigilance and pressure, constant changes in consumer lifestyles, uncontrolled greed, inordinate attachment to power, unfair labor demands and strikes, credit crunch, and other unprecedented challenges. Most wicked problems imply discontent and discord, confusion, lack of progress, and angst among multiple stakeholders that entertain different values and priorities. They involve issues that are complex and tangled. The problem keeps on changing the more we address it;

its challenge may not have a precedent, and there may not be a right answer or resolution to the wicked problem. Convergence of industries can also create wicked problems. For instance, the computer industry and the internet have changed the postal mail, music, sports entertainment, film, TV, radio, telephone, and the intellectual property industries radically. Similarly, computers and the internet have profoundly affected the biomedical, bioinformatics, and biometric industries.

Similarly, the recent phenomenon of corporate fraud, deceptive financial reporting practices, subprime mortgage crisis, and the subsequent Wall Street meltdown are not simple but complex, unstructured, involved, circular, iterative, recursive, and often not solvable wicked problems. In the past two decades, as global markets have grown increasingly opaque, competitive, and globally connected through the internet and the social media, the world has seen record numbers of corporations dramatically restructure their assets, operations, and capital resources.

Charles Perrow (1974, 1994) classified problems based on the nature of their outcomes:

- Type I: problems with known outcomes and fixed sequences – these are deterministic systems.
- Type II: problems with known outcomes and known probabilities associated with sequences – these are stochastic systems.
- Type III: problems with known outcomes and unknown probabilities associated with sequences that make them uncertain systems.
- Type IV: problems with unknown, unanticipated, or unimagined outcomes with unknown probabilities that render them emergent systems on the horizon.

Conventional methods of risk assessment and risk management apply best to Type I and II problems. Thus, we could understand auto, home, and life insurances as Type I and Type II systems with known outcomes and known fixed or probabilistic sequences. On the other hand, safety of high-speed vehicles, carbon emissions, and modern nuclear plants are Type III problems, where our current level or degree of ignorance is high owing to what Perrow (1984) calls "interactive complexity" and "coupling." Interactive complexity is a measure of the degree to which we cannot foresee all the ways things can go wrong – this is because there are too many interactions that we cannot or could not foresee, understand, and manage. Coupling is a measure of the degree to which we cannot stop an impending disaster once it starts – this is because we do not have enough resources, time, knowledge, or technologies to do so.

Structure of Problems in Free Enterprise Capitalism

In general, literature on problems (e.g., King, 1993; Rittel & Webber, 1973) distinguishes several basic types of problems (see Table 5.1).

Table 5.1. Characterizing Problems.

Is There a Definite Problem Formulation?	Is There is a Definitive Problem Solution?	
	Yes	**No**
Yes	Simple problems	Complex problems
	Simple scientific (e.g., mathematical, chemistry, physics, economics, or engineering) problems that have potentially clear problem formulations and equally clear solutions.	Complex or unstructured scientific problems (e.g., biosocial, biochemical, bioengineering, ecological) that have potentially clear problem formulations but no definitive solutions.
	Examples: Most trivial problems, puzzles, mazes and conundrums, most academic homework problems, most home economics problems, and simple business production and growth problems. All game problems such as in chess, bridge, and gambling.	*Examples*: Stem cell research, abortion, euthanasia, physician-assisted suicide, carbon emissions, water/air/land pollution, personal bankruptcy, corporate bankruptcy, nationalization, privatization, government bankruptcy, widening trade deficit, increasing federal deficit, trade inequities, trade embargoes, international law, international courts, international patent law, and labor law.
No	Unstructured problems	Wicked problems
	Socially complex or unstructured economic and political problems (e.g., cancer, auto safety, teenage violence) that are not formulated clearly, but politicians and social activists offer and market several potentially "feasible" solutions.	Socially complex or unstructured economic and political problems (e.g., terrorism, corporate fraud, corporate greed, consumer overspending) that have no known clear problem formulations and no known, clearly "viable," and "feasible" solutions.

Table 5.1. *(Continued)*

Is There a Definite Problem Formulation?	Is There is a Definitive Problem Solution?	
	Yes	No
	Examples: Cancer, AIDS, autism, Down syndrome, impulse buying, pathological addictions, exorbitant executive compensation, price gouging, preventive wars, collateral damage, regime change, nuclear détente, balkanization, global income inequalities, and command economies.	*Examples*: Global climate change, tsunami, hurricanes, global peace, global racial harmony, ethnic cleansing, genocide, global poverty, pandemic disease, global terrorism, internet pornography, cyber fraud, executive fraud, merchant fraud, consumer fraud, avarice, and greed.

Source: Compiled by the authors based on Rittel and Webber (1973).

Simple Problems
Both the problem and the solution are known. This is a problem with a clear goal, and one can easily map it onto a feedback loop of method/action and measure/ test. These are "tame" problems that are manageable with known algorithms for arriving at correct solution. Solution presupposes clear user goals, a bounded solution space, and there is a stopping condition with the right answer or solution. Problem–solution is a user-centered design. These problems are "puzzles" (Ack- off, 1974). For example, COVID-19 started out as a puzzle but quickly evolved being more complex, unstructured, and unresolvable.

Complex Problems
The problem is known, but the solution is not. Or, there could be multiple solutions. The goal is not yet clear, but it is possible to agree on it, and agreeing transforms it into a simple problem. The major task is to do some planning such that your major stakeholders buy in into its goals. Resolution presupposes several agreed-on goals. Problem–solution is a multiuser-centered design of planning, agreement, and deliberation. For example, you need to define COVID-19 and quickly arrive at an effective vaccine. The problem is clear if we can agree on "virology," but understanding how to contain viruses is far from clear. Partial solutions can be derived if we organize ourselves to solve COVID-19 as tamed problems and deal with it through research specialization groups of universities or pharmaceutical corporations using cross-disciplinary approaches. That is, deriving solutions to complex problems often requires "organizational learning" (Senge, 1990).

Pseudo Problems

The problem is not known or formulated, but the solutions are freely generated and marketed. For instance, you "carve out" a piece of a problem and find a solution to that piece disregarding other pieces of the problem. Such an approach could lead to problems such as deception: you deceive the innocent public that such a solution "solves" or "tames" the problem. Deception raises issues of morality – the morality of deceiving people into thinking something (e.g., a solution) is true when it is not. This can be a serious moral issue when one deceives the public that something is safe (e.g., a new drug, a new procedure, a new vaccine) when it is highly dangerous (Churchman, 1974). For instance, currently, the American healthcare problem, which leaves over 100 million citizens either uninsured or underinsured, has failed to be formulated. Nevertheless, different vested groups are offering solutions ranging from a totally privatized healthcare plan to a totally nationalized healthcare solution model.

Similarly, we have no definite formulation of the cancer problem, but we have a multiplicity of beneficial solutions such as chemotherapy, radiation, importing white cells, and the like. In the auto world, we have no clear definitions of the driver or passenger safety problem but have numerous partial solutions (e.g., seatbelts, airbags, or heavier metal doors). Likewise, we have not yet defined the problem of increasing teenager crime and violence in the United States but have offered many inefficient solutions (e.g., gun control, more police, metal detectors in schools, juvenile courts, stricter sentencing, and increasing prisons). This procedure could be tantamount to what Tukey (1972) described as solving the wrong problem. Therefore, the solutions proposed create further problems and exacerbate the original problem. Proposed solutions often turn out to be worse than the symptoms. In our turbulent world, it is almost a strategic necessity to solve such problems (King, 1993).

Wicked Problems

The problem and the solution are both not known. Here, you cannot agree on goals, and hence, a wicked problem cannot be converted into a complex problem, unless you reframe the problem and innovate its goals-realization, for instance, global poverty and multiple stated goals for its eradication or alleviation. Stakeholders have multiple viewpoints about wicked problems, their goals, and their consequences. There may not be any agreement on the problem, its nature, goals, or consequences among its multiple stakeholders. All may be equally expert or ignorant – a "symmetry of ignorance." Any potential problem resolution presupposes consensual sympathy or compromise about the different sets of goals. The problem–resolution design implies much teamwork, conversation, argument, discourse, debate, dialogue, rhetoric, and deliberation, for example, global poverty, teenager high school dropout, and crime. Team members leverage information and knowledge to create value and consensus. The whole process may be political and ideological. Wicked problems force us to work "outside the box." Problem definition and identification may require much dialogue between relevant stakeholder teams. We do not really "solve" wicked problems; rather we "design" more or less partially effective solutions based on how we define the problem.

Critical Thinking Exercise 5.1

Apply critical thinking (see footnote 3 in Chapter 1) to the consideration of why we confront so many wicked problems, and what are the origins of wicked problems in the Master in Business Administration (MBA) program, curriculum, and delivery. Do they enable better understanding, explanation, prediction, and resolution of the wicked problems in the MBA program, curriculum, and pedagogy in the business schools of today, and if yes, why? Accordingly, formulate your strategy for taming wicked problems in your business school.

Redesigning MBA Curriculum: Content Challenges

Literature suggests that here are many reasons why we confront so many wicked problems:

- The world is becoming more turbulent with things happening faster, bigger, and beyond our control (e.g., wars, global terrorism, genocide, political power crisis, global energy crisis, healthcare crises, teenager student suicide, financial market turbulence).
- We do not know what we want. Should we build an economic and political infrastructure predicated on the belief that we will need more energy or more conservation? Which policy will provide us with more flexibility and adaptability, more simplicity and well-being, more health and global peace? Such policy decisions will determine significant aspects of our future.
- We cannot easily predict our energy needs, our political needs, our ecology needs, our healthcare needs, our safety/security needs, and the needs of our consumptive lifestyles.
- We cannot predict our possible futures other than a few aspects of these futures.
- Most of these problems are characterized by human ignorance – what we do not know we do not know, and many do not know that they do not know (see Chapter 6 of Volume I).
- We just cannot foresee all the ways things can go wrong – this is the chaos theory.
- While we cannot easily predict our future, what we choose to do affects our future. For example, our current extractive and technology choices may have some unanticipated consequences (such as global warming, climate change, ocean acidity, etc.).
- It is *a loss of orientation* that most directly gives rise to divergent ideological activity, an inability, for lack of usable models, to comprehend the universe of civic rights and responsibilities in which one finds oneself located (Geertz, 1973).

- "Wickedness occurs when people confer immutability on value assumptions and ideological considerations" (King, 1993, p. 113).
- Different stakeholders in wicked problems hold diverse values – what satisfies one may be abhorrent to another, and what comprises problem solution for one is problem generation for another. Under such circumstances, and in the *absence of an overarching social theory or an overarching special ethic*, there is no determining which group is right and which group or problem is wrong, which needs to serve and which needs to be served (Rittel & Webber, 1973).
- "All we have are endless fragments of theory that account for bits and pieces of individual, organizational and economic behavior. But we have no overarching or truly interconnecting theories, especially none that accounts for human behavior in turbulent times" (Michael, 1985, p. 95).
- The new mathematics of complexity raises an even more disturbing question: Can there be an economic policy at all? Or is the attempt to control the "weather" of the economy, such as recessions and other cyclical fluctuations, foredoomed to failure? (Drucker, 1989, p. 167).
- There are no grounds to suspect things could be better in principle. There are no sound reasons to claim that the technological, social, and political sciences are going to mature or evolve to the point that we can more accurately predict and control our future (King, 1993, p. 111).

Challenges in Resolution of Wicked Problems

Wickedness in wicked problems occurs when people attribute metaphysical immutability to value assumptions and ideological considerations (consider Nazism and the Holocaust; Russian obduracy and the war on Ukraine; financial market opacity and subsequent 2008 October global financial meltdown). In such cases, wicked problems can easily degenerate into tyranny or chaos (King, 1993, p. 113). Type IV problems are "wicked" problems that cannot be resolved by known analytical or scientific methods. As Rittel and Webber (1973, p. 162) point out, they can only be resolved through logical argumentation and inter-scholar consensus.

The process of resolving Type IV wicked problems is elaborate and argumentative. It is a second-generation systems approach based on a model of planning as an argumentative process in the course of which an image of the problem and of the solution emerges gradually among participants, as a product of incessant judgment, subject to critical argument. In terms of participants, we need to build on diversity, cross-functionality, and interdisciplinary expertise. We need to build on adaptability, resilience, rapid response times, flexibility, reversibility, and even "redundancy" such that when confronted by undesirable and unanticipated outcomes, we have fallback positions. We must learn how to learn and unlearn, think about how we think, and we need to build learning organizations (Senge, 1990).

Above all, we need common sense – that is, common ground. Establishing common ground is a strategic necessity in our turbulent times (Bellah et al., 1991;

Hunter, 1991). Common ground essentially means that we realize that our differences are less significant and profound than what we share in common, and that this common sense represents the beginnings of wisdom (King, 1993, p. 114).

Next, given this multi-specialization stakeholders, in taming such wicked problems, we need to carefully draw boundaries such that we can sort out different "images" of the problem, tame different pieces of the original wicked problem, generate hypotheses specific to a piece of the problem, and converge toward emergent resolutions. Perhaps, following one of the fundamental tenets of Edwards Deming, we should shift from strategies that focus on results, outcomes, or objectives to strategies that focus on continuously improving processes. This strategic shift needs a profound change in mindset for managers and executives. We also need real listening and engaging in "dialogue." We need both dialogue and listening to "mapmaking." Listening, dialogue, and mapmaking are needed for mapping the boundaries and learning to recognize patterns of interaction – this is the crux in sorting messes. Real listening is also essential in establishing trust, and trust is absolutely necessary when working together. "Trust is a fundamental strategy for collectively coping with wicked problems ... mistrust is the dark heart of wicked problems" (King, 1993, pp. 112–114).

Problems, however, rarely fall neatly into neat and clean categories. Rittel and Webber's classification (see Table 5.1) describes a continuous spectrum, one end of which are simple tame problems, and the other end of each are nontamable wicked problems. Wicked problems should not be recast as tame categories in order to solve them. Treating wicked problems as tame misdirects energy and resources, resulting in ineffective solutions, and often such solutions create more difficulty.

Critical Thinking Exercise 5.2

Apply critical thinking (see footnote 3 in Chapter 1) to Table 5.1 and classify the major problems of your business world today. Does classification enable better understanding, explanation, prediction, and resolution of the problems – and if so, why? Accordingly, formulate your strategy for taming these problems in your organization.

Tame problems – the opposite of "wicked problems" – may also be quite complex, but they lend themselves to analysis and solutions by known techniques. Traditional linear processes are sufficient to produce a solution to a tame problem in an acceptable period of time, and it is clear when a solution emerges. This is not true of wicked problems. For wicked problems, the problem statement changes, its constraints keep changing, its stakeholders keep increasing and their goals and targets are constantly moving, (i.e., its requirements are volatile), and accordingly, stakeholder resistance to the problem resolutions keeps mounting. Such is the case with current wicked problems such as eradicating global poverty, global terrorism, controlling violence and crime in schools and university campuses, making cars safer, locating new freeways, prisons, and homeless shelters, controlling corporate fraud and greed, saving subprime mortgage markets, and bailing out collapsed financial markets.

Defined thus, typical examples of wicked problems are city planning, city revitalization, crime prevention and control, wealth creation and equitable distribution, building new expressways connecting populous cities, applying the doctrine of eminent domain, fair trial, fair elections, and the like. Other social wicked problems include rebuilding broken urban neighborhoods or ghettoes, reforming public education, creating and maintaining environmentally sustainable communities, reducing drug abuse, reducing teenage pregnancy, reducing abortions, and reducing teenage suicides. Most of these problems are linked with horizontal and vertical cross-cutting dimensions, multiple stakeholders, trade-offs between values, and quality of family life. Wicked problems are linked and have ramifications on larger constituents. Thus, one could link the wicked problem of terrorism to some nations unjustifiably seeking superpower over others. Possibly, we could connect the wicked problem of health care in the United States to the inordinate profit-seeking goals of healthcare systems such as the pharmaceutical companies, health insurance companies, and the medical professions. Most public issues in the world today (e.g., poverty, income inequality, genocide, and global climate change) stem from and create wicked problems of avarice and exploitation.

Wicked problems, as opposed to simple mechanical problems, are voluble and volatile, stubborn and obstinate, subtle and mysterious, and complex and dissensual. Wicked problems are ill-defined, ambiguous, and associated with strong moral, political, and professional issues. Since they are strongly stakeholder-dependent, there is often little consensus about what the problem is and its solution (Ritchey, 2005). Most major public projects today (e.g., constructing freeways, subways, bridges, and industrial parks; offshore oil or natural gas mining; controlling and containing crime and violence in schools) have a significant wicked component. Major problems of uncertainty, risk, and ambiguity arise along all the steps in their resolution. The process, far from linear, is highly iterative, forcing going back and forth between all six steps before the leverage value of any information becomes known. The value of any piece of information along each step remains unknown until the desired outcome is achieved. Often wicked problems deal with complex emerging social market issues such as uncertainty and turbulence, information explosion, cultural value monism versus pluralism and diversity, social and ethnic anarchy, and multiracial discrimination. They are also often triggered by structures of social injustice, inequity, inequality, and violence.

There is one type of problem in Perrow's categorization of problems, which have unknown, unanticipated, or unimagined outcomes accompanied by unknown probabilities – these are *emergent* systems that are future challenges. These problems are riddled with unknown sequences with unknown probabilities, leading to an unknown sequence of failures or disasters that cannot be controlled by known methods and technologies. They are "wicked" problems. Typical examples are global warming, global climate change, Arctic meltdown, global tsunami, continental hurricanes, global terrorism such as 9/11, global hacking, global cyber fraud, global invasion of privacy, global holocausts or genocide, and the October 2008 global financial market crisis. Accordingly, Table 5.2 offers a more comprehensive characterization of problems based on the nature of outcomes.

Critical Thinking Exercise 5.3

Apply critical thinking (see footnote 3 in Chapter 1) to Table 5.2 and classify the major problems of your business world today. Does your classification enable better understanding, explanation, prediction, and resolution of the problems – and if yes, why? Accordingly, formulate your strategy for taming these problems in your corporation.

Challenges in Formulation of Wicked Problems

What Makes a Problem Wicked?

Many factors generate wicked problems, but the point is not to determine if a problem is wicked or not but to have a sense of what contributes to the wickedness of a problem. The sources of problem wickedness are many (Conklin, 2006).

- The problem is complex, socially, economically, technologically and politically, and dynamic in nature.
- The problem is socially complex, involving multiple and diverse stakeholders (e.g., several companies, several government agencies, several advocacy groups) each with different sets of goals; some of these may undermine or even sabotage the project if their needs and goals are not considered.
- The fragmenting force of social complexity makes effective communication very difficult.
- The causes of the problem are many, unknown, uncertain, and ambiguous.
- The consequences of the problem are hidden, social, complex, political, and universal.
- Information and knowledge about the problem are chaotic; that is, perspectives, intentions, understanding, interpretation, knowledge, and experience of individuals involved with the wicked problem are fragmented.
- Each individual or stakeholder of the problems is convinced that his/her version of the problem is correct and complete.
- Each person makes incompatible tacit assumptions about the problem.

Table 5.2. Toward a Comprehensive Characterization of Problems.

	Problem Resolution			
	Known		**Unknown**	
Problem Nature	**Outcomes Known**	**Outcomes Distributions Known**	**Outcomes Unknown**	**Outcomes Distributions Unknown**
	Outcome sequences are fixed and known.	Outcome sequences are probabilistic with known probabilities.	Outcome sequences are known with unknown probabilities.	Outcome sequences are unknown with unknown Probabilities.
Knowledge Status	Deterministic	Stochastic	Uncertain	Divergent/ Emergent
Formulation Known	Simple problems Type I problem (Perrow, 1984)	Complex problems Type II problem (Perrow, 1984)	Messes (Ackoff, 1974) Type III problem (Perrow, 1984)	Social messes (Horn, 2001) Type IV problem (Perrow, 1984)
Examples	Classroom puzzles; science lab exercises	Most business problems; most medical problems with known diseases and known outcomes	Most sociopolitical problems with known causes but unknown outcomes (e.g., poverty, global warming)	Most medical problems with known diseases but unknown outcomes (e.g., cancer, Down syndrome)
Formulation Unknown	Created Problems Type I Error: Rejecting a true problem	Pseudo Problems Type II Error: Accepting a wrong problem	Wicked Problems Type III Error: Resolving a wrong problem	Wicked Problems Type IV Error: Resolving a wrong problem with the right solution
Examples	Created ghettoes; ghost towns;	Treating the wrong disease in medicine;	Resolving a wrong problem in	Overkill or resolving the wrong

Table 5.2. *(Continued)*

Problem Nature	Problem Resolution			
	Known		Unknown	
	Outcomes Known	**Outcomes Distributions Known**	**Outcomes Unknown**	**Outcomes Distributions Unknown**
	negative marketing; products of affluence or extravagance or billionaire enclaves	student boredom; employee malaise;	health care; traffic congestion; teenage violence; terrorism; most medical problems with known diseases but unknown outcomes	problem in preventive wars, collateral damage, cyber hacking, terrorism, or global climate change; most medical problems with unknown diseases and unknown outcomes

Source: Compiled by the authors based on Perrow (1984).

Most natural disasters are wicked problems on the geophysical level. Some wicked problems are manmade, such as labor strikes, sabotage, vandalism, gangsterism, terrorism, 9/11, consumer boycotts, and corporate fraud. Some socioeconomic problems are also wicked in nature (e.g., recession, depression, inflation, unemployment, organizational decline, massive layoffs, plant shutdowns, and personal or corporate bankruptcy). Some wicked problems arise because of hyper growth (e.g., Walmart still wanting to grow bigger and faster despite saturating retail markets; Ford, GMC, Toyota, and other automakers still wanting to sell more vehicles when the current North American auto markets are saturated and recessionary). Some wicked problems arise because of avarice and envy (e.g., corporate fraud, ethnic cleansing, genocide, most wars, preventive wars, "holy" wars, unjust aggression, and developing and building weapons of mass destruction). Some wicked problems arise because of recklessness, hatred, and retaliation (e.g., crime and violence in schools, street crime, vandalism, serial murders, terrorism, cyber-hacking, and organized crime). Reckless corporate cost-containment methods create also wicked problems (e.g., downsizing, plant shutdowns, plant relocations, massive layoffs, offshore outsourcing, sweatshops, child labor, forcing suppliers to lower prices beyond their breakeven point, and the like).

How to Recognize a Wicked Problem

A wicked problem does not have to verify all the 10 characteristics described by Rittel and Webber (1973) (see below). Moreover, a wicked problem can have several tame elements. Space research and placing a man on the moon were certainly wicked problems, but they could be defined; the solution was realized when we landed the first man on the moon and brought him home safely, and the solution could be assessed as right or wrong. Technically, we could even stop space research, but we may not want to do it as it betters our understanding of meteorology, communications via satellites, zero gravity research, and the like. That is, most wicked problems have degrees of wickedness (Conklin, 2006).

As you grapple with a problem, you come to know it is wicked if you encounter one or more of the following operational constraints (Camillus, 2008):

- The problem definition seems vague or keeps changing.
- The proposed solution creates a new, related problem unveiling new boundaries.
- There are many meetings on the project but not much progress.
- The number of stakeholders keeps increasing.
- You cannot see easily the solution at the outset.
- There are multiple solutions but no consensus and no convergence.
- The constraints on the solution keep changing.
- There are many organizational and political issues involved.
- The decision-solution has been made but not followed (i.e., it is not a real solution).
- Increasingly, today's CEOs as strategists face wicked problems for which they are ill-equipped.

Wicked projects arise when we organize to tackle a wicked problem as if it were a tame problem. For instance, a "mission-critical" project with less than half the time and resources necessary to do the job is a wicked problem called a "Death March Project" by Yourdon (1999).

- Death March Projects happen when volatile requirements, changing constraints, and stakeholder disagreements meet up against immovable deadlines.
- Such wicked problems have often occurred in the software development world as reported by a 1994 Standish Group Report (1994) that documented that about a third of software development projects get canceled, and a half do not meet their original cost projections.
- Recently, several challenging projects have been organized as wicked problems, such as designing effective workplaces (Gustafsson, 2002), closing the achievement gap (Dietz et al., 2005), classroom instructional design (Becker, 2007), canal dredging project (Blythe et al., 2008), urban streetcar parking (Kerley, 2007), and Cat's Cradling project (Hubbard & Paquet, 2007).

Characterizing Wicked Problems

Rittel and Webber (1973, pp. 161–169) believe that wicked problems have 10 characteristics, which incidentally characterize most of business problems today. We briefly describe all 10 criteria of wicked problems, as they offer compelling reasons why a redesigned MBA program should include as part of its domain and curriculum.

(1) Wicked problems are *not easily definable*. One cannot easily formulate the wicked problem of redesigning the over 150-year-old MBA program with a well-defined statement. The problem is hard to define, often including interlocking issues. The information needed to understand the problem depends upon one's idea of solving it. The process of formulating the problem and of conceiving a solution is identical; that is, *the problem cannot be defined until the solution has been found.*

(2) Wicked problems have *no stopping rules*. This follows from proposition 1. If a problem cannot be defined exhaustively, you cannot stop searching for solutions. The search for problem formulation and resolution never stops. This is also because the wicked problem is continually evolving and mutating. Since the process of solving a wicked problem such as the dated MBA program is identical to the process of understanding its nature, and since there are no criteria for sufficiently understanding the problem and there are no ends to the causal chains that link interacting open systems, there is no finished stage to the formulation and solution of the problem – it is an ongoing process. The redesigning of the MBA program that we suggest has no stopping rules – it is an ongoing process. Similarly, global poverty, global terrorism, or global warming have no stopping rules and hence cannot be defined or resolved exhaustively, as we have presumed thus far.

(3) *Solutions to wicked problems are not objectively true or false*, right or wrong but only judgmentally better or worse, good enough or bad (not good enough). With no absolute criteria for resolving a wicked problem such as the MBA program, a solution agreement may be that it is just good enough. That is, we cannot objectively assess the solutions without considering the social context in which the problems arose. The dated MBA program may have multiple competing solutions.

(4) There is *no immediate and no ultimate test of a solution* to a wicked problem. With numerous variables involved, no two wicked problems are identical, and hence, their solutions must be customized. Solutions to wicked problems generate *unexpected consequences* over time, making it difficult to measure their effectiveness. That is, there is no immediate or ultimate closure solution since any solution chosen can generate waves of consequences over extended and unbounded periods of time. We expect this to happen with the redesigning and implementing the new MBA program. Instead of a generalist program that is being standardized and globalized currently, we must regionalize the newly redesigned MBA program to suit

the domestic or regional markets and challenges – a customized solution to a given country and its specific markets. After all, all strategy is fundamentally local (Greenwald & Kahn, 2005).

(5) *Every solution to a wicked problem is a "one shot operation."* Solutions to wicked problems are not learnt by trial and error. Every attempt to reverse a decision or correct the undesired consequences of a previous solution poses yet another set of wicked problems. Contrary to this rule, the MBA program cannot be redesigned as a "one shot operation," which cannot be subjected to experiments of trial and error. As a work in progress, the MBA program needs to be dynamic – redesigned periodically and regionally to reflect volatile markets and industries.

(6) *Wicked problems do not have a well-described set of potential solutions.* While ordinary problems have a limited number of potential solutions, wicked problems do not have an exhaustively describable set of potential solutions with a well-defined set of permissible operations. We do not have criteria to prove if all resolutions to wicked problems have been identified and assessed. Any redesign of an MBA program does not nor need to have a well-described set of potential solutions – it suggests a direction to proceed given the changes in the economy, markets, and industries. Future changes may suggest other directions. The redesigned program should be flexible and resilient to address future changes. Hence, a highly standardized formulation and resolution of the wicked MBA curriculum problem is a myth; it may not exist nor be desirable.

(7) Every wicked problem is *essentially unique and novel*, while ordinary problems belong to a class of problems that one can solve in the same way. No two wicked problems are alike because of the unique social and political context in which they are embedded. A wicked problem may not have a precedent, and experience may not help you to address it. That is, wicked problems are unique in their occurrence, context, causes, resolutions, and consequences. Hence, they are not classifiable for the most part, and we do not attempt to uniquely or universally classify or benchmark our suggested redesign of the MBA program. It may be unclassifiable, continuously permutating and contextual, given new developments in the marketplace.

(8) Every wicked problem is a *symptom of another wicked problem* with which it is entwined; these problems do not have one cause. Wicked problems are not spawned in isolation; their genesis is often complex social issues or challenges that merge into a new problem. By contrast, ordinary problems are self-contained with traceable causes. Some wicked problems, accordingly, involve a good deal of mutual and circular causality, and the problem must be considered at many causal levels (Ritchey, 2005, 2006). Our suggested redesign of the MBA program may itself spawn other wicked problems, especially those of redesigning new courses, new materials, new cases, new instructional designs, new pedagogies, and the like. A radical change implies a radical departure from the status quo. Specifically, and more importantly, some of the intrinsic components of the current MBA program, such as profit maximization, wealth maximization, revenue

maximization, and cost minimization, are entwined wicked problems neither spawned nor resolved in isolation.

(9) The *cause of a wicked problem can be explained in numerous ways*. The choice of explanation determines the nature of the problem's solution. That is, the wicked problem of redesigning the MBA program *involves many stakeholders* who may have different ideas about defining the problem and tracing its causes. Thus, there is wide discrepancy in defining a wicked problem. Moreover, the nature of the problem and its solution should determine the choice of explanation.

(10) Executives confronted with a wicked problem *have no right to be wrong*; they are liable to the consequences of the actions they take to resolve the wicked problems. While scientists may play around with different hypotheses in proving or disproving a theory, social and city planners resolving social wicked problems for governments have no such theoretical luxury. They are expected to get things right at the first shot, as people and businesses rely on their resolution framework. Any redesigned MBA program, accordingly, must be well-thought through; it must address most critical problems of today as objectively as possible. We cannot afford to go wrong as lives, careers, research efforts of students, faculty, employers, and capitalist markets depend upon them. Any new MBA program must be flexible and redefinable, and be open enough to incorporate newer scopes and domains, newer properties and features, and newer directions and opportunities.

Critical Thinking Exercise 5.4

Apply critical thinking (see footnote 3 in Chapter 1) to the 10 characteristics of wicked problems identified by Rittel and Webber (1973, pp. 161–169). Do these 10 characteristics enable better understanding, explanation, prediction, and resolution of the wicked problems in the MBA program, curriculum, and pedagogy in the business schools of today, and if they do, why? Accordingly, formulate your strategy for taming wicked problems in your business school.

What Should be Avoided in Resolving Wicked Problems

Corresponding to Rittel and Webber's (1973) 10 criteria of characterizing wicked problems, Conklin (2006, pp. 10–11) suggests six ways we should avoid taming wicked problems.

(1) *Do not lock down the problem definition*: A human tendency is to *lock down* a wicked problem. That is, we restrict its domain, definition, solution space, and doable solutions. For instance, in reducing crime and violence in public schools, a locked-down solution will be to install metal detectors in all school entrances, or of increasing juvenile prison spaces. We freeze the domain and requirements of the crime problem as a way of locking it down. Federal bailing out major financial companies (e.g., Chrysler, Bear Stearns, Fannie May and Freddie Mac, or Lehman Brothers) locks down their problem, does not resolve it.

(2) *Do not assert that the problem is solved.* Since it is almost impossible to define a wicked problem, we deny there either is a problem or assert that it is solved without defining it. Autocratic politicians often adopt this process. For instance, such an attitude can deny the existence of wicked problems such as health care, fraud, greed, and recession.

(3) *Do not objectify parameters of a wicked problem to measure the success of its solution.* What is measured, officially and by definition, becomes the problem. For instance, we measure the problem of, and solution to, crime in schools by reducing deaths and injuries in school premises to zero. What if such a solution should increase crime outside the school property? The wicked problem reasserts itself in a different guise, or, the tame solution exacerbates the problem.

(4) *Do not identify current problems with previous related problems.* We cast the current wicked problem as "just like" a previous problem, and lock and resolve it accordingly. For instance, we quickly define the Mideastern countries as the "axis of evil" and resolve the problems of Iraq, Afghanistan, Pakistan, and Iran the same way. In military circles, there is a saying: "We always fight the last war," a tendency to assume the enemy will behave as in the last war. We often mistake the enemy will repeat 9/11 the same way as in 2001!

(5) *Do not give up trying to search for a good solution to the problem.* We deny or postpone resolving the problem, hoping it will resolve or disappear by itself. For example, this is how we treat the wicked problems of health care, social security, inflation, recession, unemployment, underemployment, outsourcing, migration, asylum immigration, racial discrimination, gender discrimination, crime, and poverty.

(6) *Do not declare a limited solution space to a wicked problem.* We tend to conclude that there are just a few solutions to the problem and focus on selecting from among these options. For instance, we combat terrorism by retaliation, change of regime, or by destroying countries. We refuse to negotiate. Framing wicked problems with "either/or" terms is another way of limiting the solution space. For instance, a politician may ask: Should we attack Iraq or let the terrorists take over the world?

Critical Thinking Exercise 5.5

Apply critical thinking (see footnote 3 in Chapter 1) to the six ways to handle wicked problems as suggested by Conklin (2006, pp. 10–11). Do they enable better understanding, explanation, prediction, and resolution of the wicked problems in the MBA program, curriculum, and pedagogy in the business schools of today, and if so, why? Accordingly, formulate your strategy for taming wicked problems in your business school.

Methodological Criteria for Dealing With Wicked Problems

Following the work of Rittel and Webber (1973) and Ackoff (1974), Jonathan Rosenhead (1996) of the London School of Economics suggested the following methodological criteria for dealing with wicked problems:

- Accommodate multiple alternative perspectives rather than prescribing single solutions.
- Function through group interaction and iteration rather than back-office calculations.
- Generate ownership of the problem formulation through transparency.
- Facilitate a graphic (visual, sound, color, imaging) representation of the problem for a systematic and group exploration of the solution space.
- Focus on relationships between discrete alternatives rather than continuous variables.
- Concentrate on possibility rather than probability.

Critical Thinking Exercise 5.6

Apply critical thinking (see footnote 3 in Chapter 1) to the methodological criteria for dealing with wicked problems, as suggested by Rosenhead (1996). Do these criteria enable better understanding, explanation, prediction, and resolution of the wicked problems in the MBA program, curriculum, and pedagogy in the business schools of today, and if yes, why? Accordingly, formulate your strategy for taming wicked problems in your business school.

General Morphological Analysis

Incorporating Rittel and Webber's (1973) 10 criteria for characterizing wicked problems, Ritchey (2002, 2005, 2006) describes a group-facilitated, computer-aided general morphological analysis (GMA) to handle wicked problems. Rittel and Webber (1973) suggested that in order to describe a wicked problem in sufficient detail, one has to develop an exhaustive inventory for all the conceivable solutions ahead of time. As a process, GMA goes through a number of iterative steps or phases representing cycles of analysis and synthesis in order to develop a fairly exhaustive inventory for all the conceivable solutions to a given wicked problem. GMA starts by identifying and defining the most important dimensions of the wicked problem. Each of these dimensions is then given a range of relevant (discrete) values or conditions. Together, these make up the variables or parameters of the problem complex. A morphological field is constructed by setting the parameters against each other in parallel columns, representing an n-dimensional configuration space. A particular constructed "field configuration" is designated by selecting a single value from each of the variables. This marks out a particular state or (formal) solution within the problem complex (Ritchey, 2005, p. 4).

The morphological field represents the total "problem space" that can contain thousands of possible solutions. A feasible "solution space" is derived by a process of internal cross-consistency assessment (CCA). All of the parameter values in the morphological field are compared with one another, pair-wise, in the manner of cross-impact matrix. Next, GMA analyses each pair of conditions and judges whether the pair can coexist, i.e., represent a consistent relationship. Mutual consistency is not assessed based on causality or probability but only by possibility. Using this technique, a typical morphological field can be reduced significantly, depending upon the nature of the problem. (GMA also enables "garbage detection" since poorly defined parameters and incomplete ranges of conditions surface quickly when CCA is applied.) The results of GMA would depend upon the quality of inputs provided in terms of the specificity of the total problem space and the total solution space, definitions of the parameters and the ranges of conditions, as well as CCA.

Rittel and Webber's (1973) seventh criterion states: "Part of the art of dealing with wicked problems is the art of not knowing too early which type of solution to apply." GMA calls this phenomenon "remaining in the mess," i.e., keeping one's options open long enough to explore as many relationships in the problem space as possible, before starting to formulate solutions. As many stakeholders as possible should be engaged in the work, in order to create a common terminology, common problem concept, and common modeling framework. Principal stakeholders should be involved in (a) structuring much of the problem space, (b) synthesizing solution spaces, (c) exploring multiple solutions on the basis of different drivers and interests, and (d) analyzing stakeholder structures. The different stakeholders do not have to agree on a single, common solution but must be encouraged to understand each other's positions and contexts.

Critical Thinking Exercise 5.7

Apply critical thinking (see footnote 3 in Chapter 1) to computer-aided GMA to handle wicked problems suggested by Ritchey (2002, 2005, 2006). How does GMA enable better understanding, explanation, prediction, and resolution of the wicked problems in the MBA program, curriculum, and pedagogy in the business schools of today, and why? Accordingly, formulate your strategy for taming wicked problems in your business school.

Resolving Wicked Problems: Tried and Proven Ways

Camillus (2008) suggests some tried and proven ways to resolve wicked problems:

- *Involve key stakeholders* (e.g., customers, employees, creditors, suppliers, and shareholders) in managing the wicked problem. Brainstorm and document their ideas, approaches, and hidden assumptions. Go beyond obtaining facts and figures to understand their biases and opinions. Establish ongoing inter-active communication (intranet, blogs, e-bulletins) between CEOs and key stakeholders, and among regular stakeholders. Build up collective intelligence to counteract individual cognitive biases and prejudices. The tacit knowledge of your key stakeholders may help you better tame the wicked problem.
- *Define corporate identity* and stay true to your corporate purpose and goals. Define your *values* – what is fundamentally important to your company? Assess your *competencies* – what does your company do better than your competitors do? Describe your *aspirations* – how does the company envision and measure success?
- *Focus on action.* In a world of Newtonian order, it is easy to identify causes and effects and strategize accordingly. In a world of complex and chaotic wicked problems, it is tough to gauge and link causes and effects and hence formulate one strategy. Do scenario analysis: set up 2 × 2 blocks based on meaningful vectors as a frame to provide four possible scenarios: analyze all four and see which best fits your values, goals, competencies, and aspirations. Conduct several scenario analyses. Frame your strategy to tame the wicked problem based on the convergence of your scenario analyses and resulting strategies.
- *Adopt a "feed-forward" orientation.* Under ordinary problems, an effective way of learning and refining strategies is via feedback. Feedback reflects learning from the past. Feedback is ineffective with wicked problems that do not have a clear past. The latter require executives to feed forward with insights from unfamiliar time and place, with unanticipated, uncertain, and unclear futures. With wicked problems, CEOs must envision futures and describe the set of external and internal circumstances that they would like to see in the next 10, 20, or 50 years.

Critical Thinking Exercise 5.8

Apply critical thinking (see footnote 3 in Chapter 1) to the tried and proven ways to resolve wicked problems suggested by Camillus (2008). How do they enable better understanding, explanation, prediction, and resolution of the wicked problems in the MBA program, curriculum, and pedagogy in the business schools of today, and why? Accordingly, formulate your strategy for taming wicked problems in your business school.

Wicked problems require imagination and experimentation, innovation and entrepreneurship, launching pilot programs, testing prototypes, and seeking "good enough" solutions with the least unintended consequences. Their main feature is that the problem is not understood until a solution is achieved. Often, social complexity (e.g., multiple stakeholders, their diversity and individuality, their organizational mission and goals) clouds the solution and makes the problem definition/solution method a social process with fragmented polarizations. Hence, much cooperation and collaboration, coherence and compassion is needed in defining wicked problems and identifying possible solutions.

Team effort is critical in addressing wicked problems. A good and effective team brings two benefits together: (a) diversity of backgrounds, experiences, perspectives, and knowledge will help the team's capacity to assimilate and process multiple information inputs, convert them into knowledge, and accordingly strategize resolutions; (b) the capacity of teams, over time, to be self-directed and capable of managing significant cross-disciplinary business concerns.

The traditional hierarchical and pyramidal model that puts strategy on the top, tactics in the middle, and implementation at the bottom must be abandoned. This top-down model slows information sharing and processing and knowledge generation. Instead, all three – strategy, tactics, and implementation – can be placed within the same rung as virtually indivisible activities that every team must manage. Top management may provide the overall vision, but everybody else works from the trenches. They should ensure that everybody brings commitment, empowerment, and innovation. The team culture should focus on a structure that rewards risk-taking, expects personal responsibility, and promotes high levels of trust and collaboration. Besides promoting a spirit of enquiry and creating shared displays for design, the team should create the "surround" – the whole context of learning and knowledge generation and exchange between team members (Pacanowsky, 1995).

A Synthesis of Problems

We assume that all problems, deterministic, probabilistic, uncertain, and emergent, have causes. Some of these causes are known, and hence, the problems that arise from these causes are basically known and tamable. Some of these causes are not known, and hence, the problems that arise from these unknown causes are not easily known and tamable. The complexity of unknown causes and stochastic or uncertain outcome sequences in any problem arises from several sources: demanding customers, volatile consumer behavior, demographic shifts, strong domestic competition, increasing global competition, supplier constraints, past creditor covenants, retailer behavior, employee disenchantment, Environmental Protection Agency (EPA) compliance, consumer advocacy, tough government regulation, SEC vigilance, social and political policies, and the like.

All causes have outcomes or effects. Some of these effects are known and some are not known. All outcomes or effects occur in sequences that are known or unknown. Known outcome sequences are either fixed or deterministic or not fixed with known probabilities, and hence stochastic. Unknown outcome sequences are either uncertain but estimable, or uncertain and not estimable. Hence, given that (a) causes of problems are known or unknown, (b) outcomes or effects of problems are known or unknown, and (c) under each outcome situation, the outcome sequences could be known or unknown, there is a $2 \times 2 \times 2 = 8$ cell situation that provides a more complete and realistic taxonomy of problematic situations in terms of puzzles, problems, messes and social messes, and complex puzzles, complex problems, complex messes, and complex social messes (or wicked problems). Table 5.3 presents this taxonomy with several examples under each of the eight cells. Table 5.3 assumes that "complexity" primarily occurs when the causes of problems are not known, that is, when the unknown causes of problems make them severely less tamable.

We can map Perrow's (1974) typology of Type I, Type II, Type III, and Type IV problems into Table 5.3 as indicated. Type I problems in Cell 1 have known causes; Type I problems in Cell 2 have unknown causes. Cell 3 best represents Type II problems when causes of problems are known but the outcomes sequences are stochastic. Cell 4 best describes Type III problems, the assumption being the researcher can trace the uncertain nature of outcome sequences to their unknown causes. Table 5.3 also differentiates four types of Type IV problems. All Type IV problems are "wicked" (Rittel & Webber, 1973), but the degree of wickedness differs depending upon whether the cause of the problems is known (Cells 5 and 7) or not known (Cells 6 and 8), and whether the unknown outcome sequences are estimable (Cells 5 and 6) or not estimable (Cells 7 and 8). Problems in all eight cells imply risk from small to enormous proportions. Risk could be economic, political, financial, ecological, human, social, and cultural. The source, nature, size, and outcomes of risk in each cell are different.

For instance, the risk is greater when the causes of problems are unknown (i.e., Cells 2, 4, 6, and 8) than when the causes are known (Cells 1, 3, 5, and 7). Similarly, problem complexity increases as we move from deterministic to stochastic to uncertain to divergent outcomes when the causes of the problem are

Table 5.3. Taxonomy of Problems by Causes and Effects.

Causes of the Problem	Outcomes (Effects) of the Problem			
	Known		Unknown	
	Outcome sequences known and fixed, and hence *deterministic*	Outcome sequences known, not fixed, but with known probabilities; hence *Stochastic*	Outcome sequences unknown but estimable; hence, the domain of *uncertainty*	Outcome sequences unknown and not estimable; hence, the domain of *divergence/emergence*
Known (Hence, tamable) **Examples**	Cell 1: Puzzles (Type I)+ Simple treatable diseases Simple cash flow problems Simple PR problems Simple HRD problems Consumer satisfaction Inventory management Advertising management Promotions management Accounting management Financial management	Cell 3: Problems (Type II)+ Plant shutdowns Massive layoffs Offshore outsourcing Employee motivation Union management Costing management Pricing management Cost containment Revenue management Growth management	Cell 5: Messes (Type IV)+ Droughts Famine/Blight Deforestation Tsunami Flooding Hurricanes Earthquakes Landslides and erosion Energy crisis Alternative fuels Drinking water crisis	Cell 7: Social Messes (Type IV)+ Religious bigotry Fundamentalism Ethnic cleansing Corporate greed Corporate fraud Corporate bankruptcy Home mortgage crisis Monetary crisis Financial market crisis Wall Street meltdown
Unknown (Hence, not easily tamable) Examples	Cell 2: Complex* Puzzles (Type I)+	Cell 4: Complex* Problems (Type III)+	Cell 6: Complex* Messes (Type IV)+	Cell 8: Complex* Social Messes (Type IV)+

Table 5.3. *(Continued)*

Causes of the Problem	Outcomes (Effects) of the Problem			
	Known		Unknown	
	Seasonal flu and colds	High school dropouts	Global carbon emissions	Global terrorism
	Seasonal allergies	High school violence	Global climate change	Global inequality
	Consumer dissatisfaction	Consumer obesity	Polar Arctic drift	Global poverty
	Consumer brand switching	Consumer bankruptcy	Nuclear disasters	Global injustices
	Consumer lifestyle changes	Consumer fraud	Chronic/ incurable disease	Global turbulence
	Employee malaise	Computer hacking	Trade embargoes	Global nuclear threats
	Supplier/ creditor anxiety	Cyber fraud	Global hunger and disease	Global wars
	Market rejection	Merchant fraud	Global price collusions	Global ecological damage
	Recession	Volatile interest rates	Global trade inequities	Global immigration
	Stagflation	Currency fluctuations	Global financial risk	Global revolution
	Economic depression			

Source: Compiled by the authors.

Notes: * We assume complexity arises primarily from unknown causes of the problem.[+] Type I, II, III, and IV problems refer to the categories suggested by Perrow (1984); the term "Mess" is attributed to Ackoff (1974) and "Social Messes" to Horn (2001).

known (that is, from Cell 1 to Cell 3 to Cell 5 to Cell 7) and not known (that is, from Cell 2 to Cell 4 to Cell 6 to Cell 8). In complex puzzles, complex problems, complex messes, and complex social messes, the generic risk primarily arises from unknown causes, but the risk gets differentiated by the specific nature (deterministic, stochastic, uncertainty, and divergence/emergence) of the outcomes. Thus, handling the problem situation in each cell in Table 5.3 implies unique situational dynamics and a future scenario that require a different strategy with a unique set of skills and tools.

Critical Thinking Exercise 5.9

Apply critical thinking (see footnote 3 in Chapter 1) to Table 5.3, which synthesizes what we know about wicked and other related problems. How does Table 5.3 enable you to reclassify problems you detect and identify in the current MBA program? How does your new classification enable better understanding, explanation, prediction, and resolution of the wicked problems in the MBA program, curriculum, and pedagogy in the business schools of today, and why? Accordingly, formulate your strategy for taming wicked problems in your business school.

An Alternative Design of the MBA Program to Address the World's Wicked Problems

A redesigned MBA program should address all four types of problems that are currently defining the business world. The present MBA curriculum, especially in its precore and core courses, deals mostly with simple problems with its functional "silo" disciplines of operations management, production, operations research, accounting, finance, marketing, and human resources (HR). Occasionally, some of the "electives" (e.g., advanced statistics, financial modeling, marketing research, and operations research) may invite MBA students to handle "complex" or Type II problems.

Virtually, no MBA program handles Types III and IV or unstructured and wicked problems. Given its wonted propensity for "certain" knowledge that is "proven" by statistical reliability, validity, and replicability via "scientific" research methodologies and outcomes, the real business world of market turbulence, social unrest, and unpredictable political world of unstructured, chaotic, and wicked problems escapes its narrow domain. This may be one of the reasons why the current MBA program is becoming increasingly irrelevant and incompetent to address the complex business world of wicked problems today, most of which are caused by ruthless business practices. (The domain and field of "certain" knowledge has shrunk since the manufacturing world of the last two centuries when the old MBA program was crafted.)

Table 5.4 suggests a new *design structure* for the MBA program. For convenience, we structure the MBA program along Western MBA systems of four full semesters of four–five months each, and six-semester, part-time, or weekend MBA programs can be streamlined accordingly. Each semester is characterized by five basic thematic domains of knowledge/skills/values comprising areas such as motivation management, creativity and innovation management, productivity management, revenue management, and sustainability management. These are not necessarily mutually exclusive and collectively exhaustive areas of knowledge/skills/values in business management but are domains comprehensive enough for the MBA program to begin with.

Table 5.4. A Redesigned MBA Curriculum: Problem-Centered Approach.

Semester	Problem Domain Focus	Type of Data, Knowledge/Skills/ Values Needed	Applied Entrepreneurial Content	Critical Thinking: Types and Domain	Ethical/Moral Reasoning and Imperatives
One	*Simple problems (Perrow's Type I) as opportunities and risk-free deterministic management in local and domestic corporations* [Problems of Cells 1 and 3, Table 5.3]	*Descriptive knowledge as data* mining of facts, figures, subjects, objects, properties, events, statistics, information, and inferences. Questions deal with *what, how, how often, when, where, and through whom of data.*	*Descriptive knowledge of major* entrepreneurial processes, such as creativity and innovation management, motivation management, customer management, revenue management, productivity management, and sustainability management.	*Descriptive critical thinking skills via:* identifying hidden assumptions, presumptions, suppositions presuppositions biases, prejudices and stereotypes underlying our thinking, reasoning, rationalizing, believing, choices, and actions.	*Descriptive ethical reasoning and imperatives based on* ethical theories of: teleological justice, deontological justice, distributive justice, corrective justice, nonmalfeasance justice, preventive justice, protective justice, entitlement justice (Rawls, 1971), and beneficent justice.
Two	*Complex problems (Perrow's Type II) problems as opportunities and*	*Analytical knowledge* as explaining, predicting, thinking, reasoning, risk	*Analytical knowledge of major* entrepreneurial processes such as:	*Analytical critical thinking skills via:* proactive thinking, interactive thinking,	*Analytical ethical reasoning and* imperatives via ethical theories of:

Table 5.4. (*Continued*)

Semester	Problem Domain Focus	Type of Data, Knowledge/Skills/ Values Needed	Applied Entrepreneurial Content	Critical Thinking: Types and Domain	Ethical/Moral Reasoning and Imperatives
	stochastic risk management in international and multinational environments [Problems of Cells 2 and 4, Table 5.3]	analysis, and synthesis. Questions deal *with why, why not, hence what* of data, concepts, theories, models, strategies and cases.	creativity management, innovation management, motivation management, customer management, revenue management, productivity management, and sustainability management.	inventive thinking, interpretive thinking, responsive thinking, inductive thinking, deductive thinking, and mental models.	moral rights/duties, moral virtue, trust moral claims and entitlements, moral liabilities and undeserved disadvantages. Artificial intelligence.
Three	*Unstructured problems (Perrow's Type III problems) as opportunities and uncertainty management in continental and global*	*Experiential knowledge as* experimentation imagination, intuition, creativity, innovation, incubation,	*Experiential knowledge and optimal realization of:* self-mastery, mental models, team building,	*Experiential critical thinking skills of:* questioning one's thinking, believing values, principles, convictions, biases, stereotypes,	*Experiential ethical reasoning and ethical, imperatives executive virtue/trust, faith/beliefs* executive wellness. Executive happiness,

environments [Problems of Cells 5 and 7, Table 5.3]	invention, discovery, entrepreneurship, uncertainty management.	shared vision, systems thinking, leadership skills, creativity, intuition, and talent as intangible assets management (see Senge, 2006).	assumptions, presumptions, social constructions and theories, reasoning, and rationalizing.	executive transparency, executive self-mastery, executive mindfulness, and executive shared vision.
Four *Wicked problems (Perrow's Type IV problems) as opportunities and chaos/ambiguity management in borderless global/ transnational environments* [Problems of Cells 6 and 8, Table 5.3]	*Sapiential knowledge* as wisdom and prudence, trust and trusting, discerning, with honesty and integrity, ethics and morals, for handling chaos/ambiguity management.	*Sapiential knowledge* of major entrepreneurial processes such as: creativity and innovation management, motivation management, customer management, revenue management, productivity management, and sustainability management.	*Sapiential critical thinking skills:* dialogic thinking, morality thinking, global sustainability thinking, generative thinking, divergent thinking, convergent thinking, emergent thinking, and consensual thinking.	*Sapiential ethical reasoning* and imperatives of ethical theories of: executive leadership, ethical leadership, moral leadership, executive mindfulness, servant leadership, ecological leadership in global sustainability.

Source: Compiled by the authors.

This built-in flexibility, moreover, makes the MBA program dynamic, expandable, resilient, and continually relevant. In general, all five sub-domains (that is motivation management, creativity and innovation management, productivity management, revenue management, and sustainability management) critically connect and enhance each other, thus enabling integrated business management (IBM), a much desirable quality for the MBA curriculum and program today. Subject materials suggested by Table 5.4 increase in comprehension and complexity from Semester 1 to Semester 4 reflecting the increasing nature and challenge of real business world problems chosen for course content – that is, they begin with simple (or Perrow's Type I) problems in Semester 1 to complex (Type II) problems in Semester 2, to unstructured (Type III) problems in Semester 3 to "Wicked" (Type IV) problems in Semester 4.

Concepts, constructs, theories, and paradigms of current business knowledge, such as new product development (NPD), end-to-end product value-chains, NPD development cycles such as market scanning, ideation, incubation, concept development, design testing, prototype testing, ad testing, test marketing, national product launching, entrepreneurship, creativity, discovery, invention, innovation, branding, and revenue harvesting, supply chain logistics, purchasing, upstream, midstream and downstream value chains, and so on, may be creatively imported from existing MBA programs and incorporated into the newly designed MBA program content and structure. Thus, one does not have to reinvent the wheel at every stage of the newly designed program.

The newly designed MBA program includes the following executive skills and strategic drills: (a) problem domain focus; (b) type of knowledge/skills/values generation; (c) applied entrepreneurial content; (d) critical thinking; and (e) ethical/moral reasoning, theories, and imperatives. Table 5.4 outlines the redesigned MBA curriculum for problem-entered talent and skills development. Briefly, the newly designed (Table 5.4) curriculum structure is as follows.

Semester 1
Descriptive knowledge regarding "simple" problems (Perrow's Type I deterministic problems) as business opportunities in local and national markets (see Table 5.4, row 2, columns 2–3); the problems will focus on Level 1 of five major sub-domains (not disciplines) that are critical to modern entrepreneurial business management, namely (a) creativity and innovation management, (b) motivation management, (c) customer management, (d) revenue management, and (e) sustainability management (see Table 5.4, row 2, columns 2–6 for details). Other themes could be added as per value, need, and urgency, such as productivity management, quality management, risk management, high-quality life, and global equality management, developmental technology or infrastructure management, energy management, carbon neutrality management, global human solidarity and peace management, gender-equity management, healthcare management, global supply chain management, social progress management, and so on. Each level of problem complexity will be dealt with a specific level of critical thinking and ethical imperatives (see Table 5.4, row 2, columns 5–6 for details).

Semester 2

Analytical knowledge as explanation, imagination, intuition, venture, and risk management regarding "complex" problems as business opportunities (Perrow's Type II stochastic systems) in international and multinational markets (see Table 5.4, row 3, columns 2–3); the problems will focus on Level 2 of the same five major sub-domains critical to modern entrepreneurial business management as in Semester 1 (see Table 5.4, row 3, columns 2–6 for details). This level of problem complexity will be dealt with a specifically higher level of skills (concepts, theories, strategies, paradigms) of critical thinking and ethical reasoning (see Table 5.4, row 3, columns 5–6 for details).

Semester 3

Experiential knowledge accumulated through past experience, experimentation, creation, invention, discovery, and entrepreneurship regarding "unstructured" problems as business opportunities (Perrow's Type III uncertain systems) in global and futuristic markets (see Table 5.4, row 4, columns 2–3); the problems will focus on Level 3 of the same five major sub-domains critical to modern entrepreneurial business management as in Semester 1 (see Table 5.4, row 4, columns 2–6 for details). This level of problem complexity will be dealt with a specific but still higher level of experiential thinking, trial and error thinking, critical thinking, and ethical imperatives (see Table 5.4, row 4, columns 5 and 6 for details).

Semester 4

Sapiential knowledge as wisdom, values, trust and trusting relationships, virtues and virtue habits, especially executive integrity and honesty, ethics and morals that is desperately needed to manage "wicked" problems as business opportunities (Perrow's Type IV unknown emergent systems) in transnational and borderless markets (see Table 5.4, row 5, columns 2–3); the problems will focus on Level 4 of the usual five sub-domains of modern entrepreneurial management as in Semester 1 (see Table 5.4, row 5, columns 2–4 for details).[1] Each level of problem complexity will be dealt with perhaps the highest and most demanding level of critical thinking and ethical imperatives (see Table 5.4, row 5, columns 5–6 for details).

Semester 4 will probe into the most challenging zone of "wicked" or Perrow's Type IV problems that are borderless (Ohmae, 1990) or "transnational" in scope and scale. With each semester, accordingly, the level of difficulty and challenge increases with the content of knowledge (see Table 5.4, column 2), entrepreneurial orientation (see Table 5.4, column 4), critical thinking (see Table 5.4, column 5), and ethical reasoning (see Table 5.4, column 6).

---

[1]The term "sapiential" is derived from Latin "sapientia" which translates to wisdom and wisdom-related virtues such as prudence, frugality, moral courage, moral fortitude, simplicity, abstinence, and commitment. Sapiential wisdom is both cognitive skill (e.g., distinguishing between good and evil, right and wrong, truth and falsehood, fair and unfair) and behavioral virtue (e.g., pursuing good and avoiding evil, pursuing truth and avoiding falsehood, pursuing justice and eradicating injustice).

Critical Thinking Exercise 5.10

Apply critical thinking (see footnote 3 in Chapter 1) to Table 5.4, which portrays an alternative design of the MBA program to addresses social or economic wicked problems of the world of today. How do you understand this new design? What are its assumptions, presumptions, suppositions, pre-suppositions, biases, and stereotypes, if any? How does Table 5.4 challenge you against your existing MBA program and curriculum and its pre-determining assumptions and biases? How does Table 5.4 enable better understanding, explanation, prediction, and resolution of the wicked problems, and why?

Table 5.5 sketches the redesigned MBA curriculum in terms of its content, challenges, and pedagogy with an IBM modular approach for generating global entrepreneurial knowledge, skills, and values; the latter are interactive and international in scope, scale, and domain. While Table 5.4 is focused on problem detection, research, formulation, and resolution skills, Table 5.5 focuses on problem selection, classification, integration management, especially in relation to learning and understanding of global wicked problems of distribution, social justice, and global social progress and sustainability.

Additionally, as is clear from Tables 5.4 and 5.5, all five sub-domains are integral to, and hence, integrate current compartmentalized business management disciplines such as accounting, finance, production, HR, marketing, operational research, and the like. That is, all the current disciplines of business management require varied levels of creativity and innovation management, motivation and customer management, and revenue and sustainability management. Hence, these five sub-domains provide a rich canvas for IBM education. Above all, we need to *professionalize* the current MBA program and curriculum as suggested by Khurana (2007), Podolny (2009), and others.

In general, Tables 5.4 and 5.5 describe the structure of delivering the MBA program focused on desired outcomes of knowledge/skills/values for building student learning and entrepreneurship, complemented by critical thinking and ethical reasoning skills.

Redesigned thus, the newness of the MBA program can – in content, challenge, structure, and delivery – better assure student–teacher learning. The content and structure of the new MBA program does not nullify the usefulness of current and past business knowledge, skills, and value; they need to be realigned and redefined to merge with the new MBA program. Thus, most of the current materials in business management textbooks and journal articles can be still relevant and useful, when researched, refocused, reorganized, repackaged, and redelivered differently as suggested. This serves as a great opportunity for creative originality among students, researchers, and teachers alike.

Table 5.5. A Redesigned Master in Business Administration (MBA) Curriculum: Integrated Business Management (IBM) Problem-Centered Approach.

Semester/Domain Thematic Focus	Creativity and Innovation Management	Self and Employee Motivation Management	Customer as Stakeholder Management	Revenue Management Social Growth Management	Sustainability and Equality Management
One: *Simple problems as opportunities and risk-free deterministic management in local and domestic corporations* [Problems of Cells 1 and 3, Table 5.3]	Optimal understanding of: creativity in art, drama, literature, and nature, creative skills, creative communications, quantitative skills, decision-making, team creativity, incubator research, patent, and IPR management.	Optimal realization of: self-mastery, mental models, team building, shared vision, systems thinking, leadership skills, talent as intangible assets management (see senge, 2006).	Optimal delivery of: customer motivation, worker promotions, communication, community social media advertising, community parks and malls services, services marketing, marketing research, social marketing, and socialized marketing	Optimal management of: financing strategies, purchasing inventory, cash flow payables/ receivables, product costing, product pricing, price-product bundling, cost-containment, and revenue generation.	Optimal compliance of: just business law, EPA law, conservation, reducing extraction, carbon neutrality, alternative energy, organic waste, greening, nature development.
Two: *Complex problems as opportunities and*	Optimal design for global market scanning for new	Optimal worker motivation management, labor	International management of: customer	Optimal management of: revenue	Optimal management of: land, air and water,

Table 5.5. (Continued)

Semester/Domain Thematic Focus	Creativity and Innovation Management	Self and Employee Motivation Management	Customer as Stakeholder Management	Revenue Management Social Growth Management	Sustainability and Equality Management
stochastic risk management in international and multinational environments [Problems of Cells 2 and 4, Table 5.3]	product ideation, new product design, innovation, invention and discovery, new process and production/ distribution technologies, productivity scale and scope, sustainable six-sigma quality.	welfare, worker safety, worker IPR management, worker asset ownership rights, negotiations, HR diversity, just performance appraisal, worker recognition, executive compensation.	relationships, customer financing global production, distribution and consumption cycles seasons and chains pricing/promotion, internet marketing customer satisfaction customer delight, customer experience,	generation, shareholder wealth, portfolio risk, financial models, insurance/security, global supplier chains, business turnaround, lean/clean management, transportation/ logistics e-business, global resources	eco-responsibility recycling/reuse, global energy, global nonrenewable resources, reducing extraction, carbon neutrality internet privacy cyber ethics, planetary landscape ethics.
Three: *Unstructured problems as opportunities and*	Optimal development of: creative innovation skills,	Optimal management skills for: global supply management,	Optimal management skills for: total customer experience	Optimal management skills for: global trade venture financing,	Optimal management skills for: global food management,

uncertainty management in continental and global environments [Problems of Cells 5 and 7, Table 5.3]	global conservation/ regeneration processes, global energy supply services, global life-quality management, global new markets, global blue oceans, global entrepreneurship and risk-management, global lateral thinking, global creativity management, global technology, global incubator management.	global banking, global credit, global PR, global motivation to serve one's nation, global community global NGO networks, global philanthropy, global harmony and solidarity.	management, global customer loyalty management, global brand community management, global customer involvement, global justice, customer redressal, customer development, global healthcare.	global debt and equity taming, restructuring derivatives and equity/hedge funds, global merger and acquisitions management, global due diligence management, global divestitures management, globalization management.	global clean drinking water management, global home and privacy management, global hunger and disease management, global functional literacy management, global opportunity creation/ distribution management, global income opportunity equality management.
Four: *Wicked problems as opportunities and ambiguity*	Global Creativity and Innovation Skills for: global business venture,	Optimal skills for: global relations, global servant leadership,	Optimization of: consumer value, community welfare, local	Detection/ prevention skills of: cash flow crisis, Corporate fraud,	Global elimination, reduction, and regeneration skills

Table 5.5. (*Continued*)

Semester/Domain Thematic Focus	Creativity and Innovation Management	Self and Employee Motivation Management	Customer as Stakeholder Management	Revenue Management Social Growth Management	Sustainability and Equality Management
management in borderless transnational environments [Problems of Cells 6 and 8, Table 5.3]	global joint venture, global strategic alliances, global health management, global university for global social peace and harmony management.	global citizenship, global spirituality, global happiness, global justice, global leadership for organizational change management	community, local health and fitness, international community, growth and prosperity, global unity and solidarity development.	Corporate bribery, Corporate bankruptcy, Corporate money laundering, Corporate shirking, Corporate restructuring, global crises.	of depleted earth and space/ combatting: climate change global warming, Arctic meltdown, global poverty global crime global terrorism, global fraud, global cyber fraud, sustainability of nature for her own sake.

Source: Compiled by the authors.

The starting point for each semester is not a prescribed textbook or a set of journal articles but a set of real business problems in the contemporary marketplace that are either simple, complex, unstructured, or wicked. Hence, the "official MBA curriculum" continuously reflects the ever-changing and demanding marketplace rather than any abstract theory domain of business science or discipline. The curriculum thus assures that what is learnt is relevant and is empowering students to face the business world of tomorrow. Tables 5.4 and 5.5 render the MBA program market-focused, people-relevant, and addressing the real problems of the world, thus responding to most of the criticisms of the current MBA curriculum reviewed in Chapter 4.

The mode of MBA curriculum delivery is very critical and should ensure student learning. The traditional methods and pedagogies based on textbooks, teaching, lecturing, and testing student memory of taught material by closed book in-class exams or quizzes are hardly analytic, experiential, sapiential, and postgraduate in character; much less do they assure creativity-rich graduate or postgraduate learning. As discussed earlier, learning is best assured when students are empowered to design courses and teach themselves (Ackoff & Greenberg, 2008).

The teacher or team-teachers with students registered for a given course can preselect contemporary themes and corresponding problems for that course. Next, they can together search for relevant monographs, texts, top journal articles, conference proceedings, research monographs, working papers, cases, films, video clips, websites, webinars, blogs, and social media to handle the level, scope, and nature of problem complexity dealt in that semester as it unravels during the semester. This curriculum delivery process invites continuous student–teacher interaction and involvement. The teacher learns as much as the students, if not more. With one's vast knowledge, research, and experience, each teacher can enhance, empower, and facilitate the student-learning process. Both teachers and students should periodically design instruments for tracking, metering, monitoring, and measuring their collective learning outcomes of new entrepreneurial knowledge, skills, drills, and values via discovery, design, creativity, innovativeness, entrepreneurship, and venture. The students can be graded by peer evaluation complemented by the teacher's assessment of an individual student's learning via viva voces and student presentations (see Edmondson, 2008; Garvin et al., 2008; Mascarenhas, 2009b).

Unique Features of the Redesigned MBA Program

Designed thus, the new MBA program has several desired novel features that combat existing limitations. Bennis and O'Toole (2005) warn us that we do not have to regress and convert business schools into glorified trade schools they originally were, that business schools should regain their relevance by rediscovering the best art and practice of business management while pursuing the dual roles of educating practitioners and creating new business knowledge through research. We now propose a *problem-centered curriculum with increasing problem complexity* from Semesters 1–4, as we enable students to tackle problems of increasing complexity and relevance.

- Each semester handles a distinctly higher level of problem complexity represented by real business problems from simple, complex, unstructured to wicked problems (e.g., mapped onto Perrow's Type I to Type IV problems) of the world, contemporaneous to each semester; this process ensures current market-based learning.
- Being problem-centered and not discipline-centered, the newly designed MBA program naturally predisposes to integrated business management approach that is receiving current attention among deans of business schools, as also from the Association to Advance Collegiate Schools of Business (AACSB). Every real business problem has all business aspects woven into it such as marketing, business law, accounting, finance, HR, public relations (PR), organizational behavior, and so on, thus predisposing itself to IBM, as opposed to the current highly compartmentalized and placement-determined MBA curricula. Problems segmented by business disciplines yield only truncated and myopic solutions.
- Each level of problem complexity is addressed by a specific level of critical thinking built into it (see Table 5.4, rows 2–5, column 5); this process ensures business management learning through critical thinking. Explaining each of these critical thinking processes listed in the column is beyond the scope of this chapter. For instance, most of these skills are discussed in Ackoff (1974), Ackoff and Emery (1972), Ackoff and Greenberg (2008), Mascarenhas (2009a, 2009b), Neumeier (2009), Senge (1990, 2006), and Senge et al. (1994, 1999, 2000).
- Each level of problem complexity is studied with a specific level of ethical and moral reasoning skill and categorical imperatives (see Table 5.4, rows 2–5, column 6); this process ensures business management learning through ethical and moral reasoning modules. For instance, most of these skills are discussed in Beauchamp and Childers (1989), Boatright (2003), Frankena (1973, 1980), Mascarenhas (1995, 2008, 2018, 2019), Mascarenhas et al. (2008), Rawls (1958, 1971, 1993a, 1993b), and Sen (1992, 1997). Business schools are actively pursuing ethical training in their MBA programs today (see Bisoux, 2009; BizEd, 2009).
- Each level of problem complexity is studied with an IBM approach that is anchored on five current and critical sub-domains of modern entrepreneurial management (namely, motivation management, creativity and innovation management, customer management, revenue management, and sustainability management) that impact and integrate all major value-chain components of the NPD cycle. A detailed rationale for the choice of these five sub-domains of entrepreneurial knowledge/skills/values development is again beyond the scope of this chapter, and for further details on this, see Mascarenhas (2010).
- Given features (1) to (5), MBA students should be better fortified to develop IBM skills that will empower them to address current and future business

problems, with increasing complexity and difficulty, in a systemic and holistic framework (see Senge, 1990, 2006; Senge et al., 1994, 1999, 2000).

- Given (1) to (6), MBA content, domain, and sub-domains should train MBA students into competent "professionals" rather than just management disciplinary technicians. This is because the problem orientation approach intrinsic to the newly designed MBA program leads to problem identification, specification, formulation, alternatives determination, and deciding on the best alternative, a process that transforms and upgrades the MBA to the level of other professions (e.g., medicine, law, engineering, architecture) (Mascarenhas, 2009a, 2009b, 2010).
- The redesigned MBA program with its built-in critical thinking and ethical reasoning skills can better empower students to detect, prevent, and combat corporate fraud that has infected the contemporary corporate world (Khurana, 2007).
- The redesigned MBA program renders the design of "official MBA curriculum" for business schools very flexible, totally dovetailed to contemporary and futuristic market and customer demands. No MBA program, curriculum, and delivery should be frozen beyond a year or two. The new problems that appear in the world should become the new curriculum. Each student, teacher, or teacher–student team can select their own problem set that best reflects the then industry and one's career demands. This process invites self-exploration, experimentation, creativity and innovation management, motivation and customer management, and revenue and sustainability management at all levels of learning. Thus, if properly implemented, the new MBA curriculum bears great potential for individualized, customized, high-standard, localized or globalized organizational learning (see Ackoff & Greenberg, 2008; Senge, 1990, 2006).
- Given (1) to (9), and in an age of rapid change and technological obsolescence, the newly redesigned MBA program can equip students to create resilient organizations that are focused and effective to innovate quickly, boldly, be profitable and socially responsible at the same time (see Hamel & Breen, 2007; Podolny, 2009).
- The old talent-management models failed because they were inaccurate, irrelevant, and costly in a very volatile market environment. What we need is a "fundamentally new approach to talent management that takes into account the uncertainties and ambiguities that businesses face today" (Cappelli, 2008, pp. 74–75). The new redesigned MBA program with its four-semester, four-tiered complexity dealing structure is designed precisely to respond to this challenge.
- One criticism was that the old management model was mechanical and not human, built on the deterministic assembly line model (Ackoff & Greenberg 2008; Neumeier 2009). The newly designed MBA program has nondeterministic real-world business models intrinsic to the program, such as complex problems and risk management (Semester 2), unstructured problems and uncertainty management (Semester 3), and wicked problems and ambiguity management (Semester 4).

- Marti and Scherer (2016) criticized the old MBA program for its overemphasis on scientific vigor that focused on duplicable outcomes without concentrating on market validity and relevance. The four-tiered complexity-driven management structure of the new MBA program reflects market reality and is hence better poised to deal with market validity and relevance.
- Lastly, business schools, as they stand today, are harmful to society, fostering self-interested, unethical, and even illegal behavior by their graduates (Podolny, 2009) that can result in structured levels of market mistrust and business injustice (Mascarenhas, 2009a, 2009b). The four-semester, four-tiered complexity dealing structure of the new MBA program prescribes higher levels of critical thinking and ethical and moral imperatives. This program should, other things being equal, foster law-compliant, ethical, moral, and spiritual executive development (much insisted upon by Covey, 2004; DePree, 1989; Inamori, 1985; Lencioni, 1998; O'Brien, 1989, 2006; Senge, 1990, 2006).

Problem Selection

The type of problems one chooses for one's customized MBA could be based on types of products and services, industry, country, trade region or continents, or on any other category. For instance, a person wanting to obtain a customized healthcare MBA would obviously choose healthcare-related problems of national versus private health care, public law, public subsidy, production, safety, distribution structure, distribution coverage, ethics of distribution, catastrophic care, neonatal care, intensive care, elderly care, insurance coverage, cost, price, profitability, or shareholder wealth. Whatever the specific problem chosen, the problems must increase in complexity from simple to complex to unstructured to wicked from Semester 1 to Semester 4, and each problem level must be studied from the viewpoint of motivation management, creativity and innovation management, and so on. Numerous other domains reflecting wicked problems of tomorrow offer enough challenges for years to come. In fact, global wicked problems of global poverty that violates human dignity, global unemployment that causes global income inequality, global terrorism, global greed and fraud, and imminent global wars, can offer enough serious problems for several decades to come as long as objectively investigate every wicked problem with critical thinking and ethical reasoning skills.

Semester 4 can easily focus on executive spirituality development and knowledge that is built on ethics, morals, values, virtues, and particularly on wisdom and prudence. The term "executive spirituality" is gaining much attention today, as derived from the related works of David Bollier (1997), Steven Covey (2004), Kazuo Inamori (1985), Patrick Lencioni (1998), Max DePree (1989), Bill O'Brien (1989), and Peter Senge (1990, 2006), to name a few. The content, domain, and purpose of being "spiritual" transcends any religious, sectarian, philosophical, or theological beliefs and dogmas, and concentrates on basic human dignity, integrity, and its sacred unbounded potential. According to O'Brien, the morals of the marketplace do not have to be lower than in other activities. He believes there is no fundamental tradeoff between the higher virtues in life and economic success. We believe we can have both. Over the long term, the more we practice the higher virtues of life, the more economic success we will have (O'Brien, 1989).

Concluding Remarks

We have reviewed the theory of wicked problems as stated by representative scholars such as Rittel and Webber (1973), Perrow (1974, 1984, 1994), Conklin (2006), Rosenhead (1996), Ritchey (2002, 2006), and Camillus (2008). Further, given that causes of problems are known or unknown, outcomes or effects of problems are known or unknown, and that under each outcome situation, the outcome sequences could be known or unknown, we have a fairly comprehensive and objective taxonomy in a $2 \times 2 \times 2 = 8$ cell classification of major problems sketched in Table 5.3, which we use as a major content and structure of the new MBA program design, as illustrated in Tables 5.4 and 5.5.

There are compelling reasons for learning to solve the right problems (King, 1993, p. 105). By solving the wrong problem (Type III error), we unwittingly undermine our capacity to solve the right problems. Rittel and Webber (1973) claim that wicked problems do not have a definitive formulation because in order to describe a wicked problem in adequate detail, one has to develop an exhaustive set of all conceivable solutions in advance. This may not be necessarily true. In practice, scientists or city planners consider a limited set of feasible solutions that have a larger likelihood of resolving the social or political problem. Limiting the domain of investigation is an important aspect of problem formulation-resolution methodology, even though reductionistic temporarily.

Strategies for solving simple and tame problems differ qualitatively from strategies appropriate for solving social messes and wicked problems. Messes are puzzles. Rather than solving them, we should properly frame these problems so that we can sort out their complexities and uncertainties and dissolve the barriers to consensus implicit in wicked problems. Our present inabilities of sorting and dissolving problems may be paradigmatic of things to come – more advanced technologies will empower to dissolve or resolve problems that we cannot do now.

Epistemologically and axiologically speaking, the "good" and the "bad," the "true" and the "false" are not necessarily incompatible (Bahm, 1975). A solution can be both true and good at the same time; it can even be false but good at the same time. A solution can be true and good from one perspective and false and bad from another perspective. For instance, stem cell research is good when it is based on adult cells but bad when it is solely based on embryonic cells, especially when human embryos are killed for saving victims of presently incurable diseases.

Traditionally, corporate organizations have supported people's development *instrumentally* – that is, you develop people in order to develop the organization. To view human development as an instrument of organizational development is devaluing humans and human relationships. In the type of organizations we seek to build, says O'Brien (2006), the fullest development of people is on an equal plane with financial success. Practicing the virtues of life and business success is not only compatible but enriches one another. This is, however, a far cry from the traditional marketplace morality.

The newly designed MBA program has a simultaneous focus on motivation management, creativity and innovation management, customer management, revenue management, and sustainability management, and on not using employees, customers, investors, managers, and executives instrumentally to serve principals and shareholders and suppliers of funds. It should be geared to the fullest development of all, the self, employees, and other stakeholders alike. Obviously, incorporating and realizing the newly redesigned MBA program outlined in Tables 5.4 and 5.5 may be a nightmare initially. Most of us who are specialized and comfortable in our compartmentalized disciplines will find it difficult to align with the challenging integrated business management approach. But it is worth our effort for the sake of students, faculty, and for humanity.

References

Abrahamson, E. (1997). The emergence and prevalence of employee management rhetorics: The effects of long waves, labor unions, and turnover, 1875 to 1992. *Academy of Management Journal, 40*(3), 491–533.

Abrahamson, E., Berkowitz, H., & Dumez, H. (2016). A more relevant approach to relevance in management studies: An essay on performativity. *Academy of Management Review, 41*(2), 367–381.

Abrahamson, E., & Eisenman, M. (2008). Employee–management techniques: Transient fads or trending fashions? *Administrative Science Quarterly, 53*(4), 719–744.

Abrahamson, E., & Fairchild, G. (1999). Management fashion: Lifecycles, triggers, and collective learning processes. *Administrative Science Quarterly, 44*(4), 708–740.

Ackerman, F., & Zimbalist, A. (1978). Capitalism and inequality in the United States. In R. C. Edwards, M. Reich, & T. E. Weisskopf (Eds.), *The capitalist system: A radical analysis of American Society* (pp. 297–307). Prentice-Hall.

Ackoff, R. L. (1974). *Redesigning the future.* John Wiley and Sons.

Ackoff, R. L. (1988). From data to wisdom. *Journal of Applied Systems Analysis, 16*(1), 3–9.

Ackoff, R. L., & Emery, F. E. (1972). *On purposeful systems.* Aldine Atherton.

Ackoff, R. L., & Greenberg, D. (2008). *Turning learning right side up: Putting education back on track.* Pearson Prentice-Hall.

Acton, H. B. (1971). *The morals of markets: An ethical exploration.* Longman Group Ltd.

Alchian, A. A., & Demsetz, H. (1972). Production, information costs, and economic organization. *The American Economic Review, 62*(5), 777–795.

Amis, J., Slack, T., & Hinings, C. R. (2002). Values and organizational change. *The Journal of Applied Behavioral Science, 38*(4), 436–465.

Andreasen, A. R. (1975). *The disadvantaged consumer.* The Free Press.

Andreasen, A. R. (1982). Disadvantaged Hispanic consumers: A research perspective and agenda. *Journal of Consumer Affairs, 16*(1), 46–61.

Angel, J. J., & McCabe, D. (2013). Fairness in financial markets: The case of high frequency trading. *Journal of Business Ethics, 112*(4), 585–595.

Aquinas, T. (1981/1273). *The summa theologica.* Benziger Brothers.

Arnold, D. G. (2006). Corporate moral agency. *Midwest Studies in Philosophy, 30,* 279–291.

Arnold, D. G., Audi, R., & Zwolinski, M. (2010). Recent work in ethical theory and its implications for business ethics. *Business Ethics Quarterly, 20*(4), 559–581.

Atkinson, A. B., Piketty, T., & Saez, E. (2011). Top incomes in the long run of history. *Journal of Economic Literature, 49*(1), 3–71.

Baden, D., & Higgs, M. (2015). Challenging the perceived wisdom of management theories and practice. *The Academy of Management Learning and Education, 14*(4), 539–555.

Bagozzi, R. P., Sekerka, L. E., Hill, V., & Seguera, F. (2013). The role of moral values in instigating morally responsible decisions. *The Journal of Applied Behavioral Science, 49*(1), 69–94.

Bahm, A. J. (1975). Comments: Planners' failures generate a scapegoat. *Policy Sciences, 6*(1), 103–105.

Baier, K. (1965). *The moral point of view.* Random House.

Bajaj, V. (2008, January 22). If everyone's finger–pointing, who's to blame. *New York Times.* C.1. https://www.nytimes.com/2008/01/22/business/22legal.html?smid=url-share

Baran, P. A., & Sweezy, P. M. (1966). *Monopoly capital: An essay on the American economic and social order.* Monthly Review.

Barrell, J. (1995). *The political theory of painting from Reynolds to Hazlitt: The body of the public.* Yale University Press.

Baron, P. A., & Sweezy, P. M. (1966). *Monopoly capital: An essay on the American economic and social order.* Monthly Review Press.

Bates, S. (1971). The responsibility of "random collections". *Ethics, 81*(4), 343–349.

Baumhart, R. (1968). *An honest profit: What businessmen say about ethics in business.* Holt, Rinehart and Winston.

Beauchamp, T., & Childress, J. (1989). The principles of justice. *Principles of Biomedical Ethics, 3,* 256–306.

Becker, K. (2007). Wicked ID: Conceptual framework for considering instructional design as a wicked problem. *Canadian Journal of Learning and Technology, 33*(1), n1.

Bell, D. (1973). *The coming of post-industrial society.* Basic Books.

Bell, D. (1976). *The cultural contradictions of capitalism.* Basic Books.

Bellah, R. N., Madsen, R., Sullivan, W. M., Swidler, A., & Tipton, S. M. (1985). *Habits of the heart: Individualism and commitment in American life.* University of California Press.

Bellah, R. N., Madsen, R., Sullivan, W. M., Swidler, A., & Tipton, S. M. (1991). *The good society.* Alfred A. Knopf.

Bellah, R. N., Madsen, R., Sullivan, W. M., Swidler, A., & Tipton, S. M. (1993). The good society. *Journal of Leisure Research, 25*(1), 100.

Benn, S. I., & Weinstein, W. L. (1971). Being free to act, and being a free man. *Mind, 80*(318), 194–211.

Benne, R. (1981). *The ethic of democratic capitalism.* Fortress Press.

Bennis, W. G., & O'Toole, J. (2005). How business schools have lost their way. *Harvard Business Review, 83*(5), 96–104.

Bentham, J. (1970). An introduction to the principles of morals and legislation. In J. H. Burns & H. L. A. Hart (Eds.), *The collected works of Jeremy Bentham: An introduction to the principles of morals and legislation.* Oxford University Press.

Bierly, P. E., Kessler, E. H., & Christensen, E. W. (2000). Organizational learning, knowledge and wisdom. *Journal of Organizational Change Management, 13*(6), 595–618.

Bisoux, T. (2009). Next-generation education. *BizEd, 8*(3), 24–30.

BizEd. (2009, May–June). Changing times, changing approaches: These schools are rewriting the rules of business education to make their programs more ethics–based, 29.

Blair, M. M., & Stout, L. A. (1999). A team production theory of corporate law. *Virginia Law Review, 85*, 247–303.

Blythe, S., Grabill, J. T., & Riley, K. (2008). Action research and wicked environmental problems: Exploring appropriate roles for researchers in professional communication. *Journal of Business and Technical Communication, 22*(3), 272–298.

Boatright, J. R. (2003). *Ethics and the conduct of business.* Prentice-Hall.

Bollier, D. (1997). *Aiming higher.* The American Management Association.

Bose, N. K. (1948). *Selections from Gandhi: Encyclopedia of Gandhi's thoughts.* Navajivan Publishing House. https://demolive.insightsonindia.com/wp-content/uploads/2013/07/selections-from-gandhi.pdf

Bosse, D. A., & Phillips, R. A. (2016). Agency theory and bounded self–interest. *Academy of Management Review, 41*(2), 276–297.

Bosse, D. A., Phillips, R. A., & Harrison, J. S. (2009). Stakeholders, reciprocity, and firm performance. *Strategic Management Journal, 30*(4), 447–456.

Bouckaert, L. (2015). Spirituality: The missing link in business ethics. In L. Zsolnai (Ed.), *The spiritual dimension of business ethics and sustainability management* (pp. 17–27). Springer Cham Heidelberg.

Bouckaert, L., & Zsolnai, L. (Eds.). (2007). *Spirituality as a public good.* Garant.

Bouckaert, L., & Zsolnai, L. (Eds.). (2011). *The Palgrave handbook of spirituality and business.* Palgrave Macmillan.

Boulding, K. E. (1970). *Beyond economics: Essays on society, religion and ethics.* The University of Michigan Press.

Boyd, D. (2007). Why youth (heart) social network sites: The role of networked publics in teenage social life. In D. Buckingham (Ed.), *MacArthur foundation series on digital learning: Youth, identity, and digital media volume* (Vol. 119, pp. 142).

Braham, M., & Van Hees, M. (2012). An anatomy of moral responsibility. *Mind, 121*(483), 601–634.

Braverman, H. (1974). *Labor and monopoly capital.* Monthly Review.

Bridgman, T., Cummings, S., & McLaughlin, C. (2016). Restating the case: How revisiting the development of the case method can help us think differently about the future of the business school. *The Academy of Management Learning and Education, 15*(4), 724–741.

Bridoux, F., & Stoelhorst, J. W. (2014). Microfoundations for stakeholder theory: Managing stakeholders with heterogeneous motives. *Strategic Management Journal, 35*(1), 107–125.

Bridoux, F., & Stoelhorst, J. W. (2016). Stakeholder relationships and social welfare: A behavioral theory of contributions to joint value creation. *Academy of Management Review, 41*(2), 229–251.

Brooks, D. (2010). *Bobos in paradise: The new upper class and how they got there.* Simon & Schuster.

Buchanan, A. E. (1985). *Ethics, efficiency, and the market.* Oxford University Press.

Buchanan, J. M. (1962). Politics, policy, and the Pigovian margins. In *Classic papers in natural resource economics* (pp. 204–218). Palgrave Macmillan.

Budde, M. L., & Brimlow, R. (2002). *Christianity incorporated: How big business is buying the Church.* Brazos.

Cabantous, L., & Gond, J. P. (2011). Rational decision making as performative praxis: Explaining rationality's Éternel Retour. *Organization Science, 22*(3), 573–586.

Calhoon, R. P. (1969). Niccolo Machiavelli and the twentieth century administrator. *Academy of Management Journal, 12*(2), 205–212.

Callon, M. (2007). What does it mean to say that economics is performative? In D. MacKenzie, F. Muniesa, & L. Siu (Eds.), *Do economists make markets? On the performativity of economics* (pp. 311–357). Princeton University Press.

Camillus, J. C. (2008). Strategy as a wicked problem. *Harvard Business Review, 86*(5), 98–101.

Cappelli, P. (2008). Talent management for the twenty-first century. *Harvard Business Review, 86*(3), 74.

Casey, P. (2014). *The greatest company in the world? The story of Tata.* Penguin.

Chamberlain, J. (1959). *The roots of capitalism.* D. Van Nostrand Company.

Chandler, A. D. Jr. (1977). *The visible hand: The managerial revolution in American business.* Harvard University Press.

Chandy, R. K., & Tellis, G. J. (1998). Organizing for radical product innovation: The overlooked role of willingness to cannibalize. *Journal of Marketing Research, 35*(4), 474–487.

Chandy, R. K., & Tellis, G. J. (2000). The incumbent's curse? Incumbency, size, and radical product innovation. *Journal of Marketing, 64*(3), 1–17.

Chiva, R., & Alegre, J. (2005). Organizational learning and organizational knowledge: Towards the integration of two approaches. *Management Learning, 36*(1), 49–68.

Christensen, C. M., Baumann, H., Ruggles, R., & Sadtler, T. M. (2006). Disruptive innovation for social change. *Harvard Business Review, 84*(12), 94–103.

Christensen, C. M., Grossman, J. H., & Hwang, J. (2009). *The innovator's prescription: A disruptive solution for health care.* McGraw-Hill.

Christie, R., & Geis, F. L. (1970). *Studies in Machiavellianism.* Academic Press.

Churchman, C. W. (1974). Philosophical speculations on systems design. *Omega, 2*(4), 451–465.

Cobb, A. J. (2016). How firms shape income inequality: Stakeholder power, executive decision making, and the structuring of employment relationships. *Academy of Management Review, 41*(2), 324–348.

Collins, P. (1998). *Changing ideals in modern architecture, 1750–1950.* McGill-Queen's Press-MQUP.

Conklin, J. E. (2006). *Dialogue mapping: Building shared understanding of wicked problems.* Wiley & Sons.

Constantinescu, M., & Kaptein, M. (2015). Mutually enhancing responsibility: A theoretical exploration of the interaction mechanisms between individual and corporate moral responsibility. *Journal of Business Ethics, 129*, 325–339.

Covey, S. R. (2004). *The 8th habit from effectiveness to greatness.* Simon & Schuster.

Cox, R., Goodman, C. S., & Fichandler, T. C. (1965). *Distribution in a high-level economy.* Prentice-Hall.

Dalton, G. (1974). *Economic systems and society: Capitalism, communism, and the third world.* Penguin Book.

Daniels, E. (1970). From mercantilism to imperialism: The Argentine case Part 2. *Nacla Newsletter, 4*(6), 1–12.

Danley, J. (1990). Corporate moral agency: The case for anthropological bigotry. In W. M. Hoffman & J. M. Moore (Eds.), *Business ethics* (2nd ed., pp. 202–203). McGraw.

Davis, G. F. (2015). What is organizational research for? *Administrative Science Quarterly, 60*(2), 179–188.

Davis, J. E. (2006). How medicalization lost its way. *Society, 43*(6), 51–56.

Davis, J. H., Schoorman, F. D., & Donaldson, L. (1997). Davis, Schoorman, and Donaldson reply: The distinctiveness of agency theory and stewardship theory. *Academy of Management Review, 22*(3), 611.

De George, R. T. (1981). Ethical responsibilities of engineers in large organizations: The Pinto case. *Business & Professional Ethics Journal, 1*(1), 1–14.

De George, R. T. (1999). Business ethics and the information age. *Business and Society Review, 104*(3), 261–278.

Deming, W. E. (1994). *The new economics for industry, government, education* (2nd ed.). Cambridge: Mas MITT.

Deming, W. E. (2006). Letter sent to Peter Senge concerning Senge's book. In P. Senge (Ed.), *The fifth discipline* (pp. xii). Random House. https://vitalentusa.com/links/pdfs/deming_revisited-Vitalo.pdf

DePree, M. (1989). *Leadership is an art.* Bantam Doubleday Dell Publishing Group.

Dhiman, S., & Marques, J. (2016). *Spirituality and sustainability.* Springer International Publishing.

Dietz, M., Barker, S., & Giberson, N. (2005). Solving a "wicked" problem. *Leadership, 34*(3), 20–23.

Dixit, A. K., & Stiglitz, J. E. (1977). Monopolistic competition and optimum product diversity. *The American Economic Review, 67*(3), 297–308.

Donaldson, T. (1980). Moral agency and corporations. *Philosophy in Context, 10*, 54–70.

Donaldson, T. (1982). *Corporations and morality.* Prentice-Hall.

Dorfman, R. (1972). *Prices and markets* (2nd ed.). Prentice-Hall.

Drèze, J. (2019). *Sense and solidarity: Jholawala economics for everyone.* Oxford University Press.

Drucker, P. F. (1989). *The new realities.* Harper & Row.

Dublin, T. (1979). *Women at work: The transformation of work and community in Lowell, Mass, 1826–1860.* Columbia University Press.

Eckstein, O., Sweezy, P. M., Green, M., Rustin, B., Keyserling, L. H., & Love, S. (1974). The future of capitalism: A symposium. *Business and Society Review* (Summer), 4–21.

Economist. (2015a). Better than it looks. *Economist,* June 13. https://www.economist.com/briefing/2015/06/13/better-than-it-looks

Economist. (2015b). Watch out: It is only a matter of time before the next recession strikes. The rich world is not ready. *Economist,* June 13. https://www.economist.com/leaders/2015/06/13/watch–out

Edmondson, A. C. (2008). The competitive imperative of learning. *Harvard Business Review, 86*(7–8), 60–67.

Edwards, R. C., Reich, M., & Weisskopf, T. E. (1978). *The capitalist system: A radical analysis of American society.* Prentice-Hall.

Enz, C. A. (1988). The role of value congruity in intraorganizational power. *Administrative Science Quarterly, 33*(2), 284–304.

Farmer, P. (2003). *Pathologies of power: Health, human rights, and the new war on the poor*. University of California Press.

Faulhaber, G. R., & Baumol, W. J. (1988). Economists as innovators: Practical products of theoretical research. *Journal of Economic Literature, 26*(2), 577–600.

Fehr, E., & Gächter, S. (2000). Fairness and retaliation: The economics of reciprocity. *The Journal of Economic Perspectives, 14*(3), 159–182.

Fehr, E., & Gintis, H. (2007). Human motivation and social cooperation: Experimental and analytical foundations. *Annual Review of Sociology, 33*, 43–64.

Ferraro, F., Pfeffer, J., & Sutton, R. I. (2005). Economics language and assumptions: How theories can become self-fulfilling. *Academy of Management Review, 30*(1), 8–24.

Fiske, A. P. (1991). *Structures of social life: The four elementary forms of human relations: Communal sharing, authority ranking, equality matching, market pricing*. Free Press.

Fiske, A. P. (1992). The four elementary forms of sociality: Framework for a unified theory of social relations. *Psychological Review, 99*(4), 689.

Fiske, A. P. (2004). Relational models theory 2.0. In N. Haslam (Ed.), *Relational models theory: A contemporary overview* (pp. 3–25). Lawrence Erlbaum.

Fiske, A. P. (2012). Metarelational models: Configurations of social relationships. *European Journal of Social Psychology, 42*(1), 2–18.

Fiske, A. P., & Haslam, N. (2005). The four basic social bonds: Structures for coordinating interaction. In M. W. Baldwin (Ed.), *Interpersonal cognition* (pp. 267–298). Guilford Press.

Forbes. (2002, July 25). Recent accounting frauds. *Forbes*. www.Forbes.com. accountingtracker.html

Fortune. (2002, September 2). Recent corporate scams. *Fortune*, 64–74.

Frankel, C. (1968). Meaning of political murder. *Saturday Review, 51*, 22.

Frankena, W. (1973). *Ethics*. Prentice-Hall.

Frankena, W. (1980). *Thinking about morality*. University of Michigan Press.

Frank, R. H., Gilovich, T., & Regan, D. T. (1993). Does studying economics inhibit cooperation? *The Journal of Economic Perspectives, 7*(2), 159–171.

Frederick, W. C. (1995). *Values, nature, and culture in the American corporation*. Oxford University Press.

Freeman, R. E. (1984). *Strategic management: A stakeholder approach*. Pitman.

Freeman, R. E., Harrison, J. S., Wicks, A. C., Parmar, B. L., & De Colle, S. (2010). *Stakeholder theory*. Cambridge: Cambridge University Press.

French, P. A. (1975). Types of collectivities and blame. *The Personalist, 56*(2), 160–169.

French, P. A. (1979). The corporation as a moral person. *American Philosophical Quarterly, 16*(3), 207–215.

French, P. A. (1982). Crowds and corporations. *American Philosophical Quarterly, 19*(3), 271–277.

French, P. A. (1984). *Collective and corporate responsibility*. Columbia University Press.

French, P. A. (1995). *Corporate ethics*. Harcourt Brace.

French, P. A. (2016). Complicity: That moral monster, troubling matters. *Criminal Law and Philosophy, 10*, 575–589.

Frey, B. S., & Meier, S. (2005). Selfish and indoctrinated economists? *European Journal of Law and Economics, 19*(2), 165–171.

Friedman, M. (1962). *Capitalism and freedom.* University of Chicago Press.

Furnham, A. (2010). *The elephant in the boardroom: The causes of leadership derailment.* Palgrave Macmillan.

Galbraith, J. K. (1956). *American capitalism: The theory of countervailing power.* Houghton Mifflin.

Galbraith, J. K. (1958). *The affluent society.* Houghton Mifflin.

Galbraith, J. K. (1967). The new industrial state. *Antitrust Law and Economic Review, 1*, 11.

Galbraith, J. K. (1973). *Economics and the public purpose.* Houghton Mifflin.

Galbraith, J. K. (1976). The dependence effect. In J. K. Galbraith (Ed.), *The affluent society.* Houghton Mifflin.

Galbraith, J. R. (1968). Environmental and technological determinants of organization design: A case study (pp. 352–368). *Boeing Research Project.* Library of the Massachusetts Institute of Technology.

Gans, H. J. (1988). *Middle American individualism: The future of liberal democracy.* Oxford University Press.

Garcia–Parpet, M.-F. (2007). The social construction of a perfect market: The strawberry auction at Fontaines-en-Sologne. In D. MacKenzie, F. Muniesa, & L. Siu (Eds.), *Do economists make markets? On the performativity of economics* (pp. 163–189). Princeton University Press.

Gardner, H. (2007). The ethical mind. A conversation with psychologist – Howard Gardner. *Harvard Business Review, 85*(3), 51–56.

Garvin, D. A., Edmondson, A. C., & Gino, F. (2008). Is yours a learning organization? *Harvard Business Review, 86*(3), 109.

Geertz, C. (1973). *The interpretation of cultures: Selected essays.* Basic Books.

Ghoshal, S. (2005). Bad management theories are destroying good management practices. *The Academy of Management Learning and Education, 4*(1), 75–91.

Ghoshal, S., & Moran, P. (1996). Bad for practice: A critique of the transaction cost theory. *Academy of Management Review, 21*(1), 13–47.

Ghoshal, S., & Moran, P. (2005). Towards a good theory of management. In J. Birkinshaw & G. Piramal (Eds.), *Sumantra Ghoshal on management* (pp. 1–27). Pearson FT Press.

Gladwin, T. N., Kennelly, J. J., & Krause, T. S. (1995). Shifting paradigms for sustainable development: Implications for management theory and research. *Academy of Management Review, 20*(4), 874–907.

Gomber, P., Arndt, B., Lutat, M., & Uhle, T. (2011). *High-frequency trading* (Working Paper). Goethe Universität Frankfurt am Main, Frakfurt aM.

Goode, J. G., & Maskovsky, J. (Eds.). (2001). *The new poverty studies: The ethnography of power, politics, and impoverished people in the United States.* New York University Press.

Goodpaster, K. E. (1983). The concept of corporate responsibility. *Journal of Business Ethics, 2*, 1–22.

Goodpaster, K. E., & Matthews, J. B. Jr. (1982, January 1). Can a corporation have a conscience? *Harvard Business Review on Corporate Responsibility*, 132–141.

Graham, C., & Pettinato, S. (2001). Happiness, markets, and democracy: Latin America in comparative perspective. *Journal of Happiness Studies, 2*, 237–268.

Green, R. M. (1991). When is "everyone's doing it" a moral justification? *Business Ethics Quarterly, 1*(1), 75–93.

Greenleaf, R. K. (2002). *Servant leadership: A journey into the nature of legitimate power and greatness.* Paulist Press.

Greenwald, B., & Kahn, J. (2005). All strategy is local. *Harvard Business Review, 83*(9), 94–104.

Gregg, S. (2007). *The commercial society: Foundations and challenges in a global age.* Lexington.

Griffin, J. H. (2004). *Black like me.* Wings Press.

Griffin, R. C. (2016). *Water resource economics: The analysis of scarcity, policies, and projects.* MIT Press.

Griffin, J. J., & Mahon, J. F. (1997). The corporate social performance and corporate financial performance debate: Twenty-five years of incomparable research. *Business & Society, 36*(1), 5–31.

Gustafsson, C. (2002). From concept to norm: An explorative study of office design management from an organizational perspective. *Facilities, 20*(13/14), 423–431.

Gutman, R. (1966). Site planning and social behavior. *Journal of Social Issues, 22*(4), 103–115.

Habermas, J. (1971). *Knowledge and human interests.* Beacon Press.

Habermas, J. (1991). *The structural transformation of the public sphere: An inquiry into a category of bourgeois society.* MIT Press.

Habermas, J. (1998). Three normative models of democracy. In J. Habermas (Ed.), *The inclusion of the other: Studies in political theory* (pp. 239–252). MIT Press.

Habermas, J. (2003). *Truth and justification.* MIT Press.

Hamel, G. (2006). The why, what, and how of management innovation. *Harvard Business Review, 84*(2), 72–84.

Hamel, G. (2009). Moon shots for management. *Harvard Business Review, 87*(2), 91–98.

Hamel, G., & Breen, B. (2007). *The future of management.* Harvard Business School Press.

Hamel, G., & Prahalad, C. K. (1994). Competing for the future. *Harvard Business Review, 72*(4), 122–128.

Hamel, G., & Valikangas, L. (2003). The quest for resilience. *Harvard Business Review, 81*(9), 52–65.

Hammond, A. L. (2001). Digitally empowered development. *Foreign Affairs, 80*, 96. https://www.jstor.org/stable/pdf/20050067.pdf

Hammond, A. L., & Prahalad, C. K. (2004). Selling to the poor. *Foreign Policy, 142*, 30–37.

Hammond, J. S., Keeney, R. L., & Raiffa, H. (1998). The hidden traps in decision making. *Harvard Business Review, 76*(5), 47–58.

Harrison, J. S., Bosse, D. A., & Phillips, R. A. (2010). Managing for stakeholders, stakeholder utility functions, and competitive advantage. *Strategic Management Journal, 31*(1), 58–74.

Haslam, N. (2004). *Relational models theory: A contemporary overview.* Laurence Erlbaum Associates.

Hasnas, J. (2010). Where is Flex Cohen when we need him: Transcendental nonsense and the moral responsibility of corporations. *Journal of Law and Policy, 19*(1), 55.

Hasnas, J. (2012). Reflections on corporate moral responsibility and the problem solving technique of Alexander the Great. *Journal of Business Ethics, 107*, 183–195.

Hasnas, J. (2017). Does corporate moral agency entail corporate freedom of speech? *Social Theory and Practice, 43*(3), 589–612.

Hayek, F. A. V. (1989, December). The pretense of knowledge. *The American Economic Review*, 3–7.

Heilbroner, R. L. (1970). *Between capitalism and socialism: Essays in political economics* (Vol. 365). Vintage Books.

Held, V. (1970). Can a random collection of individuals be morally responsible? *The Journal of Philosophy, 67*(14), 471–481.

Higgs, M. (2012). Leadership, narcissism, ethics and strategic change: Is it time to revisit our thinking about the nature of effective leadership? In R. T. By, B. Burnes, & M. Hughes (Eds.), *Organizational change, leadership and ethics* (pp. 57–74). Routledge.

Hiller, J. S. (2013). The benefit corporation and corporate social responsibility. *Journal of Business Ethics, 118*(2), 287–301.

Hirschman, A. O. (1976). *The passions and the interests*. Princeton University.

Hofstadter, R. (1955). *Social Darwinism in American thought* (Vol. 16). Beacon Press.

Hook, S. (1967). *Human values and economic policy*. Paper presented at the New York University Institute of Philosophy, 1966: Washington Square.

Horn, R. E. (2001, July). Knowledge mapping for complex social messes. In *A Presentation to the "Foundations in the Knowledge Economy" at the David and Lucile Packard Foundation Conference*. https://faculty.washington.edu/farkas/TC510–Fall2011/HornKnowledgeMapping.pdf

Hubbard, R., & Paquet, G. (2007). *Gomery's blinders and Canadian federalism*. University of Ottawa Press.

Hunter, J. D. (1991). *Culture wars: The struggle to define America*. Basic Books.

Hunt, S. D., & Morgan, R. M. (1995). The comparative advantage theory of competition. *Journal of Marketing, 59*(2), 1–15.

Inamori, K. (1985, June 5). *The perfect company: Goal for productivity*. Speech given at Case Western Reserve University.

Inman, P. (2013, October 24). Economics students aim to tear up free–market syllabus. *The Guardian*. https://www.theguardian.com/business/2013/oct/24/students-post-crash-economics

Inman, P. (2014, May 4). Economics students call for shakeup of the way their subject is taught. *The Guardian*. https://www.theguardian.com/education/2014/may/04/economics-students-overhaul-subject-teaching

Jacoby, N. H. (1973). *Corporate power and social responsibility*. Simon & Schuster.

Jashapara, A. (2005). The emerging discourse of knowledge management: A new dawn for information science research? *Journal of Information Science, 31*(2), 136–148.

Jensen, M. C. (2002). Value maximization, stakeholder theory, and the corporate objective function. *Business Ethics Quarterly, 12*(2), 235–256.

Jensen, M. C., & Meckling, W. H. (1976). Theory of firm: Managerial behaviour, agency costs and ownership structure. *Journal of Financial Economics, 3*(4), 305–360.

Jones, T. M. (1995). Instrumental stakeholder theory: A synthesis of ethics and economics. *Academy of Management Review, 20*(2), 404–437.

Jones, T. M., Donaldson, T., Freeman, R. E., Harrison, J. S., Leana, C. R., Mahoney, J. T., & Pearce, J. L. (2016). Management theory and social welfare: Contributions and challenges. *Academy of Management Review*, *41*(2), 216–228.

Jones, T. M., & Felps, W. (2013a). Shareholder wealth maximization and social welfare: A utilitarian critique. *Business Ethics Quarterly*, *23*(2), 207–238.

Jones, T. M., & Felps, W. (2013b). Stakeholder happiness enhancement: A neo-utilitarian objective for the modern corporation. *Business Ethics Quarterly*, *23*(3), 349–379.

Jones, T. M., Felps, W., & Bigley, G. A. (2007). Ethical theory and stakeholder-related decisions: The role of stakeholder culture. *Academy of Management Review*, *32*(1), 137–155.

Jones, T. M., & Freeman, R. E. (2013). *Sustainable wealth creation*. Working Paper. University of Washington, Seattle.

Jones, T. M., & Wicks, A. C. (1999). Letter to AMR regarding "convergent stakeholder theory". *Academy of Management Review*, *24*(4), 621–623.

Jung, L. S., Machan, T. R., & Marcus, S. A. (1983). Commercialization and the professions [with commentaries]. *Business & Professional Ethics Journal*, *2*(2), 57–91.

Kahn, H., Brown, W., & Martel, L. (1976). *Next 200 years: A scenario for America and the world*. Morrow.

Kahneman, D., Knetsch, J. L., & Thaler, R. (1986). Fairness as a constraint on profit seeking: Entitlements in the market. *The American Economic Review*, *76*(4), 728–741.

Karakas, F. (2010). Spirituality and performance in organizations: A literature review. *Journal of Business Ethics*, *94*(1), 89–106.

Keeley, M. (1979). Organizations as non-persons. *The Journal of Value Inquiry*, *15*, 149–155.

Kelman, M. (1987). *A guide to critical legal studies*. Harvard University Press.

Kerley, R. (2007). Controlling urban car parking: An exemplar for public management? *International Journal of Public Sector Management*, *20*(6), 519–530.

Khurana, R. (2007). *From higher aims to hired hands: The social transformation of business schools and the unfulfilled promise of management as a profession*. Princeton University Press.

Khurana, R., & Nohria, N. (2008). It's time to make management a true profession. *Harvard Business Review*, *86*(10), 70–77.

Kieser, A., Nicolai, A., & Seidl, D. (2015). The practical relevance of management research: Turning the debate on relevance into a rigorous scientific research program. *The Academy of Management Annals*, *9*(1), 143–233.

Kim, W. C., & Mauborgne, R. (2004, October). Blue ocean strategy. *Harvard Business Review*, 76–85.

King, J. B. (1993). Learning to solve the right problems: The case of nuclear power in America. *Journal of Business Ethics*, *12*, 105–116.

Kotter, J. B. (1996). *Leading change*. Harvard Business School Press.

Kotter, J. B. (2007, January). Leading change: Why transformation efforts fail. *Harvard Business Review*, 96–103.

Kramar, R. (2014). Beyond strategic human resource management: Is sustainable human resource management the next approach? *International Journal of Human Resource Management*, *25*(8), 1069–1089.

Ladd, J. (1970). Morality and the ideal of rationality in formal organizations. *The Monist, 54*(4), 488–516.

Ladd, J. (1984). Corporate mythology and individual responsibility. *International Journal of Applied Philosophy, 2*(1), 1–21.

Lagarde, C. (2014, May 27). *Economic inclusion and financial integrity: An address to the Conference on Inclusive Capitalism.* https://www.imf.org/external/np/speeches/2014/052714.htm

Lasch, C. (1978). *The culture of narcissism: American life in an age of diminishing expectations.* Norton.

Laudan, L. (1977). *Progress and its problems: Towards a theory of scientific growth.* University of California Press.

Layard, R. (2011). *Happiness: Lessons from a new science.* Penguin Books.

Lencioni, P. M. (1998). *The five temptations of a CEO: A leadership fable* (1st ed.). John Wiley and Sons, Inc.

Locke, E. A. (1991). The motivation sequence, the motivation hub, and the motivation core. *Organizational Behavior and Human Decision Processes, 50*(2), 288–299.

Locke, J. (1689). Of property. In *Second treatise.* The University of Chicago Press. https://press-pubs.uchicago.edu/founders/documents/v1ch16s3.html

Lourenço, F. (2013). To challenge the world view or to flow with it? Teaching sustainable development in business schools. *Business Ethics: A European Review, 22*(3), 292–307.

Luthans, F., & Avolio, B. J. (2003). Authentic leadership development. *Positive Organizational Scholarship, 241*(258), 1–26.

Machan, T. R., & Uyl, D. J. D. (1987). Recent work in business ethics: A survey and critique. *American Philosophical Quarterly, 24*(2), 107–124.

MacKenzie, D. (2006). Is economics performative? Option theory and the construction of derivatives markets. *Journal of the History of Economic Thought, 28*(1), 29–55.

MacKenzie, D. (2007). Is economics performative? Option theory and the construction of derivatives markets. In D. MacKenzie, F. Muniesa, & L. Siu (Eds.), *Do economists make markets? On the performativity of economics* (pp. 54–86). Princeton University Press.

MacKenzie, D. (2015). Mechanizing the merc: The Chicago Mercantile Exchange and the rise of high-frequency trading. *Technology and Culture, 56*(3), 646–675.

MacKenzie, D., Muniesa, F., & Siu, L. (Eds.), (2007). Do economists make markets? In *On the performativity of economics* (pp. 54–86). Princeton University Press.

Mackey, J., & Sisodia, R. (2014). *Conscious capitalism: Liberating the heroic spirit of business.* Harvard Business Review Press.

Ma, D. K., & Eliot, T. S. (2006). Destructive creation: The covenantal crisis of capitalist society. *Theology Today, 63*(2), 150–164.

Mahoney, J. T., Huff, A. S., & Huff, J. O. (1994). Toward a new social contract theory in organization science. *Journal of Management Inquiry, 3*(2), 153–168.

Mariappanadar, S. (2003). Sustainable human resource management: The sustainable and unsustainable dilemmas of downsizing. *International Journal of Social Economics, 30*(8), 906–923.

Mariappanadar, S. (2012). The harm indicators of negative externality of efficiency focused organizational practices. *International Journal of Social Economics, 39*(3), 209–220.

Mariappanadar, S. (2014). Stakeholder harm index: A framework to review work intensification from the critical HRM perspective. *Human Resource Management Review, 24*(4), 313–329.

Mariappanadar, S. (2016). Health harm of work from the sustainable HRM perspective: Scale development and validation. *International Journal of Manpower, 37*(6), 924–944.

Mariappanadar, S., & Aust, I. (2018). The dark side of overwork: An empirical evidence of social harm of work from a sustainable HRM perspective. *International Studies of Management & Organization, 47*(4), 372–387.

Mariappanadar, S., & Kramar, R. (2014). Sustainable HRM: The synthesis effect of high performance work systems on organisational performance and employee harm. *Asia-Pacific Journal of Business Administration, 6*(3), 206–224.

Marti, E., & Scherer, A. G. (2016). Financial regulation and social welfare: The critical contribution of management theory. *Academy of Management Review, 41*(2), 298–323.

Marx, K. (1959). Capital: A critique of political economy. In *The process of capitalist production as a whole* (Vol. 3). Progress Publishers.

Marx, K., & Engels, F. (1970). *The German ideology* (Vol. 1). International Publishers Co.

Mascarenhas, O. (2019). *Corporate ethics for turbulent markets: Executive response to market challenges.* Emerald Publishing Limited.

Mascarenhas, O. A. (1995). Exonerating unethical marketing executive behaviors: A diagnostic framework. *Journal of Marketing, 59*(2), 43–57.

Mascarenhas, O. A. (2018). *Corporate ethics for turbulent markets: The market context of executive decisions.* Emerald Publishing Limited.

Mascarenhas, O. A. J. (1988a). Can we humanize consumption? Tasks and models. In *AMA Winter Theory Conference Proceedings.* San Diego, CA: American Marketing Association.

Mascarenhas, O. A. J. (1988b). Towards a meta satisfaction macro consumer behavior model. In *AMA Winter Theory Conference Proceedings.* San Diego, CA: American Marketing Association.

Mascarenhas, O. A. J. (2008). *Responsible marketing: Concepts, strategies, models, theories and cases.* Roval Publishing Co.

Mascarenhas, O. A. J. (2009a). Rethinking Jesuit business education: New paradigms of business faith that does business justice. In *Conference paper presented at the 15th Annual International Association of Jesuit Business Schools (IAJBS) World Forum,* XLRI, Jamshedpur, India, June 8.

Mascarenhas, O. A. J. (2009b). Rethinking business learning: New paradigms of innovative learning. In *Commencement Motivational Address at the Inauguration of the 2009 Academic Year,* XLRI, Jamshedpur, June 15.

Mascarenhas, O. A. J. (2010, October). Towards redesigning the MBA business curriculum: A problem centered approach for integrated business management. In *Keynote Address at the National Seminar on Redesigning the MBA Curriculum,* held at AIMIT/MBA, Beeri Campus.

Mascarenhas, O. A., Kesavan, R., & Bernacchi, M. D. (2004). Customer value-chain involvement for co-creating customer delight. *Journal of Consumer Marketing, 21*(7), 486–496.

Mascarenhas, O. A., Kesavan, R., & Bernacchi, M. D. (2005a). Governmental and corporate roles in diffusing development technologies: Ethical macromarketing imperatives. *Journal of Nonprofit & Public Sector Marketing, 13*(1&2), 271–292.

Mascarenhas, O. A., Kesavan, R., & Bernacchi, M. D. (2005b). Progressive reduction of economic inequality as a macromarketing task: A rejoinder. *Journal of Nonprofit & Public Sector Marketing, 13*(1&2), 313–318.

Mascarenhas, O. A., Kesavan, R., & Bernacchi, M. D. (2005c). Global marketing of lifesaving drugs: An analogical model. *Journal of Consumer Marketing, 22*(7), 404–411.

Mascarenhas, O. A., Kesavan, R., & Bernacchi, M. D. (2008). Buyer-seller information asymmetry: Challenges to distributive and corrective justice. *Journal of Macromarketing, 28*(1), 68–84.

May, L. (1983). Vicarious agency and corporate responsibility. *Philosophical Studies: An International Journal for Philosophy in the Analytic Tradition, 43*(1), 69–82.

May, L. (1987). *The morality of groups: Collective responsibility, group-based harm, and corporate rights.* University of Notre Dame Press.

May, L., & Hoffman, S. (Eds.). (1991). *Collective responsibility: Five decades of debate in theoretical and applied ethics.* Rowman & Littlefield Publishers, Inc.

McKenna, M. (2006). Collective responsibility and an agent meaning theory. *Midwest Studies in Philosophy, 30*, 16–34.

McMahon, C. (1995). The ontological and moral status of organizations. *Business Ethics Quarterly, 5*(3), 541–554.

McRae, H. (2003, January 15). Like them or not, supermarkets have improved our quality of life. *The Independent.* https://www.independent.co.uk/voices/commentators/hamish-mcrae/like-them-or-not-supermarkets-have-improved-our-quality-of-life-124190.html

Melé, D. (2016). Re-thinking capitalism: What we can learn from Scholasticism? *Journal of Business Ethics, 133*(2), 293–304.

Mellema, G. (2006). Collective responsibility and qualifying actions. *Midwest Studies in Philosophy, 30*, 168–175.

Michael, D. N. (1985). With both feet planted firmly in mid-air: Reflections on thinking about the future. *Futures, 17*(2), 94–103.

Michalos, A. (1982). Editorial: Purpose and policy. *Journal of Business Ethics, 1*(3), 255.

Miller, D. (1999). *Principles of social justice.* Harvard University Press.

Miller, D. (2003). *Political philosophy: A very short introduction* (Vol. 97). Oxford University Press.

Miller, S. (2001). *Social action: A teleological account.* Cambridge: Cambridge University Press.

Mintzberg, H. (2004). *Developing managers not MBAs.* FT Prentice-Hall.

Mitchell, R. K., Weaver, G. R., Agle, B. R., Bailey, A. D., & Carlson, J. (2016). Stakeholder agency and social welfare: Pluralism and decision making in the multi-objective corporation. *Academy of Management Review, 41*(2), 252–275.

Mitroff, I. I. (2016). *Spirituality and sustainability: New horizons and exemplary approaches.* Springer.

Molander, E. (1980). *Responsive capitalism*. McGraw-Hill.

Molthan-Hill, P. (2014). *The business student's guide to sustainable management: Principles and practice*. Greenleaf.

Monbiot, G. (2000). *Captive state: The corporate takeover of Britain*. Macmillan.

Monbiot, G. (2004). *The age of consent*. Harper Collins.

Moyer, R., & Hutt, M. D. (1978). *Macro marketing*. John Wiley & Sons.

Nesteruk, J. (1992). The moral status of the corporation: Comments on an inquiry. *Business Ethics Quarterly, 2*(4), 461–463.

Neumeier, M. (2009). *The designful company: How to build a culture of nonstop innovation*. New Riders.

Newman, C. J. H. (1982). *The idea of a university*. University of Notre Dame Press.

Newsweek. (2009, January 20). *Newsweek* feature: Barack Obama. Commemorative Inaugural Edition.

Novak, M. (1982). *The spirit of democratic capitalism*. American Enterprise Institute: Simon and Schuster.

Novak, M. (2001). *Three in one: Essays on democratic capitalism, 1976–2000*. Rowman & Littlefield Publishers.

Nozick, R. (1974). *Anarchy, state, and utopia*. Basic Books.

Nussbaum, M. C. (1992). Human functioning and social justice: In defense of Aristotelian essentialism. *Political Theory, 20*(2), 202–246.

O'Brien, B. (1989). *Advanced maturity*. Hanover Insurance.

O'Brien, B. (2006). *Character and the corporation*.

O'Connor, A. (2001). *Poverty knowledge: Social science, social policy, and the poor in twentieth-century U.S. history*. Princeton University Press.

Ohmae, K. (1990). *The borderless world*. Harper Publishers.

Okun, A. M. (1975). *Equality and efficiency: The big tradeoff*. Brookings Institution.

Orr, D. W. (1990). Environmental education and ecological literacy. *The Education Digest, 55*(9), 49.

Orr, D. (1991). What is education for? Six myths about the foundations of modern education and six new principles to replace them. *Context: A Quarterly of Humane Sustainable Culture, 27*, 59–64.

Otsuka, M. (1998). Self-ownership and equality: A Lockean reconciliation. *Philosophy & Public Affairs, 27*(1), 65–92.

Ozar, D. (1979). The moral responsibility of corporations. In T. Donaldson & P. Werhane (Eds.), *Ethical issues in business: A philosophical approach* (1st ed., pp. 294–300). Prentice-Hall.

Pacanowsky, M. (1995). Team tools for wicked problems. *Organizational Dynamics, 23*(3), 36–51.

Packard, V. (1957). *The hidden persuaders*. David McKay Company.

Palusek, J. L. (1977). *Will the corporation survive?* Reston Publishing Company, Inc.

Parker, M. (Ed.). (1998). *Ethics and organization*. SAGE Publications.

Parker, M., & Pearson, G. (2005). Capitalism and its regulation: A dialogue on business and ethics. *Journal of Business Ethics, 60*(1), 91–101.

Pearson, G. (1995). *Integrity in organizations: An alternative business ethic*. McGraw-Hill.

Pearson, G., & Parker, M. (2001). The relevance of ancient Greeks to modem business? A dialog on business and ethics. *Journal of Business Ethics, 31*, 341–353.

Penley, L. E. (2009). It's time to shape the future of education. *BizEd, 8*(3), 32–36.

Perrow, C. (1974). Is business really changing? *Organizational Dynamics, 3*(1), 31–44.

Perrow, C. (1984). *Normal accidents: Living with high-risk technologies.* Basic Books.

Perrow, C. (1994). The limits of safety: The enhancement of a theory of accidents. *Journal of Contingencies and Crisis Management, 4*(2), 212–220.

Pettit, P. (1995). The cunning of trust. *Philosophy & Public Affairs, 24*(3), 202–225.

Pettit, P. (2007). Responsibility incorporated. *Ethics, 117*(2), 171–201.

Phillips, M. J. (1992). Corporate moral personhood and three conceptions of the corporation. *Business Ethics Quarterly, 2*(4), 435–459.

Phillips, M. J. (1995). Corporate moral responsibility. *Business Ethics Quarterly, 5*(3), 555–576.

Phillips, R. (2003). *Stakeholder theory and organizational ethics.* Berrett-Koehler Publishers.

Piketty, T. (2014). *Capital in the twenty-first century.* Harvard University Press.

Podhoretz, N. (1981, March–April). The new defenders of capitalism. *Harvard Business Review,* 96–106.

Podolny, J. M. (2009). The buck stops (and starts) at business school. *Harvard Business Review, 87*(6), 62–67.

Porter, M. E. (1996). What is a strategy? *Harvard Business Review, 74*(6), 61–78.

Porter, M. E. (2015). The competitive advantage of the inner city. In R. T. LeGates & F. Stout (Eds.), *The city reader* (pp. 358–371). Routledge.

Porter, M. E., & Kramer, M. R. (2011). Creating shared value. *Harvard Business Review, 89*(1/2), 62–77.

Porter, L. W., & McKibbin, L. E. (1988). *Management education and development: Drift or thrust into the 21st century?* McGraw-Hill Book Company.

Post, J. E., Preston, L. E., & Sachs, S. (2002). Managing the extended enterprise: The new stakeholder view. *California Management Review, 45*(1), 6–28.

Prahalad, C. K. (2004, November). The poor can be profitable. *Fortune, 17,* 70–72.

Prahalad, C. K. (2005). *The fortune at the bottom of the pyramid: Eradicating poverty through profit and enabling dignity and choice through markets.* Wharton School.

Prahalad, C. K., & Hamel, G. (1994). Strategy as a field of study: Why search for a new paradigm? *Strategic Management Journal, 15,* 5–16.

Prahalad, C. K., & Hammond, A. (2002). Serving the world's poor, profitably. *Harvard Business Review, 80*(9), 48–59.

Price, D. J. de S. (1964). Automata and the origins of mechanism and mechanistic philosophy. *Technology and Culture, 5*(1), 9–23.

Priem, R. L. (2007). A consumer perspective on value creation. *Academy of Management Review, 32*(1), 219–235.

Pruzan, P. (2011). Spirituality as the context for leadership. In L. Zsolnai (Ed.), *Spirituality and ethics in management* (pp. 3–21). Springer.

Pruzan, P. (2014). The source of ethical competency: Eastern perspectives provided by a Westerner. In K. J. Ims & L. J. P. Cheltenham (Eds.), *Business and the greater good: Rethinking business ethics in the age of economic crisis* (pp. 117–148). Edward Elgar Publishers.

Pruzan, P. (2015a). Spiritual-based leadership: A paradox of pragmatism. In L. Zsolnai (Ed.), *The spiritual dimension of business ethics and sustainability management* (pp. 169–173). Springer.

Pruzan, P. (2015b). Further reflections on spirituality and spiritual-based leadership. In L. Zsolnai (Ed.), *The spiritual dimension of business ethics and sustainability management* (pp. 191–198). Springer.

Pursell, C. W. (1979). Government and technology in the Great Depression. *Technology and Culture, 20*(1), 162–174.

Rafalko, R. J. (1989). Corporate punishment: A proposal. *Journal of Business Ethics, 8*, 917–928.

Rajan, R. (2010). *Fault lines: How hidden fractures still threaten the world economy.* Princeton University Press.

Rajan, R. G., & Zingales, L. (1998). Power in a theory of the firm. *Quarterly Journal of Economics, 113*(2), 387–432.

Rajan, R., & Zingales, L. (2003). *Saving capitalism from the capitalists: How open financial markets challenge the establishment and spread prosperity to rich and poor alike.* Currency.

Rajan, R., & Zingales, L. (2014). *Saving capitalism from the capitalists: Unleashing the power of financial markets to create wealth and spread opportunity.* HarperCollins India.

Rand, A. (1964). *The virtue of selfishness.* Penguin.

Ranson, S., Hinings, B., & Greenwood, R. (1980). The structuring of organizational structures. *Administrative Science Quarterly, 25*(1), 1–17.

Rawls, J. (1958). Justice as fairness. *Philosophical Review, 67*, 164–194.

Rawls, J. (1971). *A theory of justice.* Harvard University Press.

Rawls, J. (1993a). *Political liberalism.* Columbia University Press.

Rawls, J. (1993b). Law of peoples. *Critical Inquiry, 20*(1), 36–68.

Rio Declaration. (2012). The future we want – Outcome document. In *United Nations Conference on Sustainable Development*, June 20–22. https://sustainablede velopment.un.org/futurewewant.html#:~:text=We%2C%20the%20Heads%20of% 20State,economically%2C%20socially%20and%20environmentally%20sustainable

Ritchey, T. (2002). Modelling complex socio-technical systems using morphological analysis. Adapted from an address to the Swedish Parliamentary IT Commission, Stockholm. https://www.swemorph.com/pdf/it–webart.pdf

Ritchey, T. (2005). Wicked problems. Structuring social messes with morphological analysis. Adapted from a lecture given at the Royal Institute of Technology in Stockholm. *Swedish Morphological Society.* http://www.swemorph.com

Ritchey, T. (2006). Problem structuring using computer-aided morphological analysis. *Journal of the Operational Research Society, 57*(7), 792–801.

Rittel, H. W., & Webber, M. M. (1973). Dilemmas in a general theory of planning. *Policy Sciences, 4*(2), 155–169.

Robinson, J. (2013). *The accumulation of capital.* Palgrave Macmillan.

Robinson, S. (2014). *Simulation: The practice of model development and use.* Palgrave Macmillan.

Rodgers, H. R. (1978). *Crisis in democracy: A policy analysis of American government.* Addison Wesley Publishing Company.

Rönnegard, D. (2013). How autonomy alone debunks corporate moral agency. *Business & Professional Ethics Journal, 32*(1/2), 77–107.

Rönnegard, D., & Velasquez, M. (2017). On (not) attributing moral responsibility to organizations. In E. W. Orts & N. C. Smith (Eds.), *The moral responsibility of firms* (pp. 123–142). Oxford University Press.

Rosenhead, J. (1996). What's the problem? An introduction to problem structuring methods. *Interfaces, 26*(6), 117–131.

Rostow, E. V. (1963). The ethics of competition revisited. *California Management Review, V*(3), 20.

Rowley, J. (2006). Where is the wisdom that we have lost in knowledge? *Journal of Documentation, 62*(2), 251–270.

Sandour, R. L. (2008, April). *Our global warming and the use of markets to solve environmental problems. The Robert P. Maxon Lecture Series* (pp. 17–31). The George Washington University School of Business.

Sawhney, M., & Zabin, J. (2002). Managing and measuring relational equity in the network economy. *Journal of the Academy of Marketing Science, 30*(4), 313–332.

Scanlon, T. M. (1998). *What we owe to each other.* The Belknap Press of Harvard University Press.

Scherer, A. G., & Palazzo, G. (2007). Toward a political conception of corporate responsibility: Business and society seen from a Habermasian perspective. *Academy of Management Review, 32*(4), 1096–1120.

Scherer, A. G., & Palazzo, G. (2011). The new political role of business in a globalized world: A review of a new perspective on CSR and its implications for the firm, governance, and democracy. *Journal of Management Studies, 48*(4), 899–931.

Schoemaker, P. J., & Gunther, R. E. (2006). The wisdom of deliberate mistakes. *Harvard Business Review, 84*(6), 108–115.

Schumacher, E. F. (1973). *Small is beautiful.* Harper and Row Publishers, Inc.

Schumpeter, J. A. (1934). *The theory of economic development: An inquiry into profits, capital, credit, interest, and the business cycle.* Harvard University Press.

Schwartz, S. H., Melech, G., Lehmann, A., Burgess, S., Harris, M., & Owens, V. (2001). Extending the cross-cultural validity of the theory of basic human values with a different method of measurement. *Journal of Cross-Cultural Psychology, 32*(5), 519–542.

Seabright, M. A., & Kurke, L. B. (1997). Organizational ontology and the moral status of the corporation. *Business Ethics Quarterly, 7*(4), 91–108.

Searle, J. R. (1980). Minds, brains, and programs. *Behavioral and Brain Sciences, 3*(3), 417–424.

Sedlacek, T. (2011). *Economics of good and evil: The quest for economic meaning from Gilgamesh to Wall Street.* Oxford University Press.

Seidman, D. (2012). *How: Why how we do anything means everything.* Wiley India Pvt Ltd.

Selnes, F., & Sallis, J. (2003). Promoting relationship learning. *Journal of Marketing, 67*(3), 80–95.

Sen, A. (1992). *Inequality reexamined.* Oxford University Press.

Sen, A. (1997). *Resources, values and development.* Harvard University Press.

Sen, A. (2009). Capitalism beyond the crisis. *New York Review of Books, 56*(5), 1–7. https://core.ac.uk/download/pdf/28930875.pdf

Senge, P. M. (1990). *The fifth discipline: The art and practice of the learning organization.* Doubleday.

Senge, P. M. (2006). *The fifth discipline: The art and practice of the learning organization.* Broadway Business.

Senge, P. M., Cambroon-McCabe, N., Lucas, T., Smith, B., Dutton, J., & Kleiner, A. (2000). *Schools that learn: A fifth discipline fieldbook for educators, parents, and everyone who cares about education.* Doubleday.

Senge, P. M., Kleiner, A., Roberts, C., Ross, R., Roth, G., & Smith, B. (1999). *The dance of change: The challenge of sustaining momentum in learning organizations.* Doubleday.

Senge, P. M., Kleiner, A., Roberts, C., Ross, R., & Smith, B. (1994). *The fifth discipline fieldbook: Strategies and tools for building a learning organization.* Doubleday.

Sepinwall, A. J., & Orts, E. W. (2017). Blame, emotion, and the corporation. In E. W. Orts & N. C. Smith (Eds.), *The moral responsibility of firms* (pp. 143–166). Oxford University Press.

Shapiro, D. L., & Rynes, S. L. (2005). The role of management scholarship in the public sector. *Academy of Management Journal, 48*(6), 989–998. https://doi.org/10.5465/amj.2005.19573105

Sheppard, B. H., & Tuchinsky, M. (1996a). Interfirm relationships: A grammar of pairs. *Research in Organizational Behavior, 18,* 331–373.

Shrivastava, P. (2010). Pedagogy of passion for sustainability. *The Academy of Management Learning and Education, 9*(3), 443–455.

Shrivastava, P., Schumacher, G., Wasieleski, D. M., & Tasic, M. (2017). Aesthetic rationality in organizations: Toward developing a sensitivity for sustainability. *The Journal of Applied Behavioral Science, 53*(3), 369–411.

Sidgwick, H. (1907). *The methods of ethics.* Macmillan.

Skoll World Forum. (2015, April 15–17). The great paradigm shift. In *The 12th Skoll World Forum on social entrepreneurship.* https://s12982.pcdn.co/wp–content/uploads/2015/04/2015-Skoll-World-Forum-Program.pdf

Smith, A. (1776). *An inquiry into the nature and causes of the wealth of nations* (Vol. I). W. Strahan and T. Cadell.

Smith, A. (1976). An inquiry into the nature and causes of the wealth of nations. In R. H. Campbell (Ed.), *The works and correspondence of Adam Smith.* Oxford University Press.

Soares, C. (2003). Corporate versus individual moral responsibility. *Journal of Business Ethics, 46,* 143–150.

Sonenshein, S. (2005). Business ethics and internal social criticism. *Business Ethics Quarterly, 15,* 475–498.

Sonenshein, S. (2006). Crafting social issues at work. *Academy of Management Journal, 49,* 1158–1172.

Sonenshein, S. (2007). The role of construction, intuition, and justification in responding to ethical issues at work: The sensemaking-intuition model. *Academy of Management Review, 32,* 1022–1040.

Sonenshein, S. (2009). Emergence of ethical issues during strategic change implementation. *Organization Science, 20,* 223–239.

Sonenshein, S. (2014). How organizations foster the creative use of resources. *Academy of Management Journal, 57*(3), 814–848.

Sonenshein, S. (2016). How corporations overcome issue illegitimacy and issue equivocality to address social welfare: The role of the social change agent. *Academy of Management Review*, *41*(2), 349–366.

Sonenshein, S., DeCelles, K. A., & Dutton, J. E. (2014). It's not easy being green: The role of self-evaluations in explaining support of environmental issues. *Academy of Management Journal*, *57*(1), 7–37.

Spector, M., & Kitsuse, J. I. (1977). *Constructing social problems*. Cummings.

Steiner, J. F., & Steiner, G. A. (1991). *Business, government and society: A managerial perspective* (6th ed.). McGraw-Hill, Inc.

Sternberg, R. J. (1998). A balance theory of wisdom. *Review of General Psychology*, *2*(4), 347–365.

Sternberg, R. J. (2001). How wise is it to teach for wisdom? A reply to five critiques. *Educational Psychologist*, *36*(4), 269–272.

Sternberg, R. J. (2003). *Wisdom, intelligence, and creativity synthesized*. Cambridge University Press.

Stiglitz, J. (2015). *The great divide*. Penguin.

Sugden, R. (1998). The metric of opportunity. *Economics and Philosophy*, *14*(2), 307–337.

Sundaram, A. K., & Inkpen, A. C. (2004). Stakeholder theory and "The corporate objective revisited": A reply. *Organization Science*, *15*(3), 370–371.

Surber, J., & French, P. A. (1983). Individual and corporate responsibility: Two alternative approaches [with commentary]. *Business & Professional Ethics Journal*, *2*(4), 67–91.

Taleb, N. N. (2004). *Fooled by randomness: The hidden role of chance in life and in the markets*. Random House Inc.

Taleb, N. N. (2010). *The Black Swan: The impact of the highly improbable*. Random House.

The Standish Group. (1994). *Charting the sea of information technology—Chaos*. The Standish Group International.

Thompson, P. B. (1986). Collective responsibility and professional roles. *Journal of Business Ethics*, *5*, 151–154.

Trout, J. (2004). *Trout on strategy: Capturing mindshare, conquering markets*. Tata McGraw-Hill Education.

Tukey, J. W. (1972). Data analysis, computation and mathematics. *Quarterly of Applied Mathematics*, *30*(1), 51–65.

Van Lange, P. A., Joireman, J., Parks, C. D., & Van Dijk, E. (2013). The psychology of social dilemmas: A review. *Organizational Behavior and Human Decision Processes*, *120*(2), 125–141.

Vann, J. W., & Kumcu, E. (1995). Achieving efficiency and distributive justice in marketing programs for economic development. *Journal of Macromarketing*, *15*(2), 5–22.

Velasquez, M. G. (1983). Why corporations are not morally responsible for anything they do. *Business & Professional Ethics Journal*, *2*(3), 1–18.

Velasquez, M. G. (1985). Why corporations are not morally responsible for anything they do. In J. R. DesJardins & J. J. McCall (Eds.), *Contemporary issues in business ethics* (pp. 114–125). Wadsworth.

Velasquez, M. (2003). Debunking corporate moral responsibility. *Business Ethics Quarterly*, *13*(4), 531–562.

Vlasic, B. (2016, January 4). *GM chief Mary Barra is named chairwoman, affirming her leadership*. https://www.nytimes.com/2016/01/05/business/gm–chief–is–named–cha irwoman–affirming–her–leadership.html?searchResultPosition=1

Walsh, J. P., Weber, K., & Margolis, J. D. (2003). Social issues and management: Our lost cause found. *Journal of Management, 29*(6), 859–881.

Walt, S., & Laufer, W. S. (1991). Corporate criminal liability and the comparative mix of sanctions. In K. Schlegel & D. Weisburd (Eds.), *White-collar crime reconsidered* (pp. 309–332). Northeastern University Press.

Warnock, M. (Ed.). (1962). *Utilitarianism*. Collins.

Warren, C. (1930). Federal and state court interference. *Harvard Law Review, 43*(3), 345–378.

Watson, G. (2004). *Agency and answerability: Selected essays*. Clarendon Press.

Weber, M. (1930). *The protestant ethic and the spirit of capitalism*. Routledge.

Werhane, P. H. (1985). *Persons, rights, and corporations*. Prentice-Hall.

Werhane, P. H. (1989). Corporate and individual moral responsibility: A reply to Jan Garrett. *Journal of Business Ethics, 8*, 821–822.

Werner, R. A. (2012). Towards a new research programme on 'banking and the economy'—Implications of the quantity theory of credit for the prevention and resolution of banking and debt crises. *International Review of Financial Analysis, 25*, 1–17.

Whitley, R. (1992). Societies, firms and markets: The social structuring of business systems. In R. Whitley (Ed.), *European business systems: Firms and markets in their national contexts* (pp. 5–45). SAGE Publications.

Wilk, R. R., & Cliggett, L. (2007). *Economies and cultures: Foundations of economic anthropology*. Westview Press.

Williams, R. (1983). Capitalism. In *Keywords: A vocabulary of culture and society*. Oxford University Press.

Williams, C. A. (1999). The Securities and Exchange Commission and corporate social transparency. *Harvard Law Review, 112*(6), 1197–1311.

Williamson, O. E. (1975). Markets and hierarchies: Analysis and antitrust implications: A study in the economics of internal organization. *University of Illinois at Urbana–Champaign's Academy for Entrepreneurial Leadership Historical Research Reference in Entrepreneurship*.

Winner, L. (1977). *Autonomous technology: Technics-out–of-control as a theme in political thought*. MIT Press.

Woods, P. A. (2001). Values-intuitive rational action: The dynamic relationship of instrumental rationality and values insights as a form of social action. *British Journal of Sociology, 52*(4), 687–706.

Wray-Bliss, E., & Parker, M. (1998). Marxism, capitalism and ethics. In M. Parker (Ed.), *Ethics and organizations* (pp. 30–52). SAGE Publications.

Wyma, K. (1997). Moral responsibility and leeway for action. *American Philosophical Quarterly, 34*(1), 57–70.

Yelvington, K. (1995). *Producing power: Ethnicity, gender, and class in a Caribbean workplace*. Temple University Press.

Yourdon, E. E. (1999). *Death march projects: The complete software developer's guide to surviving "mission impossible" projects*. Prentice-Hall.

Zohar, D., & Marshall, I. (2000). *SQ: Connecting with our spiritual intelligence*. Bloomsbury Publishing.

Zohar, D., & Marshall, I. (2004). *Spiritual capital: Wealth we can live by.* Berrett-Koehler Publishers.

Zsolnai, L. (2015). Spirituality, ethics and sustainability. In L. Zsolnai (Ed.), *The spiritual dimension of business ethics and sustainability management* (pp. 1–12). Laszlo Springer Cham Heidelberg.

Index

www.ingramcontent.com/pod-product-compliance
Lightning Source LLC
Jackson TN
JSHW011917131224
75386JS00004B/233